God Have Mercy

The Life of

John Fisher

of

Rochester

God Have Mercy

Michael Macklem

The Life of John Fisher of Rochester

You shall be led to the place from whence you came, and from thence shall be drawn through the city to the place of execution at Tyburn, where your body shall be hanged by the neck, and being half alive you shall be cut down and thrown to the ground, your bowels to be taken out of your body and burnt before you being alive, your head to be smitten off and your body to be divided into four quarters, and after, your head and quarters to be set up where the King shall appoint:

and God have mercy upon your soul!

Oberon Press

PUBLISHED BY
OBERON PRESS, OTTAWA, CANADA

PRINTED AND BOUND BY
HAZELL WATSON AND VINEY LIMITED, AYLESBURY, ENGLAND

For my wife Anne

Acknowledgments

The writing of this book was made possible by the generosity of the Canada Council, whose award of a Research Fellowship enabled me to spend several months during the winters of 1965 and 1966 in the United Kingdom examining manuscripts and early printed books. I am especially thankful also for the kindness of the librarians of the British Museum, the Bodleian and the Cambridge University Library. The Master of St. John's College, J. S. Boys Smith, and the librarian of Christ's College, Dr. A. L. Peck, were particularly helpful, as was the President of Queens'. At Rochester I was given free access to the episcopal registers by H. S. Wharton of the Diocesan Registry. The Keeper of Prints and Drawings at The Royal Library, Windsor Castle, Miss Helen Scott-Elliot, answered all of my many questions, as did Charles Gibbs-Smith of the Victoria and Albert Museum and the Rev. Canon Stephen Walker, Vicar of St. Mary's, Beverley. The Lord Sinclair, M.V.O., York Herald, helped me to identify the members of Fisher's family circle, though the responsibility for the conclusions I have reached is entirely my own. The Rt. Rev. Msgr. A. N. Gilbey of Fisher House in Cambridge showed me rare hospitality while freely sharing with me his knowledge of Fisher. I am also indebted to His Excellency Javier Conde, Ambassador of Spain; to Professor Arthur E. Barker of the University of Illinois, who read the work in manuscript; to my friends Nigel and Barbara Hensman; and to my son Nicholas Macklem, who allowed me to use as my own an interesting discovery he made at the age of ten.

God Have Mercy

The Life of

John Fisher

of

Rochester

Chapter 1

When John Fisher was born in 1469, the townsmen of Beverley had been living in the shadow of the Church for almost eight hundred years. A Christian settlement had been established there as early as 693 by John—later St. John—of Beverley, and from that time forward the town had belonged to the Archbishop of York. Early in the twelfth century, the Archbishop had granted the townsmen a charter of liberties which gave them the right to regulate the manufacture and sale of cloth and other commodities, and secure in the enjoyment of this privilege the town grew steadily in size and importance. It was not long before the original monastic church of St. John of Beverley was torn down and replaced by a splendid new church of Norman style, dedicated to St. John the Evangelist. The new collegiate church, nourished as it was by the piety of the men of the town and country round about, grew so rapidly in stature and wealth that the canons began in less than a hundred years to tear down their new Norman church to make way for Gothic improvements. The choir and transepts were rebuilt by about 1260, the handsome nave by 1349 and the tall, slender west front and towers by 1420. But even such an effort as this, which left the church as it stands today, did not exhaust the devotion of the Yorkshire merchants who looked to Beverley as the centre of their spiritual life. The beautiful minster they had built for the college of canons who used it to celebrate the offices of the Church. For themselves they built the parish church of St. Mary, facing the high street of the town. They built lavishly, at first in

3

the heavy, sombre style of the Normans and later, like the canons of St. John, in the lighter and more radiant Gothic. Building and rebuilding went on, despite interruptions, until the middle of the fifteenth century, when the west front and clerestories of the present church—soaring walls of glass hung in tracery of stone—were completed. All of this spoke of two things: the steadily growing wealth of the men of Beverley and their desire to express, in things the eye could see and the hand could feel, their love of God.

One day in the early summer of 1477, a merchant of Beverley died and was buried in St. Mary's. His name was Robert Fisher. He was a mercer, a man of substance, and he left bequests to the collegiate church of St. John, to the cathedral church of St. Peter at York and to the poor of Beverley. There were legacies also to various members of his family—his brother William, his sister Ellen and her husband Thomas Wykcliff, his four children and his wife Agnes.[1]

One of these children was John, at the time of his father's death a boy of seven or eight.[2]

John had grown up in the town of Beverley, probably the eldest of the family of four. Only one of the others is known to history. This was Robert, who for many years served his brother as steward at Rochester and later attended him loyally in the Tower. Ralph Fisher, one of John's debtors at the time of his attainder, may have been the third son. There was also a sister, probably the same Elizabeth who was later professed a nun at Dartford and for whom her brother while in the Tower wrote *A Spirituall Consolation* and *The Wayes to Perfect Religion*. In time, John's mother married again. Her second husband was Willus or William White, also of Beverley, and by him she had a son Edward before her own death in 1515.[3]

From an early age John and his brothers were sent to school at the minster, to which there was attached one of the oldest grammar-schools in England. There, for a fee of eight pence a term or thereabouts, boys were taught by the canons of the collegiate church. Those who had been chosen to take part in the services of the minster were trained as choristers, principally in music and song. The rest—sons of sheep-farmers and wool-merchants from the town of Beverley and the neighbouring parishes—were also taught to read and write Latin, and this meant that before they left the school they were expected not only to understand the rules of Latin grammar but also to be familiar with a wide range of classical authors, in addition to the Scriptures. The older boys went on in some cases to a study of rhetoric and logic.

John was no doubt first sent to the collegiate school soon after his father died in the summer he turned eight. He stayed there, in all probability, for five or six years, until he was fourteen. By that time his evident desire to learn and his dogged capacity for long study and hard work had convinced his teachers and his family that he must be allowed to continue what he had begun. And so it was that he left the town of his birth and boyhood, probably in the autumn of 1483, for the new world of Cambridge. It was a journey of 150 miles or more on horseback, over rough and muddy roads. It would have taken him four or five days, perhaps longer, and on the way he would have passed through such towns as Lincoln, with its superb cathedral spread against the western sky, and Peterborough, with its Benedictine monastery of St. Peter standing on the edge of the fens much as its Norman builders had left it, strong and serene, unlike anything that had been seen in Beverley since the canons of St. John had rebuilt their Norman minster 150 years before. This was no ordinary journey for the young boy. He was seldom, if ever, to see his home again, or the countryside of his boyhood. But if he looked back he kept it to himself. For what lay before him now was one of the great forming experiences of his life : Cambridge. He came to Cambridge as a boy of fourteen from the north, friendless and alone. He had already decided to study for the priesthood—it was this decision that brought him to the university. But if he learned at Cambridge to be a priest, he learned other things as well. For here he found a new kind of home, a home that nourished his mind as well as his body. He discovered that learning could light a candle in a man's life that no darkness could put out.

All this, however, was still before him as on that first day he crossed the bridge at the north end of the town. The Cambridge that greeted his eye in the autumn of 1483 was a small town of houses, shops and parish churches. As he came to the round church of the Holy Sepulchre and turned into High Street (now King's Parade), he would have seen Trinity Hall and Clare on his right, and beyond them the great foundation begun by King Henry VI forty years before, its chapel still unfinished. Behind King's the fields sloped down to the quiet river. A short distance along the riverbank stood the first court of Queens', its warm red brick looking much as it does today, and beyond that Peterhouse, not yet adorned with the classical elegance of its later sash windows. Facing it across the street was Pembroke, as yet a stranger to the graceful hand of Christopher Wren. Nearby was Gonville, at that time situated in Freeschool Lane close to Corpus Christi.

Fisher's destination was the college of Michaelhouse, which stood on ground later acquired by Henry VIII and cleared to make way for the new royal foundation of Trinity. Michaelhouse was, with the single exception of Peterhouse, the oldest of the Cambridge colleges, having been founded in 1324 by Hervey de Stanton. Its Master was William Melton and it was to him that the young Fisher had been sent.

The life that Fisher took up as a scholar of Michaelhouse was austere and arduous. Theology was the principal subject of study, though lectures were also given in logic, philosophy and mathematics. There was no Greek as yet at Cambridge and no Hebrew, but scholars had to be able to speak and understand

Latin. They were expected to be present at lectures and exercises and to attend mass regularly; they were required to rise at dawn and to be in their rooms by dusk, when the college gates were locked for the night. Misconduct with women was forbidden and less serious improprieties were punishable at the discretion of the Master. Scholars slept four to a room and took their meals in hall.

Fisher thrived on this life. Preparation for the priesthood brought him all the excitement of a high purpose while at the same time giving full scope to his desire for knowledge and his love of learning. He took his bachelor's degree in 1488 and his master's in 1491; soon afterwards he was elected a fellow of the college. In June of the same year he sought and procured from Rome a dispensation allowing him to take orders though he was not yet of canonical age.[4] He was ordained at York on 17 December, 1491 and it is likely enough that on the way there he visited his family at Beverley. He was now 22 years old and a young man of striking appearance. Tall and spare, he had a strong, lean face with dark eyes and hair, a searching gaze and a firm, austere mouth. His manner was simple and unassuming, but when he spoke his voice was clear and strong, and people listened.[5]

It was only eight years since he had left Beverley for the first time, and yet he returned to Cambridge as a fellow and a priest. While continuing his studies in theology, he was now concerned for the first time with teaching and administration as well. He was chosen a university Proctor in 1494, which meant that at the early age of 25 he was in touch with the day-to-day affairs of the university and responsible for its management only to the Vice-Chancellor. Three years later he replaced Melton himself, who had accepted a preferment in the diocese of York, and at the age of 28 became Master of his college. In 1501, the year in which he received his doctorate in divinity, he was elected Vice-Chancellor of the university.

His remarkable success at Cambridge Fisher owed, without

doubt, to the evident sincerity of his life and work. He had come to Cambridge to fit himself for the priesthood and later, as priest and fellow and then Master, he had done everything he could to make his college and the university at large answerable to the urgent need of the Church for priests of good learning and decent living. During these years he had worked patiently, with tireless attention to detail; and yet if he was serious and spare in his living, he had the tenderness and the wit to make and keep friends. It is hardly surprising that in his circle at Cambridge he earned the confidence and the affection of everyone he met.

Chapter 2

His new position sometimes took Fisher as far as London, where he was required to attend to the affairs of the university at Court and in the City. On one such occasion in 1494, he dined with the Lady Margaret Beaufort, Countess of Richmond and Derby and mother of the King. This was no doubt a chance encounter, but for all that it changed the lives of both the Countess and the priest. The Lady Margaret was an indomitable woman to whose iron will and unfailing devotion Henry VII owed the crown of England. Now 52, she was the great-great-granddaughter of Edward III through the illicit union (later declared legitimate by Act of Parliament) of John of Gaunt, Duke of Lancaster, and Catherine Swynford. At the age of twelve she had been married to Edmund Tudor, elder son of Owen Tudor and Catherine—"fair Catherine, and most fair"—widow of King Henry V. Her husband died in the following year, leaving her a widow at the age of thirteen, already quick with child. This child, whose life was from the beginning in continual

Torrigiano bust, probably of Fisher in his late thirties

danger from the jealousy of the Yorkists, she brought up first in the safety of Wales and later across the channel in Brittany, until in the fullness of time he was ready to make good his claim to the English throne. The Lady Margaret had meanwhile married her cousin Henry Stafford, son of the Duke of Buckingham. When he died in 1482, she married for the third time, Thomas Lord Stanley, whose decision to desert Richard at Bosworth gave Henry Tudor his opportunity.[1] After her son's victory in the field, which brought him to the throne as Henry VII, the Lady Margaret was established at Court and given a place of honour worthy of the gratitude of a King.

When Fisher met her in 1494 she was interested no longer in affairs of State. Her principal concern now was with her landed property and her large and splendid income, which she wished to devote to the glory of God and to the cure of souls. She was attracted to Fisher because she sensed in him an intensity that matched her own. Here was a man, she saw, who had deliberately chosen the life and work of a priest. Surrounded as she was at Court by men who regarded the Church and its revenues as the rightful property of courtiers and statesmen, this must have impressed her at once. She soon found that she could respect his opinion and trust his advice. Though she was older than he, he supported her in her faith, encouraged her devotion and guided her in the exercise of her charity. As for him, he found in the Lady Margaret a woman of wealth and rank who sought to use her position not for her own pleasure or profit but for the nourishment of knowledge and piety. She awakened in him the fond hope that England could be renewed and its faith replenished by her superb example.

In the event, each realized in large measure the hopes of the other. But this was not the work of an hour, nor did either of them suspect, when they first dined together in London, what would one day come of their meeting. In course of time, Fisher was appointed chaplain to the Lady Margaret. Soon afterwards

Richard Fitzjames, who had been her confessor, was given the
see of Rochester and Fisher was asked to take his place. Even
then he was not in daily attendance on the countess, for he continued to spend most of his time at Cambridge. From the beginning, however, he tried to interest his patron in the work of the
university. Hitherto her main interest had been the Abbey of St.
Peter in Westminster. But in the course of time Fisher managed
to persuade her that the monks of Westminster Abbey, already
lavishly endowed, had no further need of her liberality. Gradu-
ally he convinced her that the most pressing need of the Church
was for secular priests, equipped to carry the word of God to the
people outside the religious houses, the ordinary people of England. In 1503 she agreed to endow a readership in divinity at
both Oxford and Cambridge, and that September Fisher himself
was appointed reader at Cambridge. The readers, who were to
be elected every second year by the Chancellor and Vice-
Chancellor and all doctors, bachelors and candidates for a degree
in theology, were to read for an hour daily in the divinity schools
to any comer, without fee, from such works in divinity as were
chosen by the Chancellor, Vice-Chancellor and college of doctors. For this they were to be paid, out of revenues set aside by
the Lady Margaret for the purpose, a yearly fee of £13 6s. 8d.[2]
In the following year she established a preachership at Cambridge with a stipend of £10 a year. The Lady Margaret preachers, the first of whom was John Fawne, were required to preach
six sermons in each of the three years of their appointment, one
every second year at St. Paul's or St. Margaret's, Westminster
or elsewhere in London, and one every second year in the villages
of Ware and Cheshunt in Hertfordshire, Bassingbourn, Orwell
and Babraham in Cambridgeshire, and Maxey, St. James Deeping, St. John Deeping, Bourn, Boston and Swineshead in Lincolnshire. This was a modest beginning, but it shows clearly
enough what Fisher had in mind: a literate priesthood prepared
to make known the word of God wherever it was most needed.

It was now the autumn of 1504, when Fisher received the unexpected news that the King intended to give him the see of Rochester, vacated by Fitzjames' removal to the richer bishopric of Chichester: "and I thought I shulde not offende you", the King had written to his mother, "I am well myndit to promote Master Fissher your Confessour to a Busshoprich and I assure you madame ffor non other cause but for the grete and singular vertue that I knowe and se in hym aswell in conyng and naturall wisdome and specially for his good and vertuose lyving and conuersacion and by the promocion of suche a man I knowe well it shulde corage many other to lyve vertuosely and to take shuche ways as he dothe whiche shulde be a good example to many other hereafter how be it", he added with that touching solicitude for his mother that stayed with him to the end, "withowte your pleaser knowen I woll not move hym nor tempe hym therin. And therfor I beseche you that I may knowe your mynde and pleaser in that behalf whiche shalbe folowed asmuche as god will give me grace. I haue in my days promoted mony a man vnavisedly and I wolde nowe make some recompencion to promote some good and vertuose men whiche I doubte note shulde best please god who euer preserue you in good helth and long lyve." Though it is clear enough from this that Fisher did not owe his bishopric to the influence of the Lady Margaret, there can be no doubt of the answer she sent the King. The choice of Fisher must have filled her with joy.[3]

Not that the see of Rochester was a rich prize. It was the smallest diocese in England, lying as it did between Canterbury and London, and its revenues were worth only about £300 a year. The Bishop of Rochester, like all other bishops, was entitled to a place in the upper house of Convocation, the governing body of the English Church, and to a place among the spiritual peers in the House of Lords. But there he sat beside men who governed the Church with a splendour hardly equalled by Kings, who disposed of revenues five or even ten times greater than his and who looked upon their preferments as a fitting reward for services to the State.⁴ Fitzjames had stayed at Rochester for only two years on his way to the richer see of Chichester, where in the event he remained only two years longer before being given the great see of London, which he held until his death many years later. It was expected that Fisher would do the same, and in fact he is said to have been offered a choice of Lincoln, which became vacant in 1514, and Ely, vacated in the next year by the death of James Stanley. His answer—he is reputed to have said that he wouldn't change his poor old wife for the richest widow in England—showed clearly enough that he regarded Rochester, not merely as a token of the royal favour, to be exchanged for a better at the first opportunity, but as a means of putting to use the long years of study and preparation that were now behind him.⁵

Fisher was consecrated at Lambeth by William Warham, Archbishop of Canterbury, on 24 November, 1504, and two days later he was among the lords spiritual and temporal who were present in the Star Chamber when the King gave judgment in a dispute between the Merchant Adventurers and the Merchants of the Staple at Calais. He was installed by proxy in the cathedral church at Rochester the following April.⁶

Rochester was then a small town, as it still is, on the south bank of the River Medway, thirty miles east of London. The cathedral rises close above the river and to the southwest there stood the bishop's palace. The palace was already old, and though it had recently been restored such comforts as it afforded were few enough. The cathedral itself was begun by St. Augustine in 604, only seven years after he had founded the first Christian community in England at Canterbury. The church as Fisher knew it, however, was begun anew by Gundulph, bishop from 1077 to 1108. Gundulph and his successors rebuilt the cathedral in the Norman style for a community of Benedictine monks. The completed church was consecrated in 1130, but successive fires led to renewed building before the end of the century. For more than sixty years, work went on slowly in the choir, which was remodelled in the Early English manner, with steep vaulting and narrow lancet windows, set off by clusters of polished black Purbeck. The monks evidently intended to remodel the nave as well, but they broke off abruptly in the third bay from the crossing, leaving the cathedral—save for the addition of a squat tower and spire and broad clerestory windows—much as Fisher found it more than two centuries later.

Fisher had not been long at Rochester before he set out to acquaint himself with his diocese. He had manors at Halling, a few miles up the Medway from Rochester, and at Bromley, on the road to London, as well as a house in Lambeth Marsh for use during sessions of Parliament, and by staying for a time at each he was able to visit and examine every part of his diocese, even when travel on horseback was at its worst. In the spring of 1505, he began his first visitation, preaching to the people, supervising the work of the several parishes, examining the life of the religious houses, encouraging, correcting and amending as he went.[7] It was not easy work. At the very beginning, a man from the parish of St. Nicholas in Rochester was brought before him. His name was John Moress and he was accused of having declared in public that Christ "dyed nat in perfitt charite" because he did not offer himself as a propitiation for the sins of Lucifer as well as of Adam and Eve. It was whispered that Moress had also said that the Virgin Mary was nothing "but a sakk". All of this the accused agreed to forsake and abjure and the next Sunday he carried a faggot barefoot in procession to the Church of St. Nicholas.[8] Two years later there was more serious trouble in the parish of Westerham. Richard Gavell of that parish maintained that the custom of making offerings in church was conceived by priests and curates out of "theire own covetuosse myndes and singular Avayles". On one occasion, he admitted, he had caused a certain Joan Harries, also of Westerham, to withdraw her offering, to the "euyll example" of the people. He had, more-over, on many occasions refused to listen to the word of God and had instead "gon owte of the church to the ale howses"; on other occasions he had spoken ill of the priest while he was in the pulpit, saying that he did "no thyng but chide & brawell ffor I loke more on his dedes than of his wordes". And when he was denounced by the Archbishop of Canterbury for his wrongs, it was said that he had jeered at bishops and priests and boasted that he was "nat accursid of god", inviting his neighbours and friends to "ete & drynke with me for all that." Examined by the bishop at Bromley on 5 December, 1507, Gavell signed the confession and abjuration with his mark and was duly sentenced: to carry a faggot on three separate days to the parish churches at Bromley and Westerham and to the cathedral at Rochester, and to remain within the diocese for four years. Disorderly affections, disobedience, dissent—these were problems that dogged Fisher's footsteps throughout the long, patient years of his pastorate. There was Henry Potter of West Malling, who had been heard to say that he did not believe in the resurrection and would not "till I see it". There was Thomas Batman of the parish of St. Margaret's next Rochester, who refused to pray to the saints or to make offerings to images. And Paul Lombey of Gravesend, who had dared to say that the bread offered in the sacrament of the altar was "butt a cake". There was John Pylcher of the parish of Coxston, who had declared openly to any who would hear him that "my soull sshall a rise at the day of iuggement but so sshall nat my body and bones". There was John Bechyng, a priest of the parish of Ditton, who had neglected confession for half a year and who admitted that he did not believe himself bound by Scripture to make confession or to do penance for his sins. And James Dissanger, a joiner, who had repeated talk he had heard in London, where it was said that a man should worship none but God himself, for the images of saints were "but stokkes & stones". And Peter Durr, a priest of Gravesend, who had denied that the bishops and archbishops had any right to govern the Church, adding that the prayers of one man were as good as those of another.[9] To all of these, as he made his way about his diocese, Fisher listened patiently and with concern. There can be no doubt that of all those whom he sought to correct or amend during the course of his visitations, those who refused to recognize the use or necessity of the Church in bringing man to God caused him the greatest pain. For they, he felt, had rejected the love of God itself; worse than that, they sought to deprive others of the abundance and joy that was offered to them in the sacrifice of Christ upon the Cross. For this the Church existed. In the Church men could be made whole, relieved of their fear, their suffering eased, their hearts opened. It was to this that Fisher had devoted his life and this that he saw endangered by those who sought to deprive the Church of its place in the love and trust of the people. Such wilful indifference—for so it seemed to him—to the sorrows of others and the means of their relief was more than he could endure. In every man there is a point beyond which he can no longer deal in charity with his neighbours. It is easy for us to see that these poor men deserved pity and understanding. Much of what they had to say was ignorant and foolish, and yet, as we listen to their confessions, we can discern the first signs, however awkward and crude, of a new approach to the experience of God. To their contemporaries, however, they seemed little better than thieves in the night, against whom, if they persisted, the innocent and the faithful could not but close up the shutters of their hearts. Fortunately, none of the accused forced the bishop to this extremity. He reasoned with them and perhaps he convinced them. In any case, they all confessed their wrongs and were received again into the Church. They were all required to do penance: most of them carried a faggot in procession to their parish church and there stood barefoot before the people; one was confined to prison for six weeks, after which he was allowed to go free, wearing the sign of a penitent.[10]

Chapter 3

The work of a priest and bishop did not cause Fisher to forget Cambridge. Indeed, he must have been a familiar figure on the roads leading from Rochester to London and Cambridge, as he seized such opportunities as he could to revisit his home of more than twenty years. He had resigned as Master of Michaelhouse and as Vice-Chancellor of the university before he left Cambridge for Rochester. He was, however, immediately elected Chancellor, a position of honour customarily used by its incumbent to advance the interests of the university at Court. Fisher used it instead to make himself the leading spirit of the academic community. He was re-elected annually until 1514, when he himself suggested that the post be offered to Thomas Wolsey. When Wolsey declined the honour, Fisher was returned for life.[1]

Meanwhile, he had prevailed on the Lady Margaret to enlarge the scope of her interests in the university. She had already endowed a preachership at Cambridge and a readership in divinity at both universities; now she decided to establish a new college. The bulk of the work—the appropriation of suitable premises, the provision of statutes, the appointment of fellows—she left to Fisher. She could not have done better. Fisher's familiarity with all the concerns of the university and his experience at Michaelhouse, coupled with his keen enthusiasm for the new project and his tireless patience, fitted him well for the work in hand. His eye fell on a derelict foundation known as Godshouse standing in what was then Preachers' Street, opposite St. Andrew's Church, some distance to the east of the river. Godshouse had been founded in the reign of Henry VI by a priest named William Byngham. It had stood originally in Milne Street, which at that time ran northwards from what is now Queens' Lane past Clare, Trinity Hall and Michaelhouse. It was soon forced, however, to move to its new quarters to make way for the new royal foundation at King's. Intended originally for the maintenance of 24 scholars in grammar, its revenues were by now sufficient to support only the Master, John Syclyng, and four fellows. Negotiations were begun in the spring of 1505 and on 3 October, 1506, the Master and fellows signed an agreement with the Lady Margaret under which Godshouse was refounded as Christ's College, with revenues sufficient for a Master, twelve fellows and 47 scholars. The statutes, which are the work of Fisher himself, make it clear that the principal purpose of the new foundation was to train secular priests for a life of service to the Church. The fellows were required to be bachelors of arts and were obliged to be in orders at the time of their election or within a year thereafter. They were to devote themselves to the study of theology and philosophy and to the teaching of the liberal arts. Each Sunday and high day they were to sing mattins, mass and vespers and in the course of the week they were to celebrate mass at least five times. They were admonished to pray especially for the Lady Margaret, her son the King and his children forever, and for William Byngham, the first founder of the house. They were forbidden to frequent houses of ill-fame, to bear arms, to associate with loose women, to absent themselves from the college after nine in winter or ten in summer, to keep dogs or birds of prey or to play cards (except in hall at Christmastime). Scholars were required to attend at lectures and at daily masses and to serve in hall and chapel. The Master was charged with the duty of enforcing discipline and of dealing with misdemeanours committed in the college. He was allowed to hold two benefices with cure of souls in addition to his stipend, but he was required to spend at least two months in each quarter in the college and to bind himself not to seek dispensation from any of the obligations imposed by the statutes. Fisher himself was appointed visitor for life, no doubt at the wish of the Lady Margaret, with the authority to make what inquiries were necessary to see that the rules of the society were obeyed. And for his greater ease and convenience in visiting the college, she provided that the rooms set aside for her own use should in her absence be given to Fisher.[2]

For the present, however, Fisher had been provided with quarters at Queens'. For in April of 1505 he was elected by the fellows of the college, apparently at the suggestion of the Lady Margaret, to take the place of Dr. Thomas Wilkinson as President. And so it was from Queens' that he supervised the building of Christ's College, which began the next year. The old buildings of Godshouse were preserved wherever possible. The great gate belonged to Godshouse, as did the north range of the first court, which still houses the chapel. The rest of the court was finished in 1510 and provided accommodation for the fellows and scholars of the new foundation, together with a hall and lodgings for the Master. Above the Master's lodge rooms were set aside for the use of the Lady Margaret, with a private oratory looking into the chapel below. Apart from the later addition of sash windows, the buildings stand today much as Fisher left them.

The Lady Margaret was by now a frequent visitor to the university. She had first come to Cambridge in 1505, when she stayed at Queens', and it was probably on this occasion that she proposed Fisher as successor to Dr. Wilkinson, then President of the college. The King himself visited the university the same year and a year later he returned with his mother and the young Prince Henry, who was soon to succeed his father as King Henry VIII. This was the old King's last visit to Cambridge and he was welcomed by the Chancellor in a formal address delivered in the presence of the assembled dignitaries of the university. It was a moment of rare pageantry and colour, an occasion for flattery and compliment. Nevertheless, Fisher chose to speak earnestly, as he himself put it, not only of the splendour and magnanimity of the King but also of the necessitous condition of the university. He reminded the King of the great work of his predecessors, especially that of the pious, long-suffering Henry VI, last of the Lancastrians. He spoke of King Henry's foundation of Godshouse, now renewed and quickened by the liberality and devotion of the Lady Margaret, and of the magnificent chapel at King's, begun by Henry VI but still unfinished. Since the death of King Henry 35 years before, the five bays of the choir had been carried up to their full height and roofed with timber, but the seven bays to the west still stood open to the sky. It was to the work of completing this superb building that Fisher commended his royal visitor. This, he declared, would be a work worthy of a King and one that no-one but a King could hope to accomplish. The members of the university could offer nothing in return, he confessed, but their loyalty and love.[3]

Fisher's appeal was not to bear fruit for a time, but two years later, not long before his death, Henry decided to crown the achievements of his reign with a gift of unequalled splendour. At his command, work on the chapel began at once and continued for several years. The seven bays of the nave were raised to their present height and the entire chapel roofed with a vault of fan tracery which, in its daring and exuberance, the sheer abundance of spirits displayed in the stonework, had no equal anywhere in England. Next the west front and four corner towers were raised and the tall windows filled with glass. The finished building speaks eloquently of the profound influence on the old King of the devotion of his mother and of John Fisher's dream of a new England in which knowledge and the love of God might no longer be strangers at Court. But it speaks also—in the opulence of its heraldic decoration, in its vainglorious display of wealth—of the magnificence of the House of

Tudor. There is nothing here of the austerity of the man who hoped for so much from the King and from his son; nothing of his sense of the weakness of man and the remoteness of God. For the great new chapel was built above all to celebrate the splendour of the crown. Here God himself was seen to wear the red rose and the white of the House of Tudor. Here the worshipper was made to feel above all the strength, the beauty and the pride of Tudor England.

Henry VII died in the spring of 1509, followed by the Lady Margaret his mother a few weeks later, at the end of June. Fisher was appointed to preach the sermon at the funeral of the King in old St. Paul's, and at the end of July he also preached the month-mind sermon for the Lady Margaret. When he rose to praise the dead King, Fisher had little to say of the triumph of the House of Tudor. All that, he told his hearers, was nothing to the dead man but "smoke that soone vanyssheth, and a shadowe soone passynge awaye." Instead, he spoke of the repentance of the King in his last days and of his faith in the sacraments of the Church, "whiche he receyued all with meruaylous deuocion". He observed the sacrament of penance "with a meruaylous compassyon & flowe of teres, that at some tyme he wepte & sobbed by the space of thre quarters of an houre"; the sacrament of the altar he received "with so grete reuerence that all that were present were astonyed therat, for at his fyrst entre in to the closet where the sacrament was he toke of his bonet & kneled downe vpon his knees & so crept forth deuoutly tyl he came vnto the place selfe where he receyued the sacrament." Two days before his death, the King was "of that feblenes that he myght not receyue it agayn. yet neuertheles he desyred to se the monstraunt wherin it was conteyned, the good fader his confessour in goodly maner as was conuenyent brought it vnto him, he with suche a reuerence, with so many knockynges & betynges of his brest, with so quycke & lyfely a countenaunce, with so desyrous an herte made his humble obeysaunce therunto, & with soo grete humblenes & deuocyon kyssed not the selfe place where *the* blessyd body of our lorde was conteyned, but the lowest parte the fote of the monstraunt, that all that stode aboute hym scarsly myght conteyne them from teres & wepynge." For the sacrament of annealing he "made redy & offred euery parte of his body" as best he could. And as long as he had strength enough, he lifted up his hands to the crucifix held before him and kissed it. "Who may thynke", Fisher asked the hushed assembly, "that in this maner was not perfyte fayth, who may suppose that by this maner of delynge he faythfully beleued not *tha*t the eere of almighty god was open vnto hym & redy to here hym crye for mercy"?[4]

When he came, three months later, to lament the death of the Lady Margaret, Fisher spoke tenderly of the woman who had touched his life so nearly. She had, he said simply, "all *that* was praysable in a woman eyther in soule or in body." She chastened her body with plain living and quickened her spirit with much study and devotion: "euery daye at her vprysynge whiche comynly was not longe after .v. of *the* clok she began certayne deuocyons, & so after theym w*ith* one of her gentylwomen *the* matynes of our lady", after which "w*ith* her chapelayne she sayd also matyns of *the* day. And after *tha*t dayly herde .iiij. or .v. masses vpon her knees, soo contynuynge in her prayers & deuocions vnto *the* hour of dyner". After dinner she would "go her stacyons to thre aulters dayly. Dayly her dyryges & commendacyons she wolde saye. And her euensonges before souper bothe of *the* daye & of our lady, besyde many other prayers & psalters of Dauyd thrugh out *the* yere." And finally, at night, "before she wente to bedde she faylled not to resorte vnto her chapell, & there a large quart*er* of an hour to occupye her in deuocyo*n*s." She entertained strangers who came to her door and fed and clothed those who were in need. Twelve of the neediest she kept in her house, giving them food and lodging, attending them with her own hands when they were sick and comforting them when they died. All England, he said—and we can still hear the pain in his voice—had cause to weep at her death : the poor who received her alms, the students to whom she was like a mother, the priests to whom she gave comfort and succour, the great of the kingdom to whom she was a shining example. All these he asked to pray for her and "for her now at this tyme moost deuoutly to say one Pater noster", beseeching God "*with* moost entyer mindes" to "accepte *tha*t swete soule to his grete mercy".[5]

In these two sermons Fisher had more to lament than the loss of a King who had admired and befriended him, more than the loss of a woman who had been to him, as he said, more than a mother. He mourned the passing of a period in his own life and in the life of England. From now on he would find himself increasingly alone, increasingly cut off from the decisive forces that were to shape and reshape his world. He was forty years old in the summer of 1509 and in a moment, as it seemed, he was no longer young. As the years passed age was to become a part of Fisher. With most men age is an accident of time that slowly colours the qualities most distinctive of their manhood. But with Fisher age was to become essential to his style, essential to the shape and form in which he makes his appeal to history. For, as the years closed over the old King and the Lady Margaret, Fisher spoke increasingly for the past. He was a reformer still—no man of the coming generation would do more than he for the advancement of learning, none believed more firmly than he that all knowledge is knowledge of God. But at the same time he was intensely conservative : he was concerned with life as it was lived in the parish, where men and women were before all else members of the Church and children of God. He could not think of England as another and a better Eden. Others could dream of their sceptred island, set like a precious jewel in the silver sea, and find in the substance of their dream the answer to their deepest and most secret longings. But their dreams meant little to Fisher, and for this his countrymen have been slow to forgive

him. He continued to speak in a language that knew nothing of
countries and Kings, of arms and cloth of gold, but only of
suffering and joy, sin and sorrow, love and fear, God and man.
He began to sound like a stranger.

Chapter 4

But in 1509 the new King was still young—he was under
eighteen when his father died—and, though full of promise, had
not yet discovered the style he was to make his own. He admired
learning and saw himself as a defender of the faith of his
fathers. His reign began with high hopes for liberty and peace
and for progress in the arts. There was gaiety too and a lively
mind, a promise of new life, of life lived to the hilt amid a riot
of colour, good cheer and unreserved magnificence. Despite the
doubts of certain of his councillors as to the lawfulness of such a
marriage, he married Catherine, his brother Arthur's widow,
within a few weeks of his father's death. All England celebrated
the undisputed succession of a prince who united in his own
person the rival claims of Lancaster and York, and in the early
years of the new reign the King and Queen held court with a
splendour unmatched in living memory. One Christmas, the
King being at Eltham, the Master of the Revels prepared a castle
of timber in the King's hall in which William Cornish and the
Children of the Chapel Royal performed the story of Troilus
and Cressida. "After weche komedy playd and doon, an harroud
[herald] tryd and mad an oy that 3 strange knyghts were cum
to do batall with [those] of the sayd kastell; owt [of] weche
yssud 3 men of arms with punchyng spers, redy [to] do feets at
the barryers, inparylled in whyghthe saten and greeyn saten of

Bregys, lynd with gren sarsenet and whyght sarsenet, and the saten cut ther on. To the sayd 3 men of arms enterd other 3 men of arms with lyke wepuns, and inparylled in sclops of reed sarsenet and yelow sarsenet, and with speers mad sartayn strooks; and after that doon, with nakyd swerds fawght a fayer batayll of 12 strooks, and so departyd of foors. Then out of the kastell ysseud a quyen, and with her 6 ladyes, with spechys after the devyes of Mr. Kornyche; and after thys doon, 7 mynstrells inparylled in long garments and bonets to the saam of saten of Bregys, whyght and greeyn, un the walls and towrys of the said kastell played a melodyus song. Then cam out of the kastell 6 lords and gentyllmen inparelled in garments of whyght saten of Bregys and greyn, browdyrd with counterfyt stuf of Flanders making, as brochys, ouchys, spangs and seche; and allso 6 ladyes inparelld in 6 garments of ryght saten, whyght and greeyn, set with H and K of yellow saten, poynted together with poynts of Kolen golld."[1]

In such a setting the lavish figure of the King was irresistible. So great a man as Erasmus hastened to England from Italy at the invitation of his old pupil and patron, Lord Mountjoy, thinking to find a land of milk and honey. Erasmus had first visited England ten years before, when he spent several months at Oxford. There he had met John Colet, who had recently created a stir with his lectures on the epistles of St. Paul. Colet's method was strikingly new. He disregarded the multiple levels of figurative meaning that had attached themselves to the words of Scripture through centuries of interpretation, and directed the attention of his hearers to the words themselves as they were used and understood by St. Paul himself. This, however, raised a disturbing question : how could the true meaning of the Latin text of the Vulgate be determined without knowledge of the Greek original? At that time Greek was almost unknown in England. Ten years before, Thomas Linacre had gone to Italy and on his return had brought with him a knowledge of Greek

medicine and the works of Galen. William Grocyn had studied
Greek in Italy at about the same time and later had lectured in
Greek at Exeter College, Oxford. Erasmus made up his mind to
learn enough Greek to prepare a fresh translation of the New
Testament from the original. His visit to Oxford having brought
him no permanent security for the leisure he needed, he left
England for Paris during the following winter. He was back in
1505, again as a guest of Lord Mountjoy, and it was on this
occasion that he first met Fisher. Fisher, who was then in the
midst of the negotiations leading to the dissolution of Godshouse
and the foundation of Christ's College, invited him to Cambridge, where he was admitted to the degrees of bachelor and
doctor of divinity. The following spring he left again, this time
for Italy, and it was there that, three years later, he received news
of the death of Henry VII. Encouraged by the high hopes entertained by his friends for the new reign, he set out once more for
England.

He reached London in the autumn, where he stayed for more
than a year as a guest of Thomas More. More was then a young
barrister and member of Parliament, a friend of Colet, Linacre
and Grocyn. All three were now in London, Colet as Dean of
St. Paul's, Linacre as a practising physician and lecturer on medicine and Grocyn as vicar of St. Lawrence Jewry. In this congenial
company Erasmus established himself for the winter. He was
befriended by no less a person than William Warham, the Archbishop of Canterbury. There were visits from Fisher, now an old
friend. There was his work: in More's house at Bucklersbury
the *Praise of Folly* slowly took shape, its delightful ironies the
natural fruit of the charm and wit of that brilliant circle. But,
though Warham gave his friend a pension of £20 a year charged
on the living of Aldington in Kent,[2] Erasmus was disappointed
in his hopes for a place at Court or an appointment in the Church
equal to his needs.

It was in these circumstances that Fisher suggested to him

that he come to Cambridge and offer instruction in Greek. And so it was that in the autumn of 1511 Erasmus took up lodgings in Queens' College. He was appointed to the Lady Margaret chair in divinity and began the teaching of Greek. At Oxford there were many who feared that the study of Greek would lead students to question the established text of the New Testament, and they objected noisily to the new learning. Indeed, there was little done at Oxford to carry on the work begun by Linacre and Grocyn until Richard Fox, formerly of Pembroke and now Bishop of Winchester, founded Corpus Christi College in 1516, with readers in both Latin and Greek. There was opposition at Cambridge too, but the support of Fisher, who by now possessed great influence in every quarter of the university, was decisive. Erasmus, it is true, attracted few students, perhaps because he had no love for teaching. Still, he lent his great prestige, at a crucial moment, to the study of Greek. Cambridge, in its turn, gave him the shelter and security he needed to continue his work, and it was while he was at Queens' as a guest of Fisher that he finished the most important of all his books, his edition of the Greek text of the New Testament. This he took with him when he left Cambridge in 1514 and two years later it was published at Basle, to the delight of all his English friends. The Greek New Testament is in a sense the crowning achievement of Fisher's years at Cambridge. His aim was to study and examine all the available texts, to the end that the Scriptures might be more fully and exactly understood. The study of Greek and Latin was for him—as for Colet and Grocyn—the final test of truth.

The study and teaching of Greek were not, however, Fisher's only concerns during these years. Before her death, the Lady Margaret had agreed to establish a second foundation at Cambridge. Fisher's intention was to appropriate the Hospital of St. John, now derelict, and to provide it with new buildings and with revenues adequate to the needs of a second college devoted, like the first, to the training of young men for the priesthood. The Lady Margaret died on 29 June, 1509, leaving a will dated 6 June, 1508. After making various legacies and bequests, she left the residue of her estate to be applied at the discretion of her executors for her soul's health. In a codicil without date she declared her intention with respect to St. John's and directed that certain lands be used for the benefit of the college. She named eight executors of whom Fisher was one. There were also four members of the King's Council—Fox of Winchester, Lord Herbert, the King's chamberlain, Sir Thomas Lovell, treasurer of the King's household and Sir Henry Marney, Chancellor of the Duchy of Lancaster—together with three members of the Lady Margaret's household—Sir John St. John, her chamberlain, Henry Hornby, her chancellor and Sir Hugh Ashton, her comptroller. Most of the executors, however, had little to do with the negotiations that followed. Fox was busy at Oxford with his new foundation of Corpus Christi and none of the other members of the King's Council was seriously interested in the bequest to St. John's. It was Fisher who, acting in the name of the other executors, did the greater part of the work. To him and to him alone the college owes the very fact of its existence.

There were difficulties on every hand. First there was the Bishop of Ely. James Stanley was a stepson of the Lady Margaret and had promised her that he would consent to the dissolution of the Hospital of St. John, which fell within his jurisdiction as Bishop of Ely, in favour of the new college. After her death, however, he changed his mind: "because he hadde not sealide he wolde not performe his promyse and so delaide the mattere a long seasone". "This", as Fisher later recalled, "was the first sore brounte that we hadde and like to haue quailede all the mattere if it hadde not ben wiselie handelide for apon this hong all the rest. Yff this hadde ben clerelie revoikede by hyme we cudde not haue done any thing for that college according to my ladys entente & wyll." Then there were found to be defects in the papal licence that was needed to give effect to the dissolution of the hospital: "when the graunte came home it was founde of no vailow and all by the negligence off our cownsell wich devisede it for the wiche we weare fayne to make anew writinge and to haue better counsell and to sende agayne to the courte off Rome wiche was a grete hinderance and a greate tracke of tyme." There was also the delicate question of the King's licence. Henry VIII was the heir-at-law and could hardly be expected to look with favour on disbursements made out of his grandmother's estate for the benefit of the college. A licence had been obtained by the Lady Margaret, "but she dyede or euer that it was sealyd so that we were fayne to maike anew suyte"; this, as Fisher remembered afterwards, "coste me grete suyte and labor both by myself and by my frendes or that I cudde opteyn it." Even this was not the end of the matter. The executors were forced to have the Lady Margaret's will proved in the Court of Chancery as well as in the Court of Arches. Here the delays and frustrations were almost beyond endurance, for there was "myche tyme and labore" spent on "attendance and ofte resortyng to the chanceler of englonde often having our lernyde counsell to geyder often having the chef iuges advises so many writes so many *dedimus potestatem* to them that war absente that shulde beare witnes in this mattere. So herde it was to gett them to bere this witnes and to be sworne that were then present. So many suytes to the Kinges solicitor the Kinges attorney the Kinges sergeantes withouten whose assentes my lorde chauncelore wolde nothing do oonlle as thei war all presant at euery act to beare recorde. This matere", Fisher wearily recalled, "or it cudde be concludede was a yere and a half in doyng forsoth it was sore laboreos and paynfull vnto me that many tymes I was right sory that euer I toke that besones apone me". There was trouble also with the Lady Margaret's household. When the countess was dying Fisher suggested to her, out of pity for her servants, that such of them as had done her good service might be rewarded at his own discretion and that of the Bishop of Winchester, and she consented. This was later made a pretext by certain of her household for a claim to the whole remainder of the estate. "Wiche putt vs", Fisher confessed, "to a greate trobill. For all that thei cudde ymagen off evyll agaynst me thaie gaue informacion vnto the Kyng and made hime werray hevy lorde agaynst me for the wiche was moche attendance gyvyn and moche suyte I maide for myself or euer that I might be declarede." When they were disappointed in their efforts to secure the residue for themselves, the Lady Margaret's servants demanded that the executors be compelled to show cause why the King should not claim the inheritance without further delay. The revenues in the hands of the executors amounted to £400 (about $40,000) a year, and these they proposed to use to defray the expenses of building and furnishing the college. Their accounts were brought in to be examined by the King's chief auditor, who was "well pleaside with them", Fisher said, and who "thought it resonable that tyll all thinges wer performyde the profectes off the sayde landes shulde remaine vnto the college." But this was not enough. The chief auditor died and his successor reopened the case. By him the executors were, as Fisher ruefully put it, "more straitelie handelide and so long delaide and weriede and fatigate that we must nedes lett the londe go notwithstonding all the right that we hadde there vnto by the grauntes off King Edwarde and off King henry the vij and the declaracione off my ladys wyll and the putting off the sayme londes in feoffamente and allso the prof off the sayde will in the Chancery as strong as cowthe be mayde by any lernyde counsell butt all this wolde not serue vs ther was no remedy but the Kinges counsell wolde take the profectes off these londes for the Kyng".

Left with no means whatever with which to proceed with the building, Fisher was forced to cast about for an alternative source of income. At last he succeeded in obtaining the royal licence to appropriate the revenues of three religious houses, the hospital of Ospringe and the two nunneries of Higham and Bromehall. The hospital at Ospringe in Kent had been founded three hundred years before, during the reign of Henry III, for a Master, three regulars and two secular priests. It had since become derelict and for many years had been in the possession of the crown. In 1515 Henry VIII had granted its revenues to one John Underhill for life. In the next year however, Underhill was persuaded to surrender his benefice to the crown in return for a cash settlement, whereupon the revenues of the hospital, which amounted to £70 a year, were granted to St. John's. This too had been a vexatious affair: "what labor then I hadde", Fisher recalled, "with hyme that was encombent and how long or we cudde establishe and make it sure both by temporall counsell and spirituall. And how often for this matter then I roode both to Ospryng and to London and to my lorde of Canterbury or that I cowthe performe all thinges for the suyrty therof it war to long to reherse."

The two nunneries proved less troublesome. Higham was near Rochester and within Fisher's own diocese, which meant that he could deal with the case himself. It was a sad and simple story. The nunnery had been founded in the twelfth century by King Stephen for sixteen nuns. It was now reduced to three. Two of these, Elizabeth Penney and Godlife Laurence, had been debauched by the Vicar of Higham, by whom the former had borne a child. These two, together with a third, Agnes Swayne, who was apparently innocent of the grosser sins of her sisters, consented to resign their interest in the revenues of the nunnery. In return they were placed in other houses where they were maintained for life at the expense of the college. The nunnery at Bromehall was in the diocese of Salisbury, a journey of over a hundred miles from Rochester, and Fisher left most of the arrangements to the Master of the college. This too was slow work and cost "moche payne and labor", as Fisher remembered.

The Master had to make "many iorneys" to Bromehall, which was a three or four days' ride from Cambridge, and also to "my lorde [the Bishop] off Salsebury wiche was ordinary off a bene-fice to them approperde wiche thinges he dyde with moche lease charge that I cowde haue done, and therfor I dide commyt it vnto his wisdome." The negotiations were prolonged and were not completed until late in 1521, when the prioress and two re-maining sisters resigned their interest to the King, who in turn granted the revenues of the nunnery to St. John's.[3]

During all this time Fisher had much to do in Cambridge. A charter for the new college was obtained on 9 April, 1511 and Robert Shorton named first Master. Building began that same spring. The old chapel of the hospital of St. John was first re-modelled, then new buildings were added to form a court on the south side of the chapel. A great gate was built to give access to the college from the town, similar to that at Christ's but even more sumptuous. For five years the work continued until at last, one day in late July of 1516, the college was ready to be opened.

That summer day was pregnant with meaning for Fisher. As he walked in procession across the beautiful courtyard to the chapel, he knew that he had succeeded against all odds. He had fashioned an idea and made it live in flesh and blood. All around him was the tangible evidence of his triumph. The soft pink brick, warmed by the sun, spoke then as it does now of a charity and humanity made real by the very presence of such beauty.[4] For Fisher there was never to be another moment like this. Never again was he to feel the exhilaration of knowing himself equal to anything, with strength enough to shape the world after his own image. The indifference of the King and the Court to what he had sought to do at St. John's was a token of what was to come. But of that there was nothing to be seen on that splendid summer day. Fisher read out the King's licence, the royal charter and the papal bull. The chapel was consecrated, 31 fellows were sworn to obey the statutes and a new Master, Alan Percy, was named to succeed Robert Shorton.

The statutes had been drawn up by Fisher himself. Like those provided earlier for Christ's College, which they closely resemble, the statutes governing St. John's are a model of academic discipline. The three objects of the college are to encourage virtue, to nourish faith and to increase the knowledge of God. The fellows and scholars are to rise at dawn, when the great bell is to ring out every day in term. In the evening the gates are to be locked at dusk. No fellow is to leave the college except in company, nor visit a woman more than four times a quarter without permission of the Master. No women are to be admitted to chambers except to nurse the sick. No fellow is to keep hawks or dogs or to play cards or dice except in hall at Christmas. Scholars are to be fined or even whipped for missing lectures or exercises. They are to attend mass on weekdays and on Sundays and high days as well. No scholar is to eat or drink in the company of a woman unless with a fellow or by leave of the Master. Scholars must be candidates for the priesthood and they must be able to speak and understand Latin. Their assignments are to include regular lectures in arithmetic, geometry, perspective and cosmography, as well as sophistry, logic and philosophy. Theology is to be the principal study of the fellows, though Greek and Hebrew are also to be taught.[5]

In many ways St. John's, like Christ's, was a typical school of its kind. Similar schools had flourished for centuries on the Continent, from which they had been introduced into England in 1274, when Walter de Merton, also a Bishop of Rochester, had founded Merton College at Oxford. The program of studies is on the whole (except for the omission of music) much like that of the traditional quadrivium, with the addition of certain elements (such as sophistry and logic) from the trivium. But in other ways these two colleges faithfully expressed the private convictions of one man. Here is the unyielding discipline so characteristic of

Fisher, accepted almost without comment as a normal and necessary part of life. Discipline with him was the essential condition
of all learning and virtue. Living as he did among princes of the
Church who were as often as not no strangers to the delights of
the flesh they condemned in others, he was convinced of the need
to insist on rigorous conditions of life and work. Here is the un-
shakeable will and the untiring patience that formed so persistent a habit of his mind. And here also is the readiness to experi-
ment, to try new methods where the old will not do. Fisher had
introduced the study of Greek to Cambridge when he invited
Erasmus in 1511 to take up residence at Queens'; now at St.
John's he made room for the study of both Greek and Hebrew.
The importance of Hebrew to an understanding of the Scriptures had long been recognized. At the Council of Vienne in
1312 a papal constitution issued by Clement V provided for the
teaching of Hebrew and eight years later the Convocation of
Canterbury agreed to a tax of a farthing in the pound on all
benefices in the southern province for the maintenance of a lecturer in Hebrew at Oxford. In spite of this, however, Hebrew
was still almost unknown in England. The first to teach it at
Cambridge was Robert Wakefield, who began by working with
Fisher in private (perhaps about 1516) and who later gave lectures in public. It is likely enough that Wakefield came to Cambridge at Fisher's invitation; certainly he was encouraged by
Fisher in every way possible while at the university. At St. John's
there is still preserved the copy of a letter that reveals something
of the working relationship between the two men: "After my
ryght hartty Recomendacions wher master Wakfeld this berare
ys myndid to goo by yonde the sea to thentent thatt he may be
the more expolite & perfite in the tonge of hebrew I haue grantid
hyme the emolumentes of his Colleg duryng the space of two
years next ensewyng trostyng thatt at his retourne he shall be
more able to perfite other in the sayme learnyng and to doo
honoure both to your Colleg and to the hoolle reame. Thus fare

ye weale at Rochestre by your old assured frend Jo Roffes.'"[6] Not many years later, Wakefield was to place his knowledge of Hebrew at the service of the King, whose cause he chose to defend against his old friend with all the bitter envy of the ungrateful.

Chapter 5

For the time being, however, Fisher's world remained serene. Beyond the horizon, it is true, there were disturbing events that could not be altogether ignored. Pope Julius II had taken the field in the summer of 1510 against the French in Italy and the following April Louis XII of France had retaliated by calling for a general council to depose the Pope and reform the Church. On 16 May a number of disaffected cardinals, with the consent of both the Emperor Maximilian and the King of France, published an invitation to a general council to meet at Pisa on 1 September, 1511. Julius answered by summoning a Lateran Council to meet at Rome under his own auspices on 19 April, 1512. Henry VIII, still only twenty years old and in the third year of his reign, was on the best of terms with the Pope, from whom he had only that year received a golden rose, together with a cardinal's hat for Christopher Bainbridge, Archbishop of York and ambassador of England to the Holy See. He responded to the Julian bull by appointing several delegates to the Lateran Council, one of whom was Fisher.

For a man who had never been beyond the sea, who had spent his years as boy and man in the study of books, who knew nothing of England itself but the lonely moors and dales of Yorkshire, the fens of Cambridge, the farms and orchards of Kent and the cries of London, what a heady prospect of warm sun, blue skies, brilliant colour and, at the centre of it all, the symbols of adoration! Henry Hornby, the Lady Margaret's chancellor and an old friend, wrote to congratulate him on his appointment and to offer him a servant for the journey, with his best gelding to carry him.[1] Final arrangements were made : the property held by Fisher as executor for the Lady Margaret was delivered to Hornby and Ashton to administer in his absence; proxies were named to attend to the affairs of the diocese of Rochester; a grant of £800 was approved to cover an embassy of 160 days. And then suddenly, for reasons no longer known, the appointment was cancelled. Fisher never made the journey to the Holy City and took no part in the Lateran Council, which assembled in the spring of 1512 and sat until 1517.

Instead he received a summons of a different kind. Julius had made his overtures to Henry in the hope that England would renew her long-standing hostility to France and so check the French advance in Italy. He was not disappointed. On 13 November, 1511 Henry joined Ferdinand and the Republic of Venice in a Holy League to defend the papacy against France. Before the end of the month writs were issued for the first Parliament of the new reign, and on 4 February, 1512 Fisher took his seat for the first time among the spiritual peers in the House of Lords. There he learned that England was once again committed to a policy of war with France. Revenues were needed and two fifteenths and two tenths were duly granted. Fisher was one of those, together with Sir George Neville, Lord Burgavenny, and John Brooke, Lord Cobham, appointed to collect the subsidy in the fifteen hundreds of the lathe of Aylesford in Kent.[2]

That June Henry landed 10,000 men in France, where they remained before Bayonne until October, while Ferdinand took advantage of the opportunity to seize Navarre. The next spring a new army was landed in Calais and before the summer was over the King himself had led it to victory at Thérouanne and Tournai. A treaty was signed with Ferdinand and Maximilian in October, binding the three signatories to resume the war with France in 1514. But before the winter was out both Ferdinand and Maximilian were secretly negotiating with Louis and in August a treaty of peace between England and France was sealed by the marriage of Louis to Henry's sister Mary. The holy war had come to nothing. The papal states were still menaced by the French claims in Italy and England was left with little but its captive towns and the promise of a yearly indemnity.

Fisher must have been glad to turn his attention to other matters. Erasmus had been in residence at Cambridge during the two years of the French war and he relied on Fisher to relieve his needs when others failed. From his house at Lambeth, where he lived while attending at Court, Fisher found time to send his friend aid and encouragement. "I beg you", he wrote, "not to be offended at my not writing, when I sent to you the other day. The man was in a hurry to leave town, and I met him as I went out of my house. So, as I could not write, I gave him the small present which you asked; but not", he hastened to explain, "from that fund, which you suppose to be in my hands and to be of no small amount. Believe me, whatever people say, that I have no money entrusted to me, which can be applied at my own discretion. The use of that fund is so prescribed that it cannot be changed, however much we might wish it. For myself I look upon you as necessary to the University, and will not suffer you to want, so long as there is anything to spare out of my own poor means. At the same time I will endeavour, whenever an opportunity may arise, to ask for the help of others, in case my own should not be enough. Your friend,—I might say my friend,—Lord Mountjoy, I am sure, will not forget you, if he has made any promise of help, and I will willingly remind him of it, as he is now at Court ."[3] In the event Erasmus left Cambridge, as we have seen, after a stay of only three years, having gained little from the teaching of Greek or the help of his friends in high places.

It was at this time that Fisher suggested that Wolsey be offered the position of Chancellor of the university to which he himself had been elected annually since 1504. The war with France had brought little comfort to the Pope and earned the King little but the empty honour of a sword and cap of maintenance, conferred upon him by His Holiness. But one thing it had done : it had made the name of Thomas Wolsey. The planning and execution of the enterprise in all its infinite detail had been his : the buying of provisions, the making of arms, the procurement of stores and equipment of all sorts, the regulation of expenditure. He had earned the gratitude of the King and the King was not slow to repay him. In 1514 he was elevated to the rank of bishop and given the rich see of Lincoln as well as that of Tournai, now in Henry's gift as a prize of war. A few months later Cardinal Bainbridge died at Rome and the new Bishop of Lincoln was named by the King to succeed him as Archbishop of York. Even this was not enough for Wolsey, for almost at once he began negotiating at Rome for the cardinal's hat, which he received the following autumn. That same year he succeeded Warham as Lord Chancellor and began to press for an appointment (which came in 1517) as papal legate, an office that enabled him to govern the internal affairs of the Church without reference to the Archbishop of Canterbury.[4] It may have been at this time that Fisher was offered the bishopric of Lincoln, vacated by Wolsey's translation to York, but if so he refused. He had no wish to leave Rochester for the splendours of Lincoln. Nor was he reluctant to give up his position at Cambridge to make way for the royal favourite, if he thought that such a man as Wolsey, being closer than he to the ear of the King, could better serve the interests of the university. And so it was that he agreed to leave in the spring of 1514. The Vice-Chancellor had written to him on 24 May, in the name of the university, to ask his consent to the election of Wolsey. Fisher had agreed without hesitation. As it turned out, however, Wolsey was looking for a brighter jewel than Cambridge. He declined the appointment, pleading the business of the King, and Fisher resumed his former position, which he held for the rest of his life.[5]

He was soon to have another chance to walk in Wolsey's train. The red hat was despatched from Rome early in October of 1515 and arrived in Calais a month later. Great preparations were made for its reception. On 15 November the prothonotary Bonifacio, who was charged with bringing the hat from Rome, together with a ring and the bull of appointment, reached London. He was met at Westminster stairs and escorted in state to the Abbey. There he delivered the hat to the Abbot of St. Peter's, Westminster, who carried it in procession to the high altar. On Sunday the 18th the Cardinal came to the Abbey, where mass was sung by the Archbishop of Canterbury, assisted by the Bishops of Lincoln and Exeter, the Archbishops of Armagh and Dublin, the Bishops of Winchester, Durham, Norwich, Ely and Llandaff, the Abbots of Westminster, St. Albans, Bury, Glastonbury, Reading, Gloucester, Winchcombe and Tewkesbury and the Prior of Coventry. Fisher was there too in that brilliant assembly: he bore the cross before the Archbishop of Canterbury during mass. His friend Colet, Dean of St. Paul's, preached the sermon. The bull of appointment was read out by John Voysey, Dean and later Bishop of Exeter. The Cardinal prostrated himself before the altar as a sign of his submission to the will of God. The Archbishop of Canterbury raised him up and placed the hat upon his head. The *Te Deum* was sung, after which the recessional began. As he walked in solemn procession past the King and Queen, it was Wolsey of York, not Warham of Canterbury, who was preceded by the cross and mace, symbols of supreme authority in Church and State.[6]

Henry's vigorous if quixotic prosecution of the French war in support of the papacy and the elevation of Wolsey, a churchman, to the highest office in the kingdom might well have led his contemporaries to believe that the young King would prove a faithful friend to the Church. If so they were mistaken. The campaigns in France appealed more to Henry's vanity than to his piety. They were meant to show the world that he had come of age and was to be treated by the rulers of Europe as a man among men. The elevation of Wolsey was not so much a mark of respect for the Church as a compliment to the remarkable skill of the royal servant in promoting the interests of the State. An ugly incident that occurred shortly before Christmas of 1514 plainly showed the realities of the situation. Richard Hunne, a merchant tailor of London, was found on the morning of 5 December hanging by the neck, dead, in a cell in the Lollards' Tower at St. Paul's. At the time of his death, Hunne was in the custody of Richard Fitzjames, Fisher's predecessor in the see of Rochester and now Bishop of London. More than three years before, Hunne had buried an infant child in the parish of St. Mary Matfelon, Whitechapel. The parish priest, one Thomas Dryffeld, had claimed the child's bearing-sheet as a mortuary fee and Hunne had refused to let him have it. The priest brought suit and in May of 1512 was awarded the customary fee after a hearing in the archiepiscopal court at Lambeth. The following January Hunne sued William Marshall, the assistant priest of his parish, for refusing to admit him to evensong and, while this suit was still before the courts, applied for a writ of *praemunire* against Dryffeld on the ground that an action for payment in an ecclesiastical court was injurious to the royal prerogative.[7] Thereupon he was arrested on suspicion of heresy and, after a search of his house turned up a number of heretical books, he was committed for trial before the Bishop of London. He was awaiting trial when he was found dead in his cell. Eleven days later he was tried posthumously by the Bishop of London and found guilty; on the 20th his body was burned at Smithfield. Meanwhile, an inquest had been held to examine the evidence and determine the cause of Hunne's death. The coroner's jury reported that, on entering the Lollard's Tower, they found the victim hanging from a silken girdle fastened to an iron staple. There was no stool nearby that he could have used in hanging himself. Blood, they said, was found on his chest and on the floor in the corner of the room, several feet from where the body was found. His wrists were wrung and had apparently been bound. The jury concluded that Hunne had been overcome and strangled, and then strung up by his murderers to give the appearance of suicide. Suspicion pointed to William Horsey, chancellor of the Bishop of London, in whose keeping Hunne had been placed. A man named Charles Joseph, who kept watch on the prisoner, testified at the inquest that on the evening of Sunday, 4 December he accompanied Horsey and John Spaldyng, a bell-ringer who looked after the keys, to the cell in which Hunne was confined, where he saw Spaldyng and Horsey murder the prisoner and then hang him up by the neck.[8]

What really happened to Richard Hunne we shall probably never know. It is difficult to see why the bishop or his chancellor —even supposing that they had no scruples in such a case— would have troubled to murder a man they could deal with more conveniently in other ways. Hunne had already been accused of heresy and the bishop had only to give judgment against him (as in fact he did) before exposing him to the humiliation of confessing his errors in public and making due satisfaction for the wrongs he had done. If he refused, he would be punished by the secular authorities at the stake. Hunne could no doubt foresee the outcome of his trial and that being so might well have wished to anticipate the event by suicide. Nor is it surprising that a jury of London merchants, angered by undoubted injustice to one of their number—for, whatever the provocation they had to endure, the bishop and his chancellor had, in law, slight grounds for a charge of heresy—should have found the evidence necessary for a verdict of murder. However that may be, the incident was enough to inflame the citizenry of London. The charge against Horsey was dropped but that did not put an end to the matter. When a new Parliament assembled on 5 February, a bill was brought down to limit the privileges hitherto enjoyed by persons in holy orders convicted of a felony. The previous Parliament had adopted a bill providing that no person guilty of a murder or other felony should be entitled to claim benefit of clergy—that is, the right to be tried by their spiritual superiors outside the lay courts—unless they were within the orders of priest or deacon.[9] This act was now up for renewal. There was determined opposition in the House of Lords, where the spiritual peers still held a slim majority, and no action had been taken when Parliament was prorogued on 5 April. Advocates of the bill prevailed on the King, however, to take the matter into his own hands. Accordingly, a hearing was staged before the King in the great hall of the Blackfriars. The Abbot of Winchcombe spoke for the clergy, while the case for lay jurisdiction was argued by Dr. Henry Standish, Warden of the Greyfriars and later Bishop of St. Asaph. When Parliament reassembled on 12 November, Standish was summoned before Convocation and required to affirm or deny what he had said the previous April as to the jurisdiction of laymen over spiritual persons. Afraid to reaffirm the position he had taken at the Blackfriars hearing, and unwilling to deny it, Standish appealed to the King for protection. A second hearing was convened, at which Convocation was found guilty of a *praemunire*. The action of the King was decisive. Though Parliament rose on the 22nd without having renewed the act of 1512, the case against Standish was dropped and the clergy were forced in their turn to sue for the royal pardon.

Throughout these extraordinary proceedings, Fisher was in his place in the upper house, but what part if any he played in them we do not know.[10] The issues raised by the death of Richard Hunne were stark enough and the fact that the Lords had refused to renew the act of 1512 did little to alter the situation. Fisher must have been mortified by the way in which Hunne's case was handled by the Bishop of London. At the same time he must have recognized that the wrongs suffered by Hunne were little more than a pretext for those whose real purpose was not to remedy injustice but to augment the authority of the lay courts. If he felt grief and shame, he must also have felt a new and disturbing anxiety: did the King propose to revoke the customary liberties of the Church whenever he pleased, on the grounds that they were injurious to the royal prerogative?

Chapter 6

Despite these anxieties, there were still moments when the gathering forces of history could be arrested in a ritual gesture of timeless significance. One such occurred in the spring of 1516, when the King's sister Mary, widowed Queen of France and newly married to the Duke of Suffolk, gave birth to her eldest son, Henry Earl of Lincoln. The young Earl of Lincoln was fourth in line of succession to the throne of England, after his month-old cousin Mary, daughter of Henry and Catherine, and his other cousins, James V of Scotland and Margaret Douglas. Two days later, on 13 March, he was nobly christened, in the presence of the King and Queen, Cardinal Wolsey and Thomas Ruthal, Bishop of Durham. Fisher was chosen to perform the ceremony. The godmother was Queen Catherine and Wolsey and the King were the godfathers. The King himself gave the child his name.[1]

Meanwhile, in the spring of 1515, Erasmus had returned to

England for a brief stay and Fisher had invited him to Rochester. A few months later the New Testament finally made its appearance. It had been finished before Erasmus left Cambridge in 1514, but he had spent the greater part of the next two years at Basle preparing the finished work for the press. In June of 1516 Erasmus sent Fisher a copy, with a few lines explaining the dedication. He had intended to dedicate the book to Fisher, but at the last moment, he explained, he had decided that it would be wiser to present the work to Leo X, who had succeeded Julius at Rome three years before; and "such is your kindness and your wisdom too", he added, "that I do not doubt you will approve what we have done." No doubt Fisher knew as well as Erasmus the importance of Leo's interest and support; it must have saddened him nonetheless to find that the years spent by Erasmus at Cambridge, warmed and brightened as they had been by the sympathy and mutual understanding of the two friends, had been ignored. So it was that the part played by Fisher in the most important achievement of the New Learning—the preparation of accurate texts of Scripture from the Greek and Hebrew originals—was all but forgotten.[2] Fisher himself was not proficient in Greek; indeed he was at this very moment trying to prevail upon another of his friends, William Latimer of All Souls, to help him in the study of the language.[3] But he had been one of the first to see the need for improved textual criticism, and he was among the first in England to welcome the New Testament sent him by Erasmus. It arrived as Fisher was preparing to set out from Rochester for Cambridge and the opening of St. John's College, but he found time to look into the book and to send off a message full of the excitement of the moment. "Though I am hampered", he wrote, "by a great deal of business, and preparing to go to Cambridge for the opening of the College, which is to take place at last, I do not like to let your Peter go back to you without a letter from me. You have made me your debtor in a vast amount of thanks by presenting me with the New Testament translated by you out of the Greek. As soon as I received it, and had seen the notes in several places, in which you extol your Maecenas of Canterbury"—this was Warham, to whom Erasmus owed his English pension—"with such ample praises, I went off to him myself, and showed him those passages. When he had read them, he promised that he would do a great deal for you, and exhorted me, if ever I wrote to you, to persuade you to return. And indeed I do not doubt, that if you do so, he will be more liberal to you than ever." The language of compliment, whether addressed to a Pope or an Archbishop, came readily to Erasmus, but the affection and loyalty of his old friend at Rochester he knew he could have for nothing. "Take care of your health", Fisher ends, "and hasten your return to us, which will be welcome to everybody."[4] Erasmus accepted the invitation and that summer spent a few weeks in England, but though he was received at Court and handsomely entertained, he could not be persuaded to prolong his stay. Before he returned to the Continent he spent ten days at Rochester with Fisher, but even there he did not enjoy himself. No doubt his quarters in the bishop's palace were uncomfortable and ill-furnished. Fisher himself ate little and slept on a pallet on the floor. Such hardships were never congenial to Erasmus, who was always exceedingly careful of his own comforts. Soon after he arrived he wrote to a friend in London that he had often regretted his decision to stop in Rochester.[5] But if his quarters were disagreeable the company at any rate was good. He found that Fisher had made considerable progress in learning Greek, even without the help of Latimer.[6] And he enjoyed the remarkable success of his New Testament. His friends—men like Colet, Latimer, More and Fisher—were all delighted with it. The Archbishop of Canterbury had given it his approval and a number of the bishops, among whom opposition might have been expected, had received it warmly. Erasmus could hardly have asked for more.

The winter that followed was quieter than most for Fisher. Parliament had been dissolved, and was not to be recalled until 1523. The events surrounding the death of Richard Hunne and the trial of Dr. Horsey no longer disturbed the surface of public life as they had during the session of 1515. The tedious work of administering the Lady Margaret's estate had been finished at last and her colleges established on a secure footing. For the first time since his appointment as Bishop of Rochester a dozen years before, Fisher was free of care. Much of that winter he spent in his study at Rochester, where he could find shelter from the cold and the fog in the comfortable intimacy of like minds and shared ideas. More had sent him a copy of the works of Reuchlin, and not long afterwards Reuchlin himself asked Erasmus to send his friend a copy of the *De arte cabalistica*, which had appeared only that year.[7] Reuchlin was fourteen years older than Fisher and had spent most of his life in the study of Greek and Hebrew. In 1506 he had published a Hebrew grammar and lexicon that quickly became a standard authority. Fisher must at once have recognized him as one of that small group of liberal humanists who, like himself, were working to renew and purify the text of Scripture. In his last years Reuchlin became increasingly preoccupied with a system he had devised to explain the natural world as a system of signs expressing the nature of God. But what Fisher thought of these ideas, which were developed at length in the *De arte cabalistica*, we do not know, for Colet, to whom More showed the book before sending it on to Fisher, kept it to read himself—though he later admitted that he could not understand what Reuchlin was getting at.[8] Besides the works of Reuchlin there was of course the New Testament of Erasmus, which Fisher now had time to read at leisure. There was also a last visit from Erasmus himself, who spent a short time in England during April of 1517.

Fisher saw him only for a moment before he set out again for the Continent on a journey that almost ended in disaster. On 1 May Erasmus was caught in a storm off Boulogne, where he eventually reached shore in a small boat. The two friends never met again and in a few short years the world they both cherished—a world of humane learning and progressive enlightenment—was torn apart by the impatient, irresistible forces of history. But neither forgot the days and hours they had spent together, nor the delight and comfort each had given the other. "As I was sorry to hear of the danger you incurred in your voyage", Fisher wrote a few weeks later, "I am no less rejoiced at your having come out of it safe and sound. But it was only right that you should be punished for running away in such a hurry from me, with whom you might have rested secure from sea and storm.

"That Cabalistical Book, which you say was presented to me by Reuchlin, has not yet reached me. Your friend More has sent the letter, but still detains the book in his old way; as he did before with the *Oculare Speculum*. I am very much obliged to you, Erasmus, both for your kind attentions, and especially because you take such pains to keep up Reuchlin's recollection of me. I have the greatest regard for him, and beg you, in the meantime, until I have read the book and can write to him about it, to let him know, that I feel as grateful to him as I can possibly conceive.

"The New Testament, translated by you for the common benefit of all, cannot give offence to any wise person; when you have not only cleared up innumerable passages by your erudition, but have also supplied a very complete [commentary on] the whole work; so that it may now be read and understood by every one with much more satisfaction and pleasure than it could before. But I very much fear", he added tactfully, "the printer has been often napping; for in practising the reading of St. Paul according to the rules you laid down, I have myself often found, that Greek expressions, and sometimes entire sentences are omitted. I have you to thank, that I am able to some extent to guess where the Greek does not quite correspond with the Latin. I only wish I had been permitted to have you for a few months as a teacher. Farewell and be happy."[9]

In the fall of 1517 an event occurred that shattered the calm of Fisher's life and permanently changed the shape of his world. To raise money for the building of St. Peter's in Rome, Leo X issued a plenary indulgence, according to which those who sought remission of their sins were to be absolved on payment of a stated fee. The Church had long held that absolution consisted of three elements: repentance, confession and satisfaction or penance. The purchase of an indulgence, like the payment of a fine, was intended to take the place of the customary act of penance. It did not take away the need for repentance or confession. In the course of time, however, the purpose and meaning of indulgences were lost and in the minds of ordinary people the simple act of payment came to seem in itself sufficient for the remission of sin. It was this that caused reformers to cry out against the practice of selling absolution at so much a shilling. Foremost among them was Martin Luther, who on 31 October, 1517, posted his 95 theses against indulgences on the church door at Wittenberg.

Fisher was soon made to feel the significance of what had happened.[10] As Chancellor, he caused copies of the indulgence to be set up in public places throughout Cambridge. Cambridge was soon to become the centre of religious controversy, known for radicals like Thomas Bilney and Robert Barnes who met secretly at the White Horse Inn, and the announcement of the indulgence immediately aroused opposition within the university. One night someone wrote a ribald jest across a copy of the announcement. "Beatus vir", he wrote, "cuius est nomen domini spes eius, et non respexit vanitates et insanias falsas istas": blessed is he who puts his trust in God and not in vain trifles

47

like these. By adding a single word at the end, the unknown writer—believed at the time to be a radical priest named Peter de Valence—neatly adapted the Scriptural text to his own purposes. It was a piece of effrontery that might best have been ignored or overlooked. Enquiries were made, however, in an effort to discover who had committed the offence. When these proved unsuccessful, the university was assembled in convocation and the offender called upon by the Chancellor to confess his fault and seek forgiveness. His appeal was greeted with silence. Fisher had had to deal before now with acts of disobedience in his own diocese, but this was something new and disturbing. There was nothing casual or careless about it, nor did the offender appear to be ignorant or foolish. On the contrary, there was every indication that he knew very well what he was doing. His jest, if it was a jest, was of a peculiar and sinister kind. For it questioned nothing less, as Fisher must have seen at once, than the authority of the Church to absolve the penitent of his sins. How could such a question be endured, as long as the Church sought and professed to bring sinners to repentance? And so a day was appointed for the publication of a bill of excommunication against the guilty person. When the day came, Fisher appealed once again to the offender to declare himself and confess his fault. After a long silence, he took up the bill of excommunication and began to read it aloud. But before he had read more than a few lines he broke off, unable to bring himself to continue. He appointed a third day for the reading of the bill, and when that day came he rose and read it through with tears in his eyes. Never before had he been required to declare that any man was outside the community of the Church and beyond the reach of the love of God.

Such an act was, of course, no answer to the larger questions raised by the existence of dissent. Lutheranism spread rapidly in England after 1517.[11] For Fisher this was deeply shocking. All his life he had dealt with religious experience as a form of knowledge. The authority of the Church rested in the first instance on its knowledge of God and its first duty was to teach the truth to the children of men. Hence Fisher's passionate concern for teaching and his own ardent desire to learn. Everything he did at Cambridge—the endowing of a chair in divinity, the provision of lectureships in Greek and Hebrew, the founding of Christ's College and the College of St. John—was done on the strength of his underlying belief that only ignorance stood between man and his salvation.

Now for the first time he was compelled to recognize a new kind of problem. He had always believed that the New Learning would lead inward to a central body of truth, around which all men of good will could unite. They had all been convinced of this—not only Fisher and More but also men like Colet, Grocyn and Latimer, and even the urbane and sceptical Erasmus. But what if it should be otherwise than they had supposed? What if the New Learning should instead lead away from the central truths long cherished by the Church, and create a new world in which each man was free to fashion his own idols? What then should he do? For Fisher, much more was at stake than the authority, still less the prestige and revenues, of the Church. What was at stake was the communion of all believers united as children of one God.[12]

From now on Fisher was increasingly absorbed in controversy. His first work, a treatise on the seven penitential psalms, had been published at the suggestion of the Lady Margaret in 1509. In it Fisher had set forth and explained the traditional doctrine of atonement as it was taught by the Church. Absolution, he had explained, is a work that can be accomplished by the grace of God alone. But to receive what is freely offered to all men in the sacrifice of Christ, the penitent must confess and make satisfaction for the sins he has committed. This is the familiar union of sign and reality, love and faith, man and God so characteristic of traditional teaching. For the book was intended above all as a manual of instruction. In this first work, Fisher had been content to explain and to teach. But now, eight years later, the position was altogether different: for the first time he was forced to persuade and convince.

It began with a book published in 1517 by Jacques Lefèvre, or Jacob Faber as he was usually called, on the identity of Mary Magdalen. Faber, who a few years later made the first French translations of the Old and New Testament, argued that Mary Magdalen, the sinful woman who washed Jesus' feet with tears and anointed them with oil[13] and Mary the sister of Martha, were three different persons. Tradition had always held that they were one and the same person. Fisher was less concerned with the facts of the case than with the careless way in which, he felt, Faber had handled the existing authorities on the subject. During the winter of 1518 he prepared a short answer to Faber's book that was published at Paris the following February. Others were already in the field with replies that appeared at Paris in August and December while Fisher's work was in the press. During the summer of 1519 Fisher was answered by Josse van Clichtove, one of Faber's students who that year succeeded Wolsey in the bishopric of Tournai,[14] and by Faber himself. Before the end of the year Fisher published replies to them both.[15]

Despite the distractions of the controversy with Faber, Fisher managed to keep in touch with his friends. And he was still at work on his Greek. Latimer was reluctant to teach him, as before, excusing himself on the grounds that he was familiar only with the classical idiom. But he saw clearly enough the importance of Fisher's interest in Greek studies and remarked in a letter to Erasmus that with the encouragement and protection of such a man the study of Greek had nothing to fear from its detractors in England. He suggested that Fisher should send to Italy for a teacher to complete his program of studies. Erasmus, however, was of the opinion that Greek was now better taught

in England than in Italy.[16] Early in March of 1518 he wrote to
Fisher himself. He needed a good, quiet horse, he said, and he
hoped his friend would send him one. He also complained of
ill-treatment at the hands of Faber, though he was later to regret
the severity of Fisher's criticism of Faber's book on the three
Magdalens. And he hoped Fisher would help him to correct
the first edition of the New Testament, since he was about to
start work on a new printing.[17] Fisher no doubt did what he
could. He had already made note of the mistakes he had found
in the New Testament and as for the horse he had long since
learned to be patient with the innumerable wants of his friend.

Chapter 7

In the summer of 1518 Fisher was called upon to take part in
another of the gaudy and splendid pageants arranged by Wolsey to display the majesty of a cardinal of the Church of Rome.
Leo had despatched Cardinal Lorenzo Campeggio to England
as a papal legate, in the hope of enlisting the aid of Henry VIII
against the Turk. Wolsey, however, had persuaded the King to
detain Campeggio at Calais until the Pope elevated the English
cardinal to an equal rank and dignity. And so it was that, less
than three years after his elevation to the cardinalate, Wolsey
was made a legate *a latere* with sovereign authority in the English Church. It was an occasion to be celebrated with appropriate magnificence, as the arrival of the red hat had been three
years before. Campeggio landed at Sandwich on 14 July and
was received by the Bishop of Chichester, Lord Burgavenny and
others, who conducted him to Canterbury. There he was met in
the Cathedral by the Archbishop, accompanied by the Bishop

of Rochester and the Abbot of St. Alban's. He rested at Canterbury for two days, after which he rode in company to Rochester, where he dined in state with the bishop. The next day he resumed his progress towards London. Two miles outside the city he was met by representatives of Church and State, who escorted him the rest of the way, attended by a cavalcade of 4000 horse. The streets were thronged and cannon sounded in the distance. A few days later he was received by the King at Greenwich, in the presence of the leading bishops and peers of the realm. It was a splendid moment, but the splendour of the occasion deceived no-one into believing that the King was ready to take arms against the Turk. Nothing came of Campeggio's mission and he returned to Rome leaving Wolsey in sole possession of the coveted dignities of his new style and title.[1]

Wolsey knew well enough that there had been a loosening of discipline among churchmen and he knew as well as Fisher, though he had less stomach for the task, that the English Church must be schooled once again in simplicity and purity of life. A few months after the departure of Campeggio, in October of 1518, peace was concluded with France and the Cardinal found leisure at last for the less urgent matters of the spirit. An opportunity presented itself the following February. Warham had summoned a convocation of the southern province to meet at St. Paul's to consider a program of reform.[2] Wolsey at once wrote to him to complain of the affront to his dignity as a legate, asserting that the authority to summon a convocation belonged to him alone. He went so far as to demand that the Archbishop appear before him at Richmond to explain himself. Warham answered tartly that the Cardinal was interfering in matters well known to be within the jurisdiction of the Archbishop of Canterbury; and when he received a peremptory summons to appear the next day at Lambeth he answered as patiently as he could that because of the distance and his age he would need a little longer.[3] Nevertheless, Wolsey had his way and the two provinces of Canterbury and York met in a joint convocation at Westminster.

Little was accomplished in the sessions that followed. What indeed could be expected of a convocation summoned as a matter of prerogative by the very man in whom the evils the clergy were called on to condemn were grown most rank? Who could speak of discipline in the presence of a cardinal who kept a concubine and recognized a son and daughter, who was to enjoy the revenues of the see of York for sixteen years before he entered his diocese, who had held the bishopric of Tournai as a prize of war and was to make himself Abbot of St. Alban's— the richest abbey in England—though he was not a monk, who had himself made in turn Bishop of Lincoln, Bishop of Bath and Wells, Bishop of Durham and Bishop of Winchester, though he had no intention whatever of performing the duties of a bishop in any of his sees? A number of the bishops—men like Thomas Ruthal of Durham and Nicholas West, who in 1515 had succeeded James Stanley at Ely—were in fact courtiers who had earned their position in the Church by serving the interests of the King; they regarded their episcopal revenues as a reward for past services and were unlikely to question others who did the same. Many who sat in the upper house, and many in the lower house as well, were themselves too well acquainted with the evils of clerical privilege to indulge a tender conscience. There was, however, at least one man who spoke his mind freely and that was the Bishop of Rochester. Unlike so many of his peers, he had been appointed for nothing more than his learning and humanity; and after fourteen years of public life he had acquired none of the gentle vanities of privilege and place. Why should we, he asked these great and gaudy men, " 'exhort our flock*es* to eschew and shunn worldly ambition, when we our selves that be byshopps, do wholely sett our mindes to the same things we forbidd in them' "? " 'Who can willingly suffer and beare with vs' ", he went on, " 'in whom (preaching humilitie, sobrietie, and contempt of *the* world) they maie evidently perceive, hawtines in minde, pride in gesture, sumptuousnes in apparell, and damnable excesse in all worldly delicates? Truly, most reu*e*rend fathers, what this vanitie in temporall things worketh in you I know not, but sure I am that in my selfe I perceive a greate impediment to devotion, and so have felt a longe time, for sundrie times when I have setled and fully bent my self to the care of my flocke *com*mitted vnto me, to visitt my diocesse, to governe my church, and to answere the enemies of *Chr*ist, straight ways hath come a messenger for one cause or other sent from higher authoritie, by whom I have bene called to other busines and so left of my former purpose.' " He was thinking no doubt of the lavish pageantry provided for the reception of the golden rose and later the sword and cap of maintenance, which the bishop had been required to attend in solemn ceremony from Rochester to London. " 'And thus by tossing and going this waie and that way time hath passed, and in the meane while nothinge done, but attending after tryvmphs, receiving of Ambassadors, haunting of princes court*es*, and such lyke, wherby great expenses ryse that might better be spent otherwaie.' " [4]

The convocation came to nothing, in spite of Fisher's plea. His words were prophetic : he had not been long at Rochester after his return from Lambeth when he was summoned once again to appear at Court. For in March of 1520 he was appointed to attend Queen Catherine at the Field of Cloth of Gold. The peace with France had been sealed in the autumn of 1518 by the betrothal of the Dauphin to the Princess Mary, then three years old. Henry was determined to celebrate the new alliance with a gesture equal to the splendour of the occasion. So it was arranged that he would meet Francis in person near Guisnes, a few miles south of Calais, where on 7 June the two Kings embraced amid a flourish of trumpets. There followed several days of feasting and jousting before the festivities ended on the 25th.

The King of England was attended by Cardinal Wolsey, the Archbishops of Canterbury and Armagh, the Bishops of Durham, Ely, Chester and Exeter, the Dukes of Buckingham and Suffolk and the Marquis of Dorset. Fisher waited on the Queen, together with the Bishop of Hereford and the Bishop of Llandaff, her confessor.[5] Many years later he recalled the glittering spectacle that unfolded before his eyes: "was it nat a great thynge within so shorte a space, to se thre great Prynces of this worlde? I meane the Emperour"—for Henry had kept Whitsun with Charles on the way to France and met him again at Gravelines on his return—"and the kyng our mayster, and the Frenche kynge. And eche of these thre in so great honour, shewyng theyr royalty, shewyng theyr rychesse, shewyng theyr power—with eche of theyr noblesse appoynted and apparellyd in ryche clothes, in sylkes, veluettes, clothes of gold, & suche other precyouse araymentes. To se thre ryght excellent Quenes at ones togider, and of thre great realmes. That one, the noble Quene our mastresse, the very exampler of vertue and noblenesse to all women. And the Frenche Quene. And the thyrde Quene Mary, somtyme wyfe unto Lowys Frenche kynge, syster to our souereygne lorde, a ryght excellent and fayre Lady. And euery of them accompanyed with so many other fayre ladyes in sumptuouse & gorgeouse apparell—suche daunsynges, suche armonyes, suche dalyaunce, and so many pleasaunt pastymes, so curyouse howses and buyldynges, and bankettys, so delycate wynes, soo precyouse meatys, suche and soo many noble men of armes, soo ryche and goodly tentys, suche Justynges, suche tourneys, and suche feates of warre. These assuredly were wonderfull syghtes as for this worlde—and as moche as hath ben redde of in many yeres done, or in any Croncyles or Hystoryes here tofore wryten, and as great as mennes wyttes and studyes coulde deuyse and ymagyn for that season."[6] It was an incongruous setting for this plainspoken Yorkshireman who had never left England before and never would again. The sights

he saw were such as to make men marvel for many years to
come, and yet he was curiously impatient of it all. The magnificence of the setting, with its cloth of gold and precious apparel,
hardly concealed the naked realities beneath. Negotiations with
the Emperor were already under way and within two years
Fisher was to be entertaining Henry and Charles at Rochester
while the two Kings made ready once again for war with
France. He came away with a profound sense of the vanity of
the Court and the emptiness of all its glories.

On his return he was soon caught up again in the angry whirl
of controversy. Luther had just published his *De captivitate
Babylonica ecclesiae*, in which he denied the validity of all the
sacraments but those of baptism, penance and the altar. King
Henry himself made up his mind to reply and the following
summer his elegant little book on the sacraments was despatched to Rome, where it earned him the title of *Fidei Defensor*, Defender of the Faith. It was commonly supposed at the
time that the King's book had been written by either Fisher or
More, but in fact they seem to have had little to do with it. Henry
was proud of his learning and anxious to show the world what
he could do. Indeed, when More advised him to speak somewhat
more slenderly of the authority of the Holy See, he refused,
adding that he did not need to be told the truth of the matter.[7]
Meanwhile, Leo X had published a bull denouncing Luther's
work, to which Luther replied with a reassertion of the several
articles condemned by the Pope, whose bull he publicly burned
at Wittenberg on 10 December, 1520.

Fisher was in all likelihood already at work on a rejoinder to
Luther when in April of 1521 he received a message from Cardinal Wolsey: Leo had sent letters to England directing that the
books of Martin Luther should be publicly burned; would Fisher
preach in Paul's churchyard on the occasion of a ceremonial
burning of Lutheran books appointed for the twelfth of the
following month?[8]

Before the rebuilding of old St. Paul's after the Great Fire of 1666, there was a cross in the churchyard, known to generations of Londoners as Paul's Cross. Built about 1449 by Thomas Kempe, then Bishop of London, the cross resembled a lantern, with eight sides spanned by open arches surmounted by an ogee-shaped roof. Around the preacher there was room for a number of dignitaries to sit within a low enclosure. Others were seated in galleries built for the purpose along the walls of the cathedral. Below them the populace crowded into the narrow churchyard; on a great occasion like this there would be hundreds of them.[9] On the appointed day the Cardinal repaired to the cathedral, where he was received by the Dean. Under a canopy of gold borne by four men he proceeded to the high altar, where he made his oblation, after which he took his seat before the preacher. At his feet sat the Archbishop of Canterbury and the papal nuncio and on their left the Bishop of Durham and the imperial ambassador. Around them were assembled the rest of the bishops.[10]

The sermon which furnished the occasion for all this magnificence was, like the speaker, plain and direct. In setting forth his case against Luther, Fisher went directly to the heart of the matter. Though I speak with the tongues of men and of angels, he said, and have not charity, I am nothing; and though I have all knowledge and all faith, so that I could move mountains, and have not charity, I am nothing. A man without love is like a tree without fruit : "Haue a man neuer so moche lyght of faythe onlesse he haue also this hete of charyte sterynge his soule and bryngyng forthe lyfely workes he is but a deed stock & as a tree withouten lyfe. For", he explained, "though the naturall sonne shyne neuer so bryght vpon a tree. yf this tree haue in it no greneness nor puttynge forthe of buddes & lefes this tree is not alyve. So whan *the* bemes of *the* spirytuall son*n*e be spred vpon oure soules yf we fele not the sterynge hete to fruytfull workes our soules be but deed."[11] The churchman and the great heretic were, of course, more nearly in agreement than they knew, for when Luther spoke of justification by faith he had in mind the inner peace that comes from an act of love. But if Luther and his adversaries meant essentially the same thing when they spoke on the one hand of faith and on the other hand of charity, it is true that they approached this central experience in different ways. For Luther the experience of God was private and unique; it had nothing to do with the common experience of traditional belief. And since he insisted that every man is his own priest, he made little of the visible priesthood and hardly more of the Church itself. For Fisher, on the other hand, as for all those who remained faithful to the old Church, the experience of God belonged first of all to the community, to be shared with individual men and women according to their capacity for knowledge and love.

The burning of Luther's work in Paul's churchyard was a futile gesture, nothing more. The forbidden books continued to circulate in England and to attract readers in increasing numbers. It was with a heavy heart that Fisher returned to Rochester to take up the work he had begun the previous year. He had already finished a short treatise on prayer. There was also his reply to Luther's rejoinder to the papal bull issued the previous December. Then, during the summer, Luther published an answer to the King's book and Fisher felt obliged to take that in hand as well. The first of these did not make its appearance until long after Fisher's death. The two replies to Luther were finished early in 1522. One was published at Antwerp the following January; the other, a defence of the King's book, appeared at Cologne in June of 1525, together with a treatise on the priesthood.[12] In all these works Fisher sought to set forth and defend the traditional view of the Church. He refused to admit that the Scriptures alone provide knowledge of God, insisting for his own part on the importance of the customs and traditions that had grown out of the insights of generations of the faithful. He denied that the sacraments are nothing but the outward and visible sign of an inward and spiritual grace and insisted on the actual presence of God in the sacramental act. With all the pity and anger of his intense and lonely nature he cried out against what seemed to him a violation of the love and trust of the people, for whom the Church daily offered the flesh and blood of Jesus Christ in token of the unfailing love of God.

That same year, a new work by Ulrichus Velenus came to Fisher's attention. It set out to show, on the strength of the relevant Scriptural texts, that Peter the apostle had never been at Rome. From this Velenus argued that the Pope had no reason to call himself the successor of St. Peter and no right to lay claim to the authority conferred on St. Peter by Christ when he said, "thou art Peter, and upon this rock I will build my church; and the gates of hell shall not prevail against it. And I will give unto thee the keys of the kingdom of heaven : and whatsoever thou shalt bind on earth shall be bound in heaven: and whatsoever thou shalt loose on earth shall be loosed in heaven."[13] The book disturbed Fisher because it struck at the historical unity of the Church, which rested on the traditional authority of Rome, and he set to work on a reply. Velenus had quoted certain letters supposed to have been written by St. Paul to show that St. Peter, who is not mentioned in the letters, could not have been with St. Paul at the time. Fisher knew that the letters were in fact nothing but forgeries, for they had been exposed as such by Erasmus, and this he pointed out in his answer to Velenus, which was finished during the summer of 1522 and published at Antwerp on 30 October. A reply by Simon Hess appeared the next year, but Fisher ignored it.[14]

He had done enough and for a time he turned to other matters. There was much to attend to still at Cambridge. Ever since Wolsey had refused the office of Chancellor in 1514, Fisher had been anxious to secure a hearing for the university at Court.

The difficulties he had encountered in carrying out the intentions of the Lady Margaret showed how essential it was to have the ear of the King. So when More received a knighthood and a place on the council in the spring of 1521, Fisher was delighted. *"Lett, I pray you"*, he wrote to his friend, *"our* Cambridge *men haue some hope in you to be fauoured by the king's Maiestie that our schollars may be stirred up to learning by the countenance of so worthie a prince. We haue few friends in the Court"*, he added, *"which can or will commende our causes to his royall Maiestie, and amongst all we accounte you the chiefe, who haue always fauoured vs greatly, euen when you were in a meaner place; and now also shew what you can doe, being raised to the honour of knighthood, and in such great fauour with our prince, of which we greatly reioyce, and also doe congratulate your happinesse."* More was himself an Oxford man but he was eager to encourage learning at either university and he promised to do what he could.[15]

That same year Fisher had given thought for the first time to a foundation of his own at Cambridge. What he had in mind was an endowment worth perhaps £80 or £90 a year, enough to maintain four fellows and two scholars at St. John's. On 6 March, 1521 he signed the deed of gift. In addition to the maintenance of four new fellows and two new scholars, it provided increased revenues for the use of existing fellows and scholars, together with funds for the mortmain of Ospringe, at a cost of £500 in money, £100 in jewels and ornaments and lands worth £60 a year. It was a superb gift and one that cost Fisher dearly in thought and care as well as in money. Over the years Fisher kept a close watch on his foundation, anxious to find means of increasing its usefulness. The deed of gift was revised more than once, until it was put into final form on 18 April, 1525. The new indenture made allowance for additional lectures in Greek and Hebrew, providing £3 for the lecturer in Greek and £5 for the lecturer in Hebrew. It also made more elaborate provision for the purchase of trentals and the keeping of a solemn annual dirge, at a cost of eight pounds fourteen shillings, for Fisher's own benefit and for the benefit of his father and mother, King Henry VII, the Lady Margaret and all Christian souls. Nothing is too small or too unimportant to deserve his attention, not even the cost of wax for the candles. He had already made similar arrangements for the celebration of an annual mass at Christ's College and given the Master and fellows £43 with which to defray the expenses. A few months later he gave St. John's all his vestments and plate and, above all, his books, on condition that they should remain in his possession for the rest of his life. Books had been his one extravagance and his library was the envy of scholars all over Europe. It was his last word: he had given all he had to give.

Chapter 8

Meanwhile, in the spring of 1523, writs had been issued for a new Parliament. It was now more than seven years since Parliament had been in session, for except in time of war the ordinary revenues of the crown were sufficient to defray expenses, and Wolsey, still mindful of the humiliation he had endured as a result of the Hunne affair, had no wish to face Parliament again if he could avoid it. In the event, however, he had no choice. Parliament was summoned in 1523, as in 1512, to vote a subsidy for war against France. The alliance between Henry and Francis had hardly outlived the gaudy trappings of the Field of Cloth of Gold. To the ordinary Englishman, France was the familiar enemy. Moreover, Wolsey hoped to succeed Leo X (who died at the end of 1521), and he knew that Charles could do more for him in the coming election than Francis. During the summer of 1521 he negotiated a new alliance with Charles, and the following spring, despite the failure of Charles' half-hearted efforts on his behalf at Rome (where Adrian VI was elected on 19 January, 1522), treaties were arranged providing for the invasion of France and the eventual marriage of Charles to the Princess Mary. More than £350,000 had already been raised by forced loans, but more would be needed and Wolsey was compelled to resort to Parliament.

As soon as the two houses assembled on 15 April, members were asked to consent to a tax of four shillings in the pound on their lands and goods. When some were heard to murmur, Wolsey came in person to the Commons chamber and asked them the reasons for their discontent. They greeted his words with silence, whereupon Sir Thomas More, who had been elected Speaker at the beginning of the session, knelt before the Cardinal and explained that members were not accustomed to make answer, but only to consent or deny. In the end they agreed to a subsidy of £150,000, which was much less than Wolsey needed, to be paid in four yearly instalments.

There was resistance in Convocation as well. The southern province was convened by the Archbishop of Canterbury in St. Paul's on 20 April, but it was dissolved by Wolsey who then, acting in his legatine capacity as he had four years before, summoned a joint meeting of the two provinces of Canterbury and York, to assemble at Westminster on the 22nd. From the assembled clergy he demanded a moiety of their yearly income, that is, one half of the revenues of all ecclesiastical benefices in England. There were objections in both houses. Fisher and Fox spoke against the subsidy in the upper house; in the lower house there was vigorous opposition, led by Dr. Rowland Philips, prolocutor of the southern province and vicar of Croydon. Nevertheless, the clergy agreed before the end of August to the subsidy demanded by the King, though they stipulated that payment should be spread over five years.

That fall Fisher had to spend much of his time collecting the tax to which he had objected only a few months before. On Michaelmas Day (29 September) he and Warham were served with commissions requiring them to levy the tax in the county of Kent under the authority of the act of subsidy adopted by Parliament the previous summer. It took them six weeks to complete the returns. Many of those who were listed on the tax rolls were either serving in France or Scotland or waiting on the King at Court. Several of the others complained that their fortune was not equal to their loyalty.[1] Revenues came in slowly and in 1525 Wolsey had to resort to a forced loan to meet the rising costs of the war. But the so-called Amicable Grant was also a failure and had in the end to be abandoned. The stunning victory of imperial troops at Pavia in February of 1525 left Charles in control of France and the Italian states as well, but after the failure of the Amicable Grant Henry was in no position to follow up his advantage. Charles for his part had no intention of dividing the spoils of war with the English unless he had to, and in March, despite his promise to the Princess Mary, he married Isabella of Portugal. As for Wolsey, he had seen the papacy elude him for a second time when on the death of Adrian VI the Cardinal de Medici was elected, with the connivance of the imperialists, as Clement VII. The second French war, like the first, had accomplished little or nothing, and before long the Cardinal was negotiating once again with France.

Fisher took no further part in the prosecution of the war after completing the levy in his diocese during the autumn of 1523. At Cambridge he was now occupied with the preparation of a new set of statutes for St. John's. Finished in 1524, the new statutes were intended to regulate college life even more strictly than before. The following year he was carefully revising the terms governing his fellowships and scholarships at the college.

It was as if Fisher was anxious to put his house in order while there was still time. In everything he did in these years there is an increasing sense of finality. He was now 55 years old, an advanced age for the time, and during the winter of 1524 he suffered the first of many illnesses that were to dog him for the rest of his life. Already he felt himself to be living in an alien world that was becoming more difficult for him to understand with every new year that passed. The Hunne affair and the refusal of the King to uphold the jurisdiction of the ecclesiastical courts had shown clearly the profound changes that had taken place at Court since the death of Henry VII and the Lady Margaret. The professed loyalty of the young King to the Holy See had led to nothing more than a series of adventures in France that made a mockery of the title conferred by the Pope on the defender of the faith. And now a new generation openly denied the authority of the Church and dared to claim that before God each man is his own priest. It was a bold claim and it hurt Fisher deeply. He was not indifferent to the evils that flourished in the Church. On the contrary, he had raised his voice against them again and again, while over the years the austerity of his life had spoken of his sincerity more eloquently than any words. Morover, he was among the few who had recognized the importance of learning to a progressive understanding of man and his place in the world. He knew that much remained to be done, but it never occurred to him to question the supreme importance of the Church as the living centre of the religious life of the people. This, however, was the very question now being asked by the new men, and it was a question that had to be answered. The need to answer it changed the whole direction of Fisher's life. In a few short years he found himself at odds with all the dominant forces of time and circumstance. Once he had spoken for the future; now he spoke with the unmistakable accent of the past. Anxiety took the place of the quiet confidence of youth. The man who sat for Holbein

Holbein drawing of Fisher at the age of 58

in 1527 was lean and drawn, with hollow cheeks and eyes filled with pain.[2] Erasmus heard of Fisher's illness and hastened to comfort him. He advised his friend—dearer than ever to him now that he was in uncertain health—to spend less time at work in his library where the windows overlooking the Medway let in the cold, damp air off the sea. And he suggested that he should have his room panelled with boards, to keep out the chill of brick and plaster.[3]

Illness gave Fisher no respite, however, from the relentless pressure of events. In October of 1524 a regulation forbidding the importation of books was issued by Cuthbert Tunstal, now Bishop of London. The regulation, which was intended to prevent the spread of Lutheran teachings in England, provided that henceforth no book should be imported without the licence of Cardinal Wolsey, the Bishop of London or the Bishop of Rochester. The next summer Fisher received a first-hand report on the progress and spread of Lutheran agitation overseas. John Eck, the most determined and articulate of Luther's critics on the Continent, visited England in the summer of 1525. Before he returned to the Court of Bavaria, where he occupied the chair of theology at Ingoldstadt, Eck was entertained at Rochester and introduced by Fisher to the King himself.[4] Fisher for his part was by now at work on a reply to a book on the eucharist published by Iohannis Oecolampadius, a teacher at Basle and friend of Zwingli. Oecolampadius had adopted Zwingli's view of the mass, in which the elements of bread and wine are treated as symbols of the body and blood of Christ, without any spiritual significance of their own. For centuries the Church had taught that Christ was in some sense present in the bread and wine and that in the mass the sacrifice first made upon the Cross was daily re-enacted for the comfort and succour of all who would receive it. It was this view that Fisher set forth in his reply to Oecolampadius.[5] To him it was a matter of central importance. As he saw it the sacrament of the altar was the most precious possession of the Church, its very reason for existence, for in the mass alone the Church could renew the sacrifice of Christ and replenish the souls of the faithful.

Soon afterward Fisher received a summons from the Court that he could not well refuse. Anxious to display the power and strength of the established Church, Wolsey had made up his mind to arrange another public burning of unlicensed books at Paul's Cross. Early in January of 1526 he received word that the King approved of his suggestion and desired that Fisher should preach the sermon, as he had five years before.[6] It was not long before an opportunity presented itself. On Christmas Eve Robert Barnes, Prior of the Augustinian canons at Cambridge, had preached a sermon in St. Edward's Church in which he denounced the temporal possessions and secular jurisdiction of the clergy. The Vice-Chancellor at once ordered a hearing in the schools, where Barnes was examined and required to withdraw what he had said. When he refused, he was arrested and taken to London. There he was examined by Wolsey and a panel of bishops, including Fisher, Cuthbert Tunstal of London and John Clerk of Bath and Wells. Neither Fisher nor Tunstal wished to take action against Barnes, who after all was guilty of nothing worse than indiscretion. He had, among other things, objected to the practice of fasting on holy days, as to which Fisher announced flatly that he would not condemn such an opinion as heresy for £100, though he added sardonically that it was foolish to preach against fasting before all the butchers of Cambridge. Barnes observed that the King and the Cardinal did not hesitate to transact business on Sundays. "A goodly reason", Fisher remarked; "I will make you a lyke reason, the bisshop of wynchester sufferth stuys [i.e., brothels] ergo the stuys be lawful".[7] In the end Barnes agreed to abjure and on Sunday, 12 February he carried a faggot in solemn procession to St. Paul's, in company with two merchants of the Steelyard who were guilty of minor misdemeanours. Wolsey came and sat in state on a raised platform, attended by a large and splendid gathering of bishops, abbots and priors. It was an impressive display of the power and authority of the Church, as Wolsey intended it to be. The sermon was preached by Fisher, as it had been on a similar occasion at Paul's Cross five years before. He took as his text the words of Jesus to the blind beggar who came to him to be healed, "Receive thy sight: thy faith hath saved thee."[8] As long as the beggar is alone he is blind to the light of truth. To see God, he must rejoin the community of the faithful, where he will find Christ and recognize him. When Fisher had finished speaking, a fire was kindled in the churchyard and the penitents each cast their faggot upon it, as a pledge of their obedience. It was a moment of brutal irony, this ritual ceremony of burning. For of the two honest men who faced each other on the green that day, one was in the end to suffer for conscience at the stake and the other at the block. So men sacrifice each other in the name of justice and love.

For Fisher the rest of that year passed more quietly than most. His foundation at St. John's was now securely established and new statutes had been delivered to the Master and fellows. His reply to Oecolampadius on the eucharist was in the press at Cologne. The animosities stirred up by the Barnes inquiry were stilled, for the moment at least. In February Fisher was appointed, as he had been so often before, a commissioner of the peace for the county of Kent.[9] In June a formal investiture was held at Court to confer on Henry Fitzroy, the six-year-old natural son of the King by Elizabeth Blount, the title of Duke of Richmond and Somerset. This was an important event, since Henry apparently intended one day to nominate the young boy his legitimate heir and successor. More was present and took part in the ceremonial and Fisher may also have been required to attend. It is not unlikely, however, that he preferred to remain in his diocese, where in August we find him conducting a visitation of the Abbey of Lesnes.[10] During the winter negotiations were resumed between England and France and in the spring of 1527 a treaty was concluded whereby Henry and Francis confirmed the alliance of 1525. Under the terms of the treaty, the King of England finally renounced his claims to the territory of France, in exchange for the yearly payment of a cash indemnity.[11] In spite of the unchecked power of imperial arms in Italy, peace in Europe seemed more secure than ever.

In England, however, the appearance of calm was deceptive. More than sixty years of civil war in the time of their fathers and their grandfathers had taught Englishmen the supreme value of an undisputed succession. The secret of Henry's persistent appeal to the imagination of his people lay in the fact that in his own resplendent person he perfectly represented and expressed the radiant energies of a united people. But Henry and his Queen had now been married for nearly eighteen years and they had no son. Their first child, a daughter, was born dead. Three sons followed and all three died soon after their birth. Their last child was born dead like the first, and that had been eight years before. Their only surviving child was a daughter, the Princess Mary, born in 1516 and now eleven years old. For nearly four hundred years no woman had reigned as Queen in England and Henry had good reason to fear that if he left no male heir his people would once again be made to suffer the agonies of civil war.

The time had come when he needed a son more than anything else and Catherine, he had long known, could not give him one. For a time he apparently considered appointing his natural son Henry Fitzroy as his heir; he even entertained the idea of a marriage between Fitzroy and the Princess Mary. Early in 1527, however, if not before, he began to contemplate a more radical solution. When the King first considered the possibility of a divorce we do not know; nor can we be sure who first suggested it to him. Henry himself later insisted that it was the Bishop of Tarbes who had first raised doubts in his mind. In the course of negotiations between England and France during the winter of 1527, he explained, the Bishop of Tarbes, one of the French envoys, had questioned the legitimacy of the Princess Mary and had refused to consider a marriage between the Princess and the Dauphin until her place in the succession was established. There are those who believe that Wolsey, anxious to promote a French match for the King, prompted the bishop to question the validity of the marriage of Henry and Catherine. Others regard the whole story as a fabrication and take it for granted that the idea of a divorce occurred to the King himself, with or without the connivance of Longland, his confessor, or his other advisers.[12] However this may be, the divorce soon became the prime objective of English policy.

It is easy to see how Henry could have become convinced of the need for a divorce, on grounds of principle as well as policy. He knew—he had always known—of the commandment delivered to Moses and recorded in the book of *Leviticus*: "Thou shalt not uncover the nakedness of thy brother's wife: it *is* thy brother's nakedness." And he knew the punishment provided by the law: "if a man shall take his brother's wife, it *is* an unclean thing: he hath uncovered his brother's nakedness; they shall be childless."[13] Had he not married his brother's wife, and had not all his children died except one, and she a girl? Is it surprising that Henry should have come to believe that his children—the sons he so desperately needed—had died because his marriage was in fact no marriage at all, because he and the Queen were living in sin?

The story had begun nearly thirty years before, when Henry was a boy of eight. Catherine had been married by proxy to his elder brother Arthur Prince of Wales in the spring of 1499. Two years later, in the autumn of 1501, she arrived in England and on 14 November she and Arthur were married in person in St. Paul's Cathedral. Catherine was then almost sixteen years old, Arthur just fifteen.[14] They stayed for a time in the palace of the

Bishop of London and then went down together to the Welsh border country. There, at Ludlow Castle on 2 April, 1502, Prince Arthur died. Anxious to preserve the alliance, Ferdinand and Isabella sent Hernan Duque de Estrada to England to arrange a marriage between the widowed Princess and Prince Henry of York, now eleven years old. The next year Hernan Duque agreed to a draft treaty providing for the eventual marriage of the Prince and Princess. The treaty was confirmed by Ferdinand and Isabella in September, 1503, and by Henry VII the following March. It was generally believed at the time that after a marriage of less than five months Arthur had left Catherine, as he found her, a virgin. Ferdinand wrote to his agent at Rome that it was common knowledge in England that Arthur had never made Catherine his wife.[15] It was essential, however, to procure a dispensation at Rome to remove the impediment arising from the formalities of their marriage, and to place the matter beyond reasonable doubt the Spanish representatives insisted that the dispensation be so worded as to remove any objections that might arise in future if it could be made to appear that the marriage had in fact been consummated. This led to delays. Pope Alexander VI died in August, 1503; Pius III followed him in October. Julius II was elected on 1 November, but though he professed himself willing to issue the necessary bull it was not immediately forthcoming. In private he told Hadrian de Costello, the English agent at Rome, that he was not sure that he had the authority to issue a dispensation in such a case.[16] Eventually, however, the bull was ready and in the summer of 1505 it was sent to England. Meanwhile, Elizabeth of York had died and Henry VII found himself in a position to contemplate a marriage of his own. For a time he considered the widowed Queen of Naples, though he preferred Joanna of Castile, eldest daughter of Ferdinand and Isabella; he even considered Catherine herself. Prince Henry was still young and in the circumstances nothing further was done to implement the treaty of

1503. Indeed, when in 1505 the young prince became fourteen and reached the age of consent, he was required to make a public statement repudiating the treaty insofar as it obliged him to a marriage with Catherine.[17] There the matter rested until four years later Prince Henry succeeded his father as Henry VIII and married Catherine of his own choice.

That had been in the summer of 1509. Now, almost eighteen years later, Henry could wait no longer for the son he so ardently desired. He made up his mind to submit his case to a judicial inquiry for examination and judgment. It never occurred to him that the outcome of such an inquiry might be in doubt. He took it for granted that after an examination of the facts his marriage would be pronounced unlawful. No doubt he then intended to apply to the curia at Rome for a formal declaration of nullity.

Secret proceedings began on 17 May before Wolsey and Warham. The King was cited and charged to show cause why he should not be pronounced guilty of living in sin with his brother's widow. He appointed Dr. John Bell to act in his defence; Richard Wulman was appointed by the court to direct the prosecution. At the second sitting, three days later, Bell began his presentation of the case for the defence, which continued at successive sittings. At length the Julian bull was solemnly produced for the inspection of the court, whereupon the defence rested its case. On 31 May Wulman stated his objections. He pointed out that Prince Arthur had married Catherine and lived with her for nearly five months and so had presumably used her as his wife. By marrying his brother's widow, the King had disobeyed the Mosaic law set forth in the book of *Leviticus*. The Pope, as everyone knew, had the right to dispense with the canon law of the Church, but he had no right, Wulman argued, to dispense with the laws of God revealed in Scripture. And therefore, he concluded, the Julian bull was of no effect in removing the impediment to such a marriage as that of the King and Queen.[18]

Wulman's statement brought the proceedings to an end. For some reason the hearing was broken off and never resumed. It may be that Wolsey was afraid to commit himself to a positive decision in so delicate a matter without first considering its larger implications. During the course of the inquiry, news reached England of the sack of Rome some days before by imperial troops. Wolsey had little reason to expect that Clement VII, now a virtual prisoner in the Castle of San Angelo, would look with favour on a petition unfriendly to the Queen or her nephew the Emperor. He evidently decided to delay the outcome of the suit until he had more thoroughly explored the intentions of the King of France. If he could secure an acknowledgment of his own right to act, with the consent of the French cardinals, in the name of the Church, it would no doubt be possible, in spite of the captivity of the Pope, to arrange a French marriage for the King. A French marriage, Wolsey saw, would not only provide for the succession but would also unite France and England against the growing power of the Empire. In such a policy he saw the best hope for both the safety of England and his own advancement.

Chapter 9

Wolsey set out for France early in July. On the evening of the 4th he stopped at Rochester, on his way from London to the channel coast. That night he spent at the bishop's palace and while there he sounded Fisher as to the marriage of the King and Queen. Six weeks before, during the secret hearings at Westminster, he had put the case to Fisher in general terms, without revealing the identity of the persons concerned. At that time Fisher could have had no idea that the King and Queen were involved. The King had himself insisted that his intentions be kept secret and though the Spanish ambassador knew of the process begun on 17 May before Wolsey and Warham,[1] there is no reason to suppose that Catherine heard of it before 22 June, when Henry told her for the first time that he could no longer treat her as his wife. And since it was from the Queen, as he now admitted to Wolsey, that Fisher first learned of the King's suit, the news probably reached him during the last week of June, only a few days before Wolsey himself brought word of it.

So when Wolsey had first sent to him for his advice at the end of May, Fisher had considered the question, not as it touched the crown, but as it affected the Holy See and the Church. This is clear enough from the answer he sent to the Cardinal. Having considered all the evidence and weighed all the arguments on both sides, he had written, he had come to the conclusion that such a marriage was contrary to neither the law of nature nor the law of God. As for the formal impediment in canon law, that, he had pointed out, was clearly within the jurisdiction of the Holy See and could be dispensed with, for sufficient reason, by the Pope.[2]

Wolsey had sent Fisher's answer to the King early in June. The opinion of my lord of Rochester, he had observed drily, "Your Highnes shal perceyve by his original letters, which I send unto Your Grace herwith". To the Cardinal it seemed clear that Fisher must have had "som conjecture or smelling of the matier", for such an opinion as his could proceed, he was convinced, only from personal affection for the Queen.[3] How untrue this was Wolsey was to learn now that he was free to disclose the true nature of the case to Fisher in the privacy of the bishop's palace at Rochester.

This time the Cardinal told him plainly what was at stake: nothing less than the King's marriage and the succession to the crown of England. Wolsey began, as he reported next day to the

King, by asking Fisher if he had had any news of late from Court. "At which question he sumwhat stayed and pawsed", Wolsey observed; after a moment's hesitation, however, he answered that "of late oon was sent unto him from the Quenes Grace, who brought him a message oonly by mowth, without disclosure of any particularite, that certain matiers there were, bitwene Your Grace and her lately chaunced, wherin she [*would be*] glad to have his counsail, alleging that Your Highnes was content she shuld soo have". He had told the Queen that he would gladly give her advice on any matter that concerned her alone, "but in matiers concerning Your Highnes and here", Wolsey reported, he had told her "he wold nothing doo, without knowledge of your pleasour and expresse commaundement".[4]

Already, therefore, Fisher knew something of the circumstances. Now he was to hear the whole story, "as was divised with Your Highnes at Yorke Place".[5] Whether this curious phrase means that the story Wolsey told Fisher that night was a fabrication we shall never know. In any case, King and Cardinal held steadily to the same story, true or false, for the next six years. It turned on the question said to have been raised by the Bishop of Tarbes as to the legitimacy of the Princess Mary and the security of her place in the succession. To this disturbing question Wolsey traced the doubts and scruples that had since grown up in the mind of the King. If the King and Queen were living in sin in the sight of the law, was it not natural to suppose that the King's three sons had been taken away to punish him for having uncovered his brother's nakedness?[6] After raising this sinister question, Wolsey produced the Julian bull under which Henry and Catherine had been married eighteen years before, and showed it to Fisher. By now, having consulted him on that very point, Wolsey knew that Fisher considered the Pope entitled to dispense in such a case as this. More had expressed a similar opinion, and there are indications that Wolsey found several of the bishops unwilling to question the authority of the Holy See. He therefore shifted his ground. Instead of denying the right of the Pope to issue the dispensation, as Wulman had done in the first place, he now admitted that a papal dispensation could, in certain circumstances, remove the impediment to a marriage within the prohibited degrees. His present object was to show that in the existing circumstances the Julian bull was invalid. Fisher read the bull over carefully and confessed that in some respects it seemed to him imperfect. The Pope, he knew, could dispense with the law only when and where there was sufficient reason for him to do so. But in the bull as it stood no reason was given except the reputed desire of the King of England and the King and Queen of Spain for the preservation of peace—then long established and in no sort of jeopardy—between their two countries. Wolsey reported with satisfaction to the King that Fisher "gretly lamented the negligence of them, that soo handled that thing in the begynnyng; being of soo high importaunce and gret weight".[7] He pretended that the King also lamented the carelessness of the curia, and led Fisher to believe that all the King desired was proof of the sufficiency of the dispensation. Fisher was evidently deceived, for he agreed with Wolsey in blaming Catherine for taking so ill the attentions of those who proposed to examine and, as he thought, to confirm her title as Queen. He told the Cardinal that he "doubted not, but that if he might speke with her, and disclose unto her al the circumstances of the matier as afore, he shulde cause her gretly to repent, humille, and submitte herselfe unto Your Highnes; considering that the thing doon by Your Grace, in this matier, was soo necessary and expedient, and the Quenes acte herin soo perilous and daungerous".[8] In this Fisher had more to learn from Catherine than she from him, a fact of which Wolsey was only too well aware. Hurriedly, he asked Fisher to say nothing to the Queen without the King's consent, and Fisher, unaware of the reasons for Wolsey's anxiety, agreed.

For "although she be Quene of this realme, yet", as Wolsey reported to the King, "he knowelegith youe for his high Souverain Lorde and King; and wil not therfor otherwise behave himself, in al matiers, concerning or towching your personne, thenne as he shalbe by Your Grace expressely commaunded; like as he made answer unto the messanger sent from the Quene, as I have bifore writen. Wherfor there restith oonly the advertisement of your pleasour to be geven unto him, whereuppon he wil incontinently repare unto Your Highnes, and further ordre himselfe to the Quene, in wordes, maner, and facion as he shalbe by Your Grace enfourmed and instructed."[9] So the Cardinal left Fisher and continued on his way to France.

The departure of Wolsey did not end the matter for Fisher. He recognized at once that the King's proceedings were of the first importance to both Church and State. For two years and more he devoted himself to a scrupulous study of the Scriptural authorities and the opinions of the Fathers. To the end he remained convinced, as he had been ever since Wolsey first sent to him for his opinion during the secret hearings at Westminster, that the Pope had the right to dispense in such a case; he was also satisfied—whatever technical imperfections might be found in the dispensation—that the evident intention of the Julian bull was sufficient to assure the legitimacy of a marriage that had been made in good faith by both parties a full eighteen years before. Not long after Wolsey's departure, we find him writing to a friend who had sent to warn him that Robert Wakefield, his old teacher in Hebrew, had prepared a case against the Queen strong enough to convince the wavering bishops. Fisher replied that if this was true of the bishops it was a disgrace. As for himself, he wrote, he had taken great pains to arrive at the truth and he could not change his mind without injury to both his reputation and his conscience. Evidently Fisher already suspected that the King was less interested in proving the legitimacy of his existing marriage than in being set free to make another. For Kings, he remarked drily, are apt to think that whatever pleases them is right.[10]

By now the grand design was beginning to take shape. Some time before, Richard Pace had undertaken to examine the Hebrew originals of the relevant Scriptural texts, in the hope of finding evidence that such a marriage as the King's was contrary to the law of God. Wakefield, who probably knew more about Hebrew than any other man in England, had helped him finish the book, which Pace now sent to the King. Wakefield himself soon afterwards wrote to Henry offering, as he put it, "to defende your cause or question"—by which he meant that he would attempt to show that the King and Queen were not and never had been man and wife—"in all the vniuersities in christendom agaynst all men, by good and sufficiente autorite of the scripture of god and the wordes of the beste lernyd and moste excellent autors of the interpreters of the hebrewes, and the holy doctors bothe grekes and latyns in christes faythe". He confessed that he was at first of the contrary opinion, for he was not then aware that the Queen had been "carnally knowen of prince Arthure your brother". Like so many others, however, he had since changed his mind and was prepared to speak for the King against any one who took the Queen's part. Apparently Fisher had by now openly declared his opinion of the marriage, for Wakefield boasted that he would so "answer to the bysshop of Rochesters booke, that I truste he shall be asshamyd to waade or meddyll any further in the matter."[11] What this book of Fisher's was we do not know. None of his surviving tracts or broadsides relating to the divorce date from earlier than June of 1529, when he prepared two briefs in defence of the Queen for the consideration of the papal legates at Blackfriars. It may be that one of these was drawn up two years before and was known to Wakefield. Or it may be that Wakefield—using the word "book" in a sense then fairly common—was simply referring to the letter Fisher had sent Wolsey when the latter first consulted him the previous May. In any case, the promised reply was in due course published by Thomas Berthelet, printer to the King, and was followed a short time later by a second, printed by Wynkyn de Worde.[12] There was, as everyone knew, an ordinance set down in the book of *Deuteronomy* that bore directly on the case in question. "If brethren dwell together," it read, "and one of them die, and have no child, the wife of the dead shall not marry without unto a stranger : her husband's brother shall go in unto her, and take her to him to wife, and perform the duty of an husband's brother unto her."[13] Wakefield argued that this rule was intended to apply only where the woman had never been carnally known by her first husband. In the Hebrew original, he insisted, the phrase translated in the Latin of the Vulgate as *sine liberis* (without children) means without touch of woman. This interpretation was, Wakefield well knew, likely to do the King good service. That Catherine had come to Henry without child was a matter of common knowledge. That she had come to him a virgin was more doubtful, since the truth of the matter could, in the nature of the case, be known to no-one but the Queen herself.[14]

While Wakefield and Pace were at work in England, the King's cause was being pressed in the several Courts of Europe. Wolsey was already on his way to treat with Francis for an alliance that, he hoped, would secure the interests of England and deliver the Church from the intolerable dominion of Charles V. He had made a good start. On 9 July William Knight, the King's secretary, wrote to tell the Cardinal that Henry was well pleased with what he had heard of his conversations with Fisher at Rochester. As a mark of his gratitude, Henry sent the Cardinal a red deer killed by the King with his own hand.[15] A few days later, Knight warned Wolsey that Catherine had despatched Francis Phillips, a member of her household, to the Emperor with a message explaining her new position. The King asked that Wolsey arrange for Phillips' arrest, but in spite of

Wolsey's efforts Catherine's message reached Charles, who assured her that he would do what he could to protect her interests.[16] Throughout the rest of the summer and early autumn of 1527, Wolsey continued negotiations at the French Court. The treaty drafted the previous winter was confirmed and the alliance with France proclaimed. Wolsey had accomplished much of what he set out to do. But one prize escaped him. He had written to Henry at the end of July that the only hope of obtaining a favourable judgment from the Church in the matter of the King's marriage, so long as Clement was in the hands of the Emperor, lay in persuading the cardinals to assemble at Avignon under the jurisdiction of Wolsey himself.[17] And this he was, as it proved, unable to persuade them to do. In August he sent an embassy to Rome in the hope that Clement would be willing to grant him the authority denied him by the French cardinals.[18] Given this, he could himself conduct a judicial inquiry and pronounce on the legitimacy of the King's marriage with all the authority of the Holy See.

But events in England were moving rapidly and already the Cardinal, abroad since early summer, had begun to lose touch with English policy. Whether Wolsey had first proposed the divorce or had simply made use of doubts that had grown up in the mind of the King himself, we do not know. In either case, Wolsey had intended to take what advantage he could of the opportunity afforded by the King's scruples to confirm the alliance with France. Such a policy called, of course, for a French marriage. Unknown to Wolsey, however, Henry had by now made up his mind to marry Anne Boleyn, a daughter of English stock and a member of his own circle at Court. Nor was it long before Wolsey was to feel the effects of the King's choice. Early in September he found that Henry had sent Knight on a secret mission to Rome, whereupon he hastily wrote to the King, asking that the matter be allowed to remain in his hands. But his advice was disregarded and Knight was instructed to continue to Rome.[19] Knight's purpose was to persuade Clement to issue a dispensation for a second marriage as well as a commission for Wolsey to examine and annul the first. The dispensation was to be worded in such a way as to remove any impediment to a second marriage contracted, like the first, within the forbidden degrees. It is difficult to see why such a dispensation would have been considered necessary unless the King had already decided to marry Anne Boleyn, in full knowledge of the fact that he had contracted an affinity in the first degree with Anne through his relationship with her sister Mary, as indeed it was generally believed at the time.[20] Nor is it easy to see why, unless this was the case, Henry felt it necessary to conceal the dispensation from Wolsey. To ask the Pope to dispense with an impediment to the King's second marriage while at the same time asking him to annul the first on the same grounds: this is what Knight was instructed to do. To Henry this would not have seemed unreasonable. He contended that his marriage to Catherine should be annulled because he had found defects in the original dispensation. This time there would be no mistakes and his marriage to Anne would be beyond doubt or scruple. That his existing marriage could have been repaired by the same means was a possibility he did not allow himself to contemplate. Catherine was now barren and he needed a son. Like most men, Henry had little difficulty in adjusting his conscience to his interests.

Difficulties there were, however, and these arose in the first instance from the presence of imperial troops in Italy. Clement himself was a prisoner in the Castle of San Angelo and as long as he remained there Knight found it impossible to discuss the King's business with him. Wolsey, once he was back in England, sent fresh instructions to Sir Gregory Casale, head of the mission he had depatched to Rome in August, together with an urgent plea to Clement, warning him that if he neglected Henry's petition the Church of Rome would lose its place in England.[21]

On his return the Cardinal found other problems to occupy

his mind. The flow of new ideas from the Continent had scarcely been checked by the burning of Lutheran books at Paul's Cross. The Church was threatened as never before by those who questioned its exclusive possession of the keys of the kingdom. In November Wolsey, acting in his legatine capacity, appointed a special commission of bishops to examine such heretics as could be found. Fisher was among those named and he came up from Rochester to attend the hearings. The others were Warham of Canterbury, Tunstal of London, Clerk of Bath and Wells, Standish of St. Asaph, Kite of Carlisle, West of Ely, Voysey of Exeter and Longland of Lincoln. The size and character of the commission, representing as it did five great and four lesser sees, shows the importance that was attached to the work to be done. Wolsey himself attended the first two sittings, after which Tunstal took charge. The most important of the accused were Thomas Bilney and Thomas Arthur. Bilney and Arthur, along with George Joye, were summoned to appear without delay before the commission in the chapter house at Westminster. All three were associated with the radical group at Cambridge to which Thomas Cranmer also belonged. Joye escaped to the Continent, but Bilney and Arthur appeared to answer the charges against them. Bilney admitted having preached on more than one occasion against pilgrimages and the veneration of images and relics. Arthur confessed to having maintained the priesthood of all believers and to being an advocate of lay preaching. Both were at length persuaded to abjure, and on Sunday, 8 December they each bore a faggot to Paul's Cross. Bilney, considered the more serious offender, had also to serve a year in prison before being allowed to return to Cambridge.[22]

Fisher was now free to return to his diocese. As for Wolsey, he was still waiting impatiently for news from Italy. Before Christmas the news came. Clement had escaped from captivity and taken refuge at Orvieto. There at least he was allowed some semblance of liberty. He was able to see Knight and to listen to his requests. On the 16th he wrote to Henry promising to do all he could to gratify his desires.[23] The King and his council had always assumed that Clement would act, in this as in all other cases, according to his own interests. As long as he was in the hands of the imperialists, he could not be expected to do anything for Henry that would compromise the Queen's position or the alliance she represented between England and Spain. Now that he was restored to liberty, it was taken for granted that he would gratify the King if only to merit the continued aid and succour of the Defender of the Faith. That Clement would be governed or even influenced by the elementary principles of justice never occurred to either the King or his council. Nor did it occur to Charles. He never doubted for a moment that Clement would forget his friendship for Henry as soon as he was reminded of the sack of Rome. And it must be admitted that Clement encouraged both sides to think of him in these terms. It is true, of course, that he was afraid of displeasing either England or Spain. But he knew that he could not in the end avoid a decision. This being the case, he must have seen that it would be prudent to assuage Henry's anger and frustration by blaming Charles for what he himself felt bound to do. When Clement addressed the English he spoke of the imperial troops. But when he addressed his own advisers within the curia he spoke of his conscience. It is a mistake to see him as a man driven by fear for his own person and authority. His deepest anxieties were of another sort. He could see no way of preserving English obedience to the Church of Rome without giving Henry what he wanted; and he could see no way of giving Henry what he wanted without diminishing the name and authority of the Church. This, as Clement saw it, was the real problem.

Wolsey, however, could see only the need to satisfy the King before it was too late, before the King repudiated the authority of Rome and destroyed the independence of the English Church.

As soon as he heard of Clement's escape to Orvieto, he sent Casale new instructions. If the Pope objected to a commission under which Wolsey alone, as an English subject, was authorized to give judgment on the King's marriage, Casale should suggest that a second legate be joined with him in the commission. The man Wolsey had in mind was Cardinal Campeggio, who had come to England as a papal legate ten years before and, being now in Henry's debt for the see of Salisbury, could, he felt, be counted on to look with favour on the King's suit.[24]

Clement was less amenable than Wolsey had hoped. He made no difficulty about dispensing with an impediment arising out of affinity within the prohibited degrees. But he hesitated to grant a commission in the form desired. Wolsey wanted what was known as a decretal commission, which would have had the effect of requiring the legates, after establishing the facts alleged by the King, to pronounce a decree of annulment. Clement was doubtful and referred Knight and Casale to the Cardinal St. Quatuor, his principal adviser in matters of canon law, but St. Quatuor, despite a bribe of 2000 crowns, refused to advise His Holiness to sign the commission as it stood. Instead, he redrafted it in a new form for Clement's signature. On 1 January, 1528 Knight sent word to Wolsey and the King that the commission had been signed and was on its way to England.[25]

When the bulls arrived in England, however, it was found that they would not do. There was nothing in the revised commission to prevent the Queen from appealing to the curia; nor was there anything to prevent the Pope from revoking the commission at any stage in the proceedings. In the event, Knight had proven no match for the skill and experience of St. Quatuor. Within a month a new mission was despatched to the Holy See, led by Edward Fox, the King's Almoner, and Stephen Gardiner, Wolsey's secretary. Gardiner soon became the King's principal spokesman at Rome, where he laboured in the King's cause with a strength of will and honesty of purpose that make him one of the most remarkable of the King's men. He and Fox reached Rome on 20 March and began at once to press their demands on the Pope. Their object was to secure a decretal commission for Wolsey and Campeggio to conduct a judicial inquiry secure from appeal or advocation and so limited in its terms of reference as to assure a verdict favourable to the King.[26]

Chapter 10

During most of the winter Fisher had stayed away from London, where the negotiations at Rome were being watched more closely than elsewhere in the kingdom. After attending the several sittings of the commission appointed to examine Bilney and Arthur, he had returned for Christmas to the more normal and homely routines of his diocese. This was the life he had made his by his own choice. " 'Truly, most reu*e*rend fathers' ", as he had remarked ten years before in Convocation, " 'what this vanitie in temporall things worketh in you I know not, but sure I am that in my selfe I perceive a greate impediment to devotion' ", for on many a day, " 'when I have setled and fully bent my self to the care of my flocke co*m*mitted vnto me, to visitt my diocese, to governe my church, and to answere the enemies of *Chr*ist, straight ways hath come a messenger for one cause or other sent from higher authoritie, by whom I have bene called to other busines' ", such as " 'attending after tryvmphs, receiving of Ambassadors, haunting of princes court*es*, and such lyke, wherby great expenses ryse that might better be spent otherwaie.' "[1]

And so it was that soon after Christmas he was sent for again, this time by the King himself. On his arrival, he presented himself before the King in his long gallery in the palace at Westminster, in the presence of the Dukes of Norfolk and Suffolk and several others. Henry told him he wished to know the bishop's opinion as to his marriage. He professed that his conscience was troubled and added that he desired to satisfy himself as to the sufficiency of the dispensation and the security of the succession. Fisher had long suspected what the King was about, but he chose—on such an occasion he could hardly do otherwise—to take him at his word.[2] He knelt before the King and urged him in plain words to dismay himself no further with the matter, " 'nether to vnquyet or trooble your conscience for the same' ", assuring him that " 'by my advise and counsell you shall with all speed put all such thought out of your minde' ". He considered it " 'a verie perrilous and vnseemly thinge' ", he added, " 'that any Divorce should be spoken of' ".[3] He had put himself on record.

Fisher returned to Rochester, where a few days later he entertained Staphileus, Dean of the Rota and papal representative in London. Staphileus had been recalled to Rome and on his way to the coast he broke his journey, as so many did, at Rochester. While in England he had evidently been persuaded of the justice of the King's cause. No doubt he gave Fisher details of the proceedings as they then stood. We know at least that he discussed the matter with Fisher, because he sent Wolsey an account of his stay at Rochester. The bishop, we hear, was put to shame by the arguments of his visitor. So pleased, indeed, was Staphileus with his own performance that he said he wished the King and the Cardinal had been there to hear it.[4] But in spite of the eloquence of his guest, Fisher did not alter his opinion.

At Orvieto, meanwhile, Gardiner and Fox were pressing Henry's case with tireless energy. At the end of March their first reports were sent to England. They had seen the Pope for the first time on the 22nd, they told the King and Wolsey, and

since then had been granted daily audiences. Indeed, they gave
the ailing Clement no rest. First they presented a book setting
forth the reasons that had moved the King to ask for an inquiry,
a book prepared, in part at least, by the King himself.[5] Then
they offered St. Quatuor a further gift of 2000 crowns. When he
refused it they gave his secretary thirty crowns and kept the
remainder in case the Cardinal should change his mind. When
they pressed the Pope for a decretal commission authorizing the
legates to annul the marriage provided Henry could establish
the fact that Catherine had been carnally known by Prince
Arthur, Clement pointed out that unless the verdict was fair
to the Queen, the Emperor would enlist the support of the universities of Europe in her behalf. This, of course, was exactly
what Henry himself was to do two years later when the legates
refused to give judgment in his favour. Instead of the decretal
the English asked for, Clement offered a general commission
authorizing Wolsey and Campeggio to conduct a joint inquiry
and to come to a decision in the light of the evidence submitted
to them.[6] Such a commission would be little better than that
already obtained by Knight, and Gardiner and Fox were not
satisfied. They pressed for a secret decretal, together with a
written promise binding the Pope to refrain from advoking the
hearing to Rome in case of an appeal by the Queen. Apparently
their object was, by promising secrecy, to obtain a decretal commission that would compromise the Holy See if made public;
they then could count on Clement's fear that the decretal would
be published to restrain him from recognizing Catherine's
appeal. Provided the case was not advoked to Rome, they were
fairly sure that they could persuade Campeggio to consent to a
favourable verdict. Failing that, the pledge of secrecy could be
ignored and the decretal used as a basis for the hearing, in which
case a favourable verdict would be almost certain.

Early in June the general commission was signed and on the
11th Gardiner wrote to Henry VIII that Campeggio was at last

on his way. Best of all, he was carrying the secret decretal and would show it to the King and Wolsey on his arrival.[7] Gardiner had good reason to feel that he had served the King well. But in England Wolsey remained anxious and impatient. More than a year before, he had promised the King a speedy decision at Rome. He had disappointed his master and he was made to feel it. In July Henry sent him a sharp rebuke for a trifling indiscretion in the disposal of a living.[8] At about the same time, Anne Boleyn wrote to him to thank him for his pains, adding significantly that she hoped the coming of the legate would soon conclude the matter, so that she could reward the Cardinal for his services.[9] These scraps of information reveal clearly enough the direction in which events were silently moving. Wolsey's reward, which he knew to be his very survival as a public figure, would depend entirely on his ability to persuade the papal curia to serve the interests of the English crown. And on his success would depend as well the continued independence of the Church of England.

All this time Campeggio, painfully afflicted with gout, was making his slow way across France towards Calais and England. He was in no hurry, for his instructions were to delay judgment as long as possible in the hope that, given time, the situation would resolve itself. It took him three months to reach Paris and from there he wrote to Wolsey on 16 September that he would have to finish the journey on a litter as he could no longer ride. The same day he sent a despatch to the papal secretary, Giocomo Salviati, that shows the real bent of his mind. He promised to do all he could to persuade the King to relent. If he failed, he would hear the cause without prejudice and give sentence according to the law. He added that he would not sell his conscience to the King at any price.[10] Already the outlines of papal policy were beginning to emerge. Clement had chosen to risk the loss of the English Church—for he had been repeatedly warned of the risk by Wolsey and by Casale, by Gardiner and by

Fox—rather than lose the spiritual prerogatives by which the several churches of Christendom were still united under the primacy of the Holy See. For this, he knew, would be the effect of placing the Church of Rome at the service of the King of England.

It was two weeks longer before the legate reached Calais. At last, on 29 September, he crossed from Calais to Dover, where he was met by Sir Francis Brian and Robert Sherborn, the aged Bishop of Chichester. Nine days later he reached London.[11] Wolsey hurried at once to see him at Bath House, where he was staying as the guest of the Bishop of Bath and Wells. Wolsey was anxious to proceed at once to judgment and was bitterly disappointed to find that Campeggio had instructions to try first to effect a reconciliation between the King and Queen. He told Campeggio frankly that if the legates failed to satisfy the King he himself would be ruined and the English Church deprived of its liberty. The next day Campeggio visited Wolsey in his palace at Westminster, where he was formally received before a large and splendid gathering. After the customary addresses of welcome, Campeggio was admitted to a private audience with the King and the Cardinal. Henry showed little interest in the niceties of canon law. He spoke instead of the papal states, now in the hands of Charles V. He would be pleased, he said, to use his influence to restore the independence of the Holy See, if Clement would first do him justice in the matter of his marriage. On the following day Henry visited Campeggio privately. Campeggio pointed out that if the King still had any scruples as to his marriage, a new dispensation could be issued amplifying and confirming the first. Henry answered that no man could dispense with the impediment in his case, since such a marriage as his was clearly forbidden by the laws of God and nature. The King's answer marked a significant change in policy. When Wolsey first discussed the King's scruples with Fisher at Rochester, he was content to point out the supposed defects in the text of the bull. He did not question the right of the Holy See to grant the dispensation; he questioned only the sufficiency of the dispensation under which the marriage had in fact taken place. Fisher himself was doubtful about the sufficiency of the bull, as he admitted to Wolsey; he chose to oppose the King, however, because he saw that those who began by questioning the bull would end by questioning the authority of the Church. Henry's answer would have been no surprise to him. As for Campeggio, he knew well enough what to expect. He remarked in private that he doubted if an angel from heaven could change the King's mind or alter his determination to proceed with the case to the end.[12]

Having failed to dissuade the King, Campeggio made a new proposal. What if Catherine should agree to take the vows and enter a house of religion? The King would then be free to remarry without prejudice to either the Queen or the Princess Mary. The Queen could retain her rank and the Princess her place in the succession. Henry was pleased with the proposal and urged the legate to take it up with Catherine. The meeting took place the next day. The Queen listened to Campeggio's advice and then told him that she could not consent to such a step without consulting her advisers.[13]

Knowing it was likely that Henry would appoint Fisher as one of the Queen's counsel, Campeggio soon found an opportunity of sounding him on the subject. They met on the 25th, either at Lambeth or at Bath House. Until now Fisher had not been deeply involved in the working out of the King's great matter. He had been consulted, twice by Wolsey and then again by Henry. He had made no secret of his opinions but he had not as yet actively opposed the King. From now on, however, he was to be drawn ever more closely into the affair. He agreed readily enough that Catherine would do well to withdraw to a nunnery. Such a course of action would satisfy all the requirements of policy without jeopardizing the rights of the Church. The next day he found himself one of the Queen's council of advisers, which included Warham of Canterbury, Tunstal of London, West of Ely, Clerk of Bath and Wells and Standish of St. Asaph.

Meanwhile, Campeggio had spoken again to the Queen. She came to him, at her own request, to make her confession. Under the seal of confession she told him that during the five months of her first marriage she had slept with Prince Arthur no more than seven nights; and she insisted that at his death he had left her a virgin, as he found her. She protested that she had done the King no wrong and declared that she would never renounce the estate and dignity to which God had called her. Those of her advisers who urged her to withdraw to a nunnery were, she felt, merely seconding the wishes of the King. She had, it is true, good reason to suspect the motives of her counsellors; churchmen like West and Clerk, and even Tunstal, had risen to their present eminence as servants of the crown. Even Warham, a former Chancellor and now an old man, seldom dared to cross the King. In Fisher she had an adviser of another kind. Certainly she had no reason to distrust his advice, as she evidently did. But to retire now from the stage of English history was, in Catherine's eyes, to betray the very object of her life, which was, as it had always been, to unite in her own person the crowns of England and Spain. She suffered from the defects of her virtues. The proud courage that had given her the strength to serve the cause of imperial Christendom, as she saw it, through the long and lonely years she had spent in a strange country, prevented her now from recognizing the real nature of her position. She did not care for prudence; she thought only of what was expected of a Queen. She was willing, she said, to die; nothing less was worthy of her station.[14]

At this moment a fresh obstacle presented itself. A copy of a preliminary brief, issued by Julius II a year before the bull itself, was produced by Catherine and exhibited to the legates. The original had been found in Spain and a copy made and sent to England in the care of Iñigo de Mendoça, the Spanish agent in London. On his accession, Julius had for a time been reluctant to publish a dispensation for the marriage of Henry and Catherine.[15] Butwhen itwas discovered that Isabella of Castile was on the point of death he had drawn up a preliminary brief to relieve her mind and sent it to Spain. The bull itself, which like the brief was dated 26 December, 1503, finally reached England during the summer of 1505. Once the bull had been issued the brief became worthless. It had never been registered at Rome, since it was only a preliminary draft of the bull. Though copies were sent to England, no record of them was preserved among the State Papers, and the original disappeared, to be found many years later in Spain and turned over to Charles V.[16]

The importance of the brief was at once obvious, for it suffered from none of the supposed defects of the bull itself. In the bull no reason for the dispensation was given except the need to confirm the "bonde of peace and amitie" between England and Spain, though, as the English agents hastened to point out, the two countries were already united by a treaty of perpetual peace.[17] In the brief Julius gives the same reason, but adds that he is dispensing with the impediment *for this and other reasons*.[18] No argument could be effective against a general statement such as this. Since Wolsey still planned to rest Henry's case on the alleged imperfections of the bull, without raising the larger question of the authority of the Holy See over Kings and princes, the discovery of a brief that appeared to remedy these very imperfections was a serious misfortune. Nothing further could be done until the original was in the hands of the King. The council hastily drew up special instructions for Catherine's advisers. The Queen must be urged to send at once to Spain for the original, the want of which, she must be made to understand, might damage her case irreparably.[19] Accordingly the

Queen was advised to give her word that she would endeavour
to procure the brief, and this she did on 13 October before
several witnesses. The Bishop of Rochester, however, was not
among them.[20] There was, indeed, no reason to expect that the
one man who had spoken out consistently in favour of the
Queen would choose, on this occasion, to betray her interests.
For he must have known perfectly well why the Queen had
been asked to send for the brief. Catherine herself saw clearly
enough that the council wanted the brief in order to suppress it.
She wrote to Charles, as she had sworn to do, but her chaplain,
Thomas Abell, who carried the letter, also carried a message by
word of mouth, explaining that the Queen had written under
duress.[21] The brief remained in Spain.

This was a bitter disappointment for Wolsey and the King.
Further delays were now inevitable, for it was impossible to
proceed with the case until the authenticity of the brief was
determined one way or the other. For the Queen it meant that
for a few weeks or months there would be respite from the
relentless pressure of events. There was, however, one difficulty
that caused her anxiety. In the brief it was implied that she and
Arthur had been united in fact as well as in name; in the bull
the wording was altered by the insertion of the word *forsan* or
perhaps, to allow for the possibility that when Arthur died she
was still a virgin. Early in November, Catherine drew up a
statement protesting that her use of the brief in evidence was not
to be construed as an admission on her part that she had been
carnally known by Prince Arthur, which indeed she emphati-
cally denied. The affidavit was drawn up and sworn at Bridewell
in the presence of five of the bishops. Fisher was one of the witnesses and it is quite likely that in issuing her denial Catherine
was acting on his advice.[22]

It was for Henry to make the next move. His great matter was
no longer a secret and the Queen, he knew, had a loyal following among the London populace. The arrival of Campeggio had

sent rumours flying. Henry decided to show his hand. To the great chamber in Bridewell Palace, where only the day before Catherine had protested her innocence before the five bishops, he summoned the Lord Mayor of London, the aldermen and burgesses, members of the Inns of Court and privy councillors. For twenty years, he told them, they had lived more quietly and prosperously than any of their fathers before them. Everything they had gained would be lost, however, if he left no lawful heir to govern the kingdom after his death. Many learned clerks had warned him that the Princess Mary was not his lawful daughter nor the Queen his lawful wife, inasmuch as she was the widow of his brother Arthur. When a marriage was lately proposed between the Princess and the Duke of Orleans, he added, the French objected that the Princess was not the lawful daughter of the King of England, as it was well known that her begetting was contrary to the law of God. For this reason he had asked the Holy See to send him judges to determine the truth of the matter. He would gladly abide by their decision. Meanwhile, however, if any of his subjects spoke ill of him, he would make his head to fly.[23]

While Henry was proclaiming his readiness to accept the judgment of the Church in the settlement of his cause, Wolsey was working feverishly behind the scenes to make sure that the judgment was favourable to the King. He asked Clement for permission to determine the authenticity of the brief; failing that, he begged that His Holiness would himself pronounce the document a forgery.[24] He waited on the Queen with a story about certain ill-disposed persons who, he said, were conspiring against the life of the King, adding that if the Queen continued to oppose his wishes many would suspect that she was guilty of treason. He taxed her with witholding the brief from the King when she knew it would have quieted his conscience to have it. To make good the harm she had done, he urged her again to take the vows of chastity.[25] The Queen, however, was neither frightened nor deceived. Next the Cardinal turned his attention to the secret decretal that Campeggio had brought with him. It had been shown to Wolsey and the King but to no-one else. If the Pope would agree to its publication, the legates could come to a decision without further delay. Just before Christmas, however, John Casale reported to Wolsey that Clement had angrily refused to allow Campeggio to publish the decretal. Warned that if the King were denied what he asked the English Church would be lost to Rome, Clement answered that he could not disobey his conscience, nor could he knowingly commit an injustice. He pointed out to Casale that the legates were free to proceed under their existing commission to examine the evidence and give judgment on the merits of the case.[26] Clement knew well enough what Wolsey had in mind. He immediately sent his confidential secretary, Francesco Campana, to England with orders that the decretal be destroyed.

Still reluctant to act on a commission that called for a fair and open inquiry and a verdict in accordance with the law, Wolsey redoubled his efforts. In December he sent Sir Francis Brian and Knight to join the Casales and Peter Vannes at Rome. On their way they were to seek an audience with Francis in the hope of persuading him to support the King's suit. After continuing to Rome they were to explain the irregularities in the brief to His Holiness in the hope that he would agree to have it brought into the curia for examination or else declared a forgery without further formalities. Failing this, they were to seek a dispensation for the remarriage of the King on condition that the Queen agree to enter a house of religion. Finally, in case this expedient should also prove unsuccessful, they were to sound the Pope as to the propriety of the King's taking a second wife while still married to the first.[27] In January Stephen Gardiner, who had served the King so well the year before, left England once again to join the others at Rome.

They found Clement too ill to receive them. On all sides there were rumours of his death. In early February the news reached England, where Wolsey now saw a last chance to recover his position. He at once drew up instructions directing the agents at Rome to press for his own election if the rumours proved to be true.[28] But Wolsey lived in the hope for no more than a fortnight. Clement recovered. The desperate Cardinal had no choice but to renew his pleas for a decretal or at least for a more ample commission under which the case could be settled in England without risk of appeal.[29] Everyone expected Catherine to appeal to the Holy See and if such an appeal were to be admitted the legates would be unable to reach a decision in their own right. Indeed, as Wolsey well knew, the imperial agent at Rome was already pressing the Pope to revoke the legatine commission in favour of a hearing before the curia.[30]

Next the English agents turned their attention to the brief. They searched the papal registers, where no record of the document could be found.[31] The imperial archives were examined by Ghinucci and Lee, who sent Wolsey a minute description of the original, overlooking none of the suspected irregularities in the text.[32] Nevertheless, Clement persisted in refusing to pronounce on the question of authenticity until he had seen the brief itself and heard the arguments on both sides, though he did agree to send to Spain for the original so that it could be examined at Rome.[33] But in this Henry could see only another excuse for delay. Perhaps fearing that Charles would prevail upon Clement to advoke the case to Rome before anything more could be accomplished in the matter of the brief, he decided to wait no longer. He would proceed with the hearing before the legates on the strength of their existing commission. Wolsey sent at once for Brian and Gardiner to assist in preparing the King's case. Before he left Rome, however, Gardiner was to make one more effort to secure a more ample assurance from Clement that he would admit no appeal from the jurisdiction of the legates. He was to tell His Holiness that the original pollicitation had been damaged on its way to England; then, in drafting a new copy, he was to add certain "pregnant, fat, and available words" that would serve the purpose of the King. Casale, who would remain at Rome, was to deter the Pope from revoking the commission before the legates acting upon it could proceed to judgment. Peter Vannes stayed with Casale and Dr. William Benet was sent out to join them.[34]

Chapter II

A year of effort had been largely wasted. The English agents had won few concessions denied to them in the spring of 1528. The policy of the Holy See, however uncertain as to ways and means, had proved inflexible where fundamental objectives were concerned. The previous September, Sanga had written to Campeggio that if the Pope were to do as Henry wished he would compromise the Church and risk the ruin of the Holy See. He wrote again in December to say that His Holiness would be willing to endure the displeasure of the Emperor if only Henry's request were reasonable in itself. Sir Gregory Casale himself told his brother Vincent to advise Wolsey that, even if he had no reason to fear the force of imperial arms, Clement would never do what Henry asked of him.[1]

The only hope, for Wolsey and the King, was to hurry the case to a conclusion in England before Clement could revoke the legates' commission. And this they now set out to do. On 29 May, 1529, Wolsey and Campeggio sent the King a request for leave to proceed with the cause and to give sentence. The King was pleased to give his consent,[2] and on the last day of May the court was convened. It was a supreme moment. The hearings were held in the great hall of the Blackfriars in London. Contemporary accounts give a vivid impression of the scene. There were two chairs for the legates covered with cloth of gold. The floor was covered with carpets and the walls hung with arras. On the legates' right there was hung a cloth of estate behind a chair covered with rich tissue for the King, and on their left a chair for the Queen. At the first sitting, the papal commission was read out in the presence of the legates, who then appointed the Bishop of Lincoln and the Bishop of Bath and Wells to cite the King and Queen to appear before them on Friday, 18 June, between nine and ten in the morning.[3] On the 18th the legates sat again and the Bishops of Lincoln and of Bath and Wells testified that they had delivered the citations. Richard Sampson, Dean of the Chapel Royal, and Dr. John Bell appeared for the King. The Queen appeared in person and rose at once to protest against the competence of the legates, both of whom had an interest in gratifying the King, to hear and decide her cause. Thereupon the court was adjourned until Monday the 21st when Catherine was cited to appear once again to hear the decision of the legates as to her appeal.[4]

On this occasion, Henry made his first and only appearance before the legates. Opposite him sat the Queen. Between them, and facing the legates, were the Archbishop of Canterbury and the several bishops. On the right were the counsel for the King, Sampson and Bell; on the left the Queen's counsel, John Fisher, Bishop of Rochester, and Henry Standish, Bishop of St. Asaph. This, if we may trust contemporary accounts, was Fisher's first appearance before the court. In any case, there is no record of his attending either of the previous sittings. "The court being thus furnished and ordered", Cavendish tells us, "the judges commanded the crier to command silence." That done, "the crier called the King by the name of 'King Harry of England come into the court etc.' With that the King answered and said 'Here, my lords.' Then he called also the Queen by the name of

'Catherine Queen of England come into the court etc.'; who made no answer to the same, but rose up incontinent out of her chair whereas she sat and, because she could not come directly to the King, for the distance which severed them, she took pain to go about unto the King, kneeling down at his feet in the sight of all the court and assembly, to whom she said in effect, in broken English, as followeth :

" 'Sir,' quod she, 'I beseech you for all the loves that hath been between us and for the love of God, let me have justice and right; take of me some pity and compassion, for I am a poor woman and a stranger, born out of your dominion. I have here no assured friends, and much less indifferent counsel. I flee to you as to the head of justice within this realm. Alas, sir, wherein have I offended you, or what occasion of displeasure have I deserved against your will or pleasure? Intending, as I perceive, to put me from you, I take God and all the world to witness that I have been to you a true, humble, and obedient wife, ever confirmable to your will and pleasure, that never said or did anything to the contrary thereof, being always well pleased and contented with all things wherein ye had any delight or dalliance; whether it were in little or much, I never grudged in word or countenance, or showed a visage or spark of discontentation. I loved all those whom ye loved only for your sake, whether I had cause or no, and whether they were my friends or my enemies. This twenty years I have been your true wife (or more), and by me ye have had divers children, although it hath pleased God to call them out of this world, which hath been no default in me.

" 'And when ye had me at the first (I take God to be my judge) I was a true maid without touch of man; and whether it be true or no, I put it to your conscience. If there be any just cause by the law that ye can allege against me, either of dishonesty or any other impediment, to banish and put me from you, I am well content to depart to my great shame and dishonor. And if there be none, then here I most lowly beseech you let me remain in my former estate and to receive justice at your princely hands. The King your father was in the time of his reign of such estimation through the world for his excellent wisdom that he was accompted and called of all men "the second Solomon"; and my father Ferdinand, King of Spain, who was esteemed to be one of the wittiest princes that reigned in Spain many years before—who were both wise and excellent Kings in wisdom and princely behavior. It is not therefore to be doubted but that they elected and gathered as wise counsellors about them as to their high discretions was thought meet. Also, as me seemeth, there was in those days as wise, as well learned men, and men of as good judgment as be at this present in both realms, who thought then the marriage between you and me good and lawful. Therefore it is a wonder to me what new inventions are now invented against me, that never intended but honesty. And cause me to stand to the order and judgment of this new court, wherein ye may do much wrong if ye intend any cruelty; for ye may condemn me for lack of sufficient answer, having no indifferent counsel, but such as be assigned me, with whose wisdom and learning I am not acquainted. Ye must consider that they cannot be indifferent counsellors for my part which be your subjects and taken out of your own council before, wherein they be made privy, and dare not for your displeasure disobey your will and intent, being once made privy thereto. Therefore I most humbly require you in the way of charity and for the love of God (who is the just judge) to spare the extremity of this new court, until I may be advertized what way and order my friends in Spain will advise me to take. And if ye will not extend to me so much indifferent favor, your pleasure then be fulfilled, and to God I commit my case.'

"And even with that", Cavendish goes on, "she rose up, making low curtsy to the King, and so departed from thence."

Whereupon the crier called her again three times, but she refused to answer or return to her place and so was pronounced contumacious. Catherine had made an extraordinary impression on everyone who saw and heard her. After her simple assertion of human dignity and human worth, the proceedings of the court seemed suddenly sordid and shameful.

The King had now to make an effort to recover his position. He began by confessing that Catherine had been to him " 'as true, obedient, and as confirmable a wife as I could in my fancy wish or desire. She hath all the virtuous qualities that ought to be in a woman of her dignity or in any other of baser estate. Surely she is also a noble woman born, if nothing were in her but only her conditions will well declare the same.' " To satisfy those who suspected his motives, Wolsey asked the King to declare openly whether or not he had been the first mover of the affair. " 'My Lord Cardinal' ", replied the King, " 'I can well excuse you herein. Marry indeed, ye have been rather against me in attempting or setting forth thereof. And to put you all out of doubt, I will declare unto you the especial cause that moved me hereunto' "—and so the King told the court the story he had told the citizens of London the previous November, of how when a marriage was proposed between the Princess Mary and the Dauphin the French had questioned the legitimacy of the Princess and her right to the crown on the death of her father. " 'These words' ", he went on, " 'were so conceived within my scrupulous conscience that it bred a doubtful prick within my breast, which doubt pricked, vexed, and troubled so my mind, and so disquieted me, that I was in great doubt of God's indignation . . . and partly in despair of any issue male by her, it drave me at last to consider the estate of this realm, and the danger it stood in for lack of issue male to succeed me in this imperial dignity. I thought it good therefore in the relief of the weighty burden of scrupulous conscience, and the quiet estate of this noble realm, to attempt the law therein, and whether I might take another wife in case that my first copulation with this gentlewoman were not lawful; which I intend not for any carnal concupiscence, ne for any displeasure or mislike of the Queen's person or age, with whom I could be as well content to continue during my life, if our marriage may stand with God's laws, as with any woman alive. In which point consisteth all this doubt that we go now about to try by the learned wisdom and judgments of you our prelates and pastors of this realm here assembled for that purpose, to whose conscience and judgment I have committed the charge, according to the which (God willing) we will be right well contented to submit ourself, to obey the same for my part.

"'Wherein after I once perceived my conscience wounded with the doubtful case herein, I moved first this matter in confession to you, my Lord of Lincoln, my ghostly father [i.e., confessor]. And for as much as then yourself were in some doubt to give me counsel, moved me to ask further counsel of all you, my lords, wherein I moved you first my Lord of Canterbury, asking your license, for as much as you were our metropolitan, to put this matter in question. And so I did of all you, my lords, to the which ye have all granted by writing under all your seals, the which I have here to be showed.'

"'That is truth if it please your highness,' quod the Bishop of Canterbury, 'I doubt not but all my brethren here present will affirm the same.'" There was a pause while the King waited for the unspoken assent of the bishops. In the silence, however, a voice spoke out from the Queen's benches. "'No, sir, not I'", said the Bishop of Rochester, addressing the Archbishop of Canterbury, "'ye have not my consent thereto.'" The King turned on him in anger: "'look here upon this, is not this your hand and seal?' And showed him the instrument with seals. 'No, forsooth, sir,' quod the Bishop of Rochester, 'it is not my hand nor seal.' To that quod the King to my Lord of Canterbury, 'Sir, how say ye? Is it not his hand and seal?' 'Yes, sir,' quod he. 'That is not so,' quod the Bishop of Rochester, 'for indeed you were in hand with me to have both my hand and seal, as other of my lords hath already done, but then I said to you that I would never consent to no such act for it were much against my conscience, nor my hand and seal should never be seen at any such instrument (God willing) with much more matter touching the same communication between us.' 'You say truth,' quod the Bishop of Canterbury, 'such words ye had unto me, but at the last ye were fully persuaded that I should for you subscribe your name and put to a seal myself, and ye would allow the same.' 'All which words and matter,' quod the Bishop of Rochester, 'under your correction, my lord, and supportation of this noble audience, there is nothing more untrue.'"

The effect of Fisher's words must have been breathtaking. And yet they are of a piece with everything we know of the man. No-one else in the kingdom would have dared to give the lie in public to the Archbishop of Canterbury and the King.

Apparently the King had procured an affidavit of some sort from a number of the bishops before the opening of the court at Blackfriars, with the intention of displaying it, as in fact he did, before the legates. Henry had always known the value of presenting a policy in such a way as to make it appear that he was acting with the advice and consent of his subjects. If the advice that was needed could be obtained with the consent of those who gave it, so much the better. If not, other means could be found of prevailing upon a reluctant bishop who was mindful of the King's displeasure. And if this was not enough—as in Fisher's case it evidently was not—it might be necessary to resort to less honourable means. Because of his reputation for learning and integrity, Fisher was worth courting. His support would have done more for Henry's cause, both at home and abroad, than that of any other single man. That is why Wolsey had been at such pains, two years before, to enlist his support. And that is no doubt why Warham had been tempted to add his name to the affidavit Henry was to produce before the legates.[5] Confronted in public, the archbishop made no attempt to deny that Fisher was telling the truth. He let Fisher have the last word. " 'All which words and matter,' quod the Bishop of Rochester, 'under your correction, my lord, and supportation of this noble audience, there is nothing more untrue.' " Warham did not answer. Nor did the King attempt to defend him. Instead, he passed the matter over with what amounted to an admission of the truth of what Fisher had said: " 'it shall make no matter. We will not stand with you in argument herein, for you are but one man.' "[6]

When the King had finished, Campeggio rose to announce that the court had refused Catherine's appeal against the jurisdiction of the legates. Thereupon the hearing was adjourned until Friday, 25 June. The Friday came and went and the Queen still refused to appear. The next day a new citation was served on her, requiring her to appear before the legates on the following Monday.[7] Again she refused and hearings resumed in her absence. The legates called on the counsel for the King to open their case. Their first object was to show that the marriage of Catherine and Arthur had been consummated. Unless they could put that beyond reasonable doubt, they could not hope to show that Henry had ever, in fact, contracted an affinity with Catherine. And unless they could show that an impediment had actually existed they could not expect to achieve anything by questioning the validity of the bull that professed to dispense with it. It was, they admitted at the outset, only a presumption they sought to establish, for no man could ever know the truth of such a matter. Fisher, it seems, had no stomach for the disclosures made by the witnesses who were called to testify to the likely performance of the young prince as a husband. " '*Ego nosco veritatem*' ", he broke in impatiently, 'I know the truth.' " 'How know ye the truth?' quod my Lord Cardinal. 'Forsooth,' quod he, '*Ego sum professor veritatis*, I know that God is truth itself, nor He never spake but truth; which said "*Quod deus coniunxit, homo non separet.*" And for as much as this marriage was made and joined by God to a good intent, I say that I know the truth, the which cannot be broken or loosed by the power of man upon no one feigned occasion.'"[8] Fisher knew perfectly well that he was begging the question. As Wolsey pointed out, the whole object of the inquiry was to determine whether or not the marriage of the King and Queen had in fact been "made and joined by God to a good intent". To take for granted that it was so made and joined was to make nonsense of the whole proceedings. And this, no doubt, was just what Fisher intended. The marriage, as everyone admitted, had been made in good faith, with the express consent of the Holy See, more than twenty years before. To question it now upon a "feigned occasion"—for no-one could suppose that the defects discovered in the Julian bull were anything more than that—was in effect to put apart those whom God had joined together.

Fisher did not, of course, expect the court to be satisfied so easily. He was prepared to answer Wolsey on his own ground by showing that the Julian bull was sufficient to dispense with the existing impediment, regardless of whether or not Catherine had been a virgin when she married the King. He presented his case that same day, according to news sent to France by Jean Du Bellay, the French ambassador in London. Campeggio's secretary, Florian, wrote to Salviati in Rome at greater length.[9] The Bishop of Rochester, he said, reminded the legates that in a former sitting the King had told the court of his scruples and asked that his conscience be set at rest. The bishop came forward now because he believed it to be his duty to relieve the King of his perplexity. For, he declared, he could assure the King without hesitation that his marriage was pleasant in the sight of God and beyond the reproach of men. He likened himself to John the Baptist, who had given his life in the cause of marriage, even before the union of man and woman had been made holy by the shedding of Christ's blood. Before he withdrew, he submitted a written brief setting forth the several heads of his argument. A fragment of this document has survived, enough to indicate the main outlines of Fisher's case, which is set forth in six axioms. In the first of these Fisher makes it plain that there is no impediment in the laws of God or nature to the marriage of a widow and her late husband's brother. The rule in *Leviticus*, he explains, creates a judicial impediment that derives what authority it has from the ordinances of canon law, which can be dispensed with, for sufficient reason, by the Pope. The other five axioms follow naturally from the first. In issuing his dispensation for the marriage of Henry and Catherine, Julius II exercised an authority that rightfully belonged to the Church in whose name he acted. Once the impediment of affinity had been removed, there was nothing in existing law to prevent the marriage. Having been joined together according to the accustomed rites of the Church, the King and Queen were *ipso facto* united by the hand of God and so could not be put apart for any cause.[10]

Fisher was followed by Henry Standish, another of Catherine's counsellors, but he spoke without conviction and his words had little effect on the court. And so it was against Fisher that the King's advisers now directed their attack. The man chosen to reply was Stephen Gardiner, who had been summoned from Rome to help in the preparation of the case for the King. He first submitted a short statement in which he argued that even if it were admitted that the Pope had the right to dispense with the impediment of affinity, it could be shown that the existing dispensation was insufficient because of its formal irregularities.[11] So far Gardiner had confined himself to the argument set forth by Fisher in his six axioms concerning the dispensation. But the King, who took pride in the fact that any of his subjects was free to speak his mind without fear or favour, had been stung by Fisher's reference to John the Baptist. And so he had Gardiner prepare a second brief to vindicate his honour.[12] When the Bishop of Rochester was first told of the King's scruples, Gardiner announced, he had admitted that the King had reason for his anxiety and had urged him to submit the question to a judicial inquiry. Gardiner's statement must have been shown to Fisher, for there are marginal comments in his hand throughout the text. At this point he remarked drily, 'Non hec dixi certe cardinalis voluit ut hec dixissem : I said nothing of the kind, though the Cardinal wished I had." Having once confessed the need for such a hearing as this, Gardiner went on, why did the bishop now come before the court and speak of the King's scruples as if they had no real substance and could be resolved by a little study and learning? If this were so, why did he not come forward earlier and speak to the King in private and relieve him of his anxiety? This, of course, was just what Fisher had done more than a year before when he went to the King in his palace at Westminster and advised him to trouble his mind no further with doubts as to his marriage. From this pretended slight, however, Gardiner turned to another. By what token, he asked the court, had the King deserved to be likened to Herod? And by what right did the Bishop of Rochester liken himself to John the Baptist, rashly declaring that he had a juster cause to sustain than the Baptist himself? In the quiet of his study Fisher jotted down a modest question of his own : "Quid amplius ego quam cardinalis qui se comburi potius pateretur & membratim discerpi quam contra iusticiam faceret : what more did I say than the Cardinal, who claimed that he would rather be burned or torn limb from limb than act contrary to justice?" When Cardinal Wolsey professed that he would rather suffer than be untrue to himself, the King merely applauded. Why then should he be offended with the Bishop of Rochester when he used the same words? Was it because he suspected that Fisher, unlike Wolsey, might mean what he said?

At the next sitting the hearing was resumed and the legates turned to an examination of witnesses produced by the crown to show that Catherine had lain with Arthur and so contracted an affinity with the King his brother. Only two persons had ever known the truth of this question, and of these two the Queen alone was living. And the Queen had declared on many occasions, in private and in public and under the seal of confession, that when she came to Henry she was, as she put it, a true maid without touch of man. As for the King, he had often boasted in the early days of his marriage that he had found Catherine a virgin when she came to him.[13] But that was long forgotten. Now the legates were to ascertain the truth, the King's truth, from those who had it on hearsay from those who professed to know. The old Earl of Shrewsbury remembered how, almost 28 years before, he, together with the Earl of Oxford and others, had conducted the young Prince of Wales to Catherine's bedchamber. He had always supposed that the Prince had used her as his wife, the Earl testified, because he had done so himself at the same age. The Marquis of Dorset could go a little farther. He had escorted the Prince to his wife's bedchamber after their marriage and had observed Catherine there, lying under a coverlet. Arthur had a good and sanguine complexion, he added, and looked fit to make a woman his wife. When Sir Anthony Willoughby gave his evidence there must have been many in the court who did not know whether to laugh or to weep for the young Prince of long ago. Willoughby had been present when Prince Arthur went to bed on the night of his marriage in the palace of the Bishop of London. Next morning, the Prince had addressed him before several of his attendants, calling out bravely, " 'Willoughby, bring me a cup of ale, for I have been this night in the midst of Spain' ", and later he had said to them all, " 'Masters, it is good pastime to have a wife' ". Sir William Thomas and the Viscount Fitzwater had also accompanied Arthur to Catherine's chamber. Fitzwater had seen the Prince into the bed where his wife was lying, but Sir William had so far neglected his duty as to observe only that the Prince was wearing a nightshirt. Another witness remembered that Maurice St. John, who was also present, had said to the Prince at breakfast on the morrow of his wedding, " 'Sir, ye look well upon the matter' ", to which the boy had replied, " 'I look well for one that hath been in the midst of Spain.' "[14] That the young Prince, on this one occasion when his sad short life touched the pages of history, had in fact worn a nightshirt, gone to bed with his wife in the palace of the Bishop of London, and had, the next morning, boasted of his manhood and called for a cup of ale to support his courage, of this we need have no doubt. But that he ever made himself a genuine impediment to the marriage of Catherine and Henry there is no evidence whatever.

The court pressed on with all possible speed, for Wolsey knew that time was against him. Campeggio complained of the haste and did all he could to delay the proceedings.[15] Meanwhile, the English agents at Rome sought desperately to prevent Clement from admitting Catherine's appeal. On 9 July they sent messages to Wolsey and the King warning them that the Queen's appeal had arrived in Rome. Clement had told them, they reported, that he no longer had any choice but to advoke the cause to Rome for consideration by the papal curia. They had warned him of the probable consequences of such an act, but he had refused to change his mind. This they blamed on the importunity of the imperial agents, who continued to insist on a hearing at Rome, though what Clement told Benet in so many words was that he could not satisfy the King without doing an injustice to his conscience and bringing dishonour to his see.[16] Already Clement had sent word to both Wolsey and the King, explaining that he could no longer refuse to admit the Queen's appeal.[17] It was clear that unless the legates acted quickly they would not be able to act at all. At Wolsey's insistence, they pressed on with the examination of evidence.

But it was too late. On 15 July Clement revoked the commission he had given to Wolsey and Campeggio.[18] Three days later he sent letters to England to notify Wolsey and the King of his decision.[19] While this news was still on its way, however, the King demanded that the legates proceed at once to judgment. For them, the moment of decision was at hand. Campeggio well knew what was expected of him at Rome. He had been told when he left for England that he was in no circumstances to come to a decision without further instructions. And on the eve of the first sitting at Blackfriars, he had been reminded once again that he was not to pronounce sentence on his own authority.[20] As for Wolsey, he knew well enough what the King and the council expected of him. He must have realized now that, do what he could, he could no longer serve two masters at once.

At the end of July the moment came. The court was crowded with spectators who had come to hear the verdict. Cavendish says that the King was there himself. Campeggio rose to speak. " 'I come not so far to please any man' ", he began, in words that must have given small comfort to the King and his friends, " 'for fear, meed, or favor, be he King or any other potentate. I have no such respect to the persons that I will offend my conscience. I will not for favor or displeasure of any high estate or mighty prince do that thing that should be against the law of God. I am an old man, both sick and impotent, looking daily for death. What should it then avail me to put my soul in the danger of God's displeasure to my utter damnation for the favor of any prince or high estate in this world? My coming and being here is only to see justice ministered according to my conscience, as I thought thereby the matter good or bad.' " And so he announced his decision: " 'to avoid all these ambiguities and obscure doubts, I intend not to damn my soul for no prince or potentate alive. I would therefore (God willing) wade no further in this matter unless I have the just opinion and judgment with the assent of the Pope and such other of his counsel as hath more experience and better learning in such doubtful laws than I have. Wherefore I will adjourn this court for this time, according to the order of the court in Rome from whence this court and jurisdiction is derived.' "[21] The adjournment was, of course, nothing but a pretext. The case had been advoked to Rome and the sittings at Blackfriars would never be resumed.

There was consternation in the court. The King had been denied his wish. The kingdom had been forced to submit to an authority that governed its decisions by considerations other than the tangible interests of the English people. There was nothing new in this. For generations Englishmen had knelt at the shrine of Thomas Becket, a man who was remembered precisely because he had compelled an imperious King to recognize and respect the authority of the Church. But there was a difference. If the deepest aspirations of the English people had once been united in Thomas Becket, they were united now in the gilded figure of Henry VIII. When the Duke of Suffolk heard what Campeggio had to say, he stepped forward and cried out, " 'It was never . . . merry in England whilst we had Cardinals among us' ".[22] It was said that all men marvelled what he intended. Few could have foreseen the full significance of his words.

For Fisher this must have been a moment of rare elation. The Church, after long and painful hesitation, had spoken out at last. His own immediate object was achieved. For the first time in many weeks, he could return to his cathedral church at Rochester and leave behind him the mummery of the Court. He could not know then that he would soon again be sent for, or that before he was a year older the simple, sturdy and apparently changeless order of his life would be gone forever.

Chapter 12

The court at Blackfriars was adjourned at the end of July. Before a fortnight had elapsed, writs had been issued for a new Parliament, the first since 1523. This was Henry's answer to the Holy See. Wolsey had warned Clement again and again of what would happen if he did not gratify the King. Had Clement yielded, the primacy of Rome would no doubt have been preserved. But he had refused to yield and the consequences of his refusal Wolsey could foresee only too well. Denied the object of his desire by the Church, the King would make the Church his own.

Henry saw—it was the supreme insight of his reign—that the strongest feelings of his people were no longer centred on the Cross, austerely offering as it did the love of God to all men who would receive it; what stirred them most deeply now, he sensed, was something new and different, speaking in the very blood of Englishmen, speaking to them of their country, with its fields and farms, its ale-houses, its cottages and gilded palaces, its yeoman archers and its armoured knights, speaking to Englishmen as nothing else had spoken to them before of their country and of their love for it. Henry saw that if he made himself the symbol of England, Englishmen would follow him as, in story and legend, they had followed St. George against the dragon.

His first necessity was to summon Parliament. He knew that if he could concentrate attention on the grievances of the laity against the clergy, he could command broad popular support for policies aimed at secular control of the Church. Writs were issued early in August for a session to open on 3 November. Meanwhile, plans were laid to sound out the universities. Thomas Cranmer is said to have first suggested the idea to Gardiner and Fox. He proposed that the King submit his cause to a panel of divines chosen from Oxford and Cambridge. Cranmer was a member of the radical group at Cambridge that also included Bilney and Arthur and George Joye. Only two years before, Bilney and Arthur had been examined as heretics for their views on the priesthood and the Church. Now, however, such men could be of use. Cranmer was admitted at once into the service of the King. It was arranged that six divines from each university should meet at Cambridge and there give judgment as to the validity of the King's marriage. The meeting took place in September or October. Cranmer himself did not attend and perhaps for that reason the divines felt free to decide in favour of the Queen. When Cranmer heard of the verdict, he set to work with such a will that he succeeded in prevailing upon five of the Cambridge divines to change their minds. His success soon brought him to the attention of the King. He was summoned to Greenwich and encouraged to set forth his opinions in writing. It was decided that he should spend the next three or four months at Durham House, the London home of the Earl of Wiltshire, preparing his case. While he was at work, the King decided to follow up his success at Cambridge by consulting the leading theologians on the Continent as well.

Meanwhile, negotiations continued at Rome. Henry refused to accept a citation to appear, either in person or by proxy, to argue his case before the papal curia. He insisted that the case be heard in England and nowhere else. Already he spoke like a man who recognized no superior, under God, but his own will and the will of his people. When the advocation arrived in England and was brought to the King with a message from the Pope exhorting him to submit, he remarked with ill-concealed irony, "See how his Holiness only exhorts when he could command."[1]

Campeggio took his leave on 7 October but before he embarked at Dover on the 8th he was subjected to the rough indignity of a search. If the King's agents were looking for the decretal the legate had brought with him to England, they were disappointed. Had it been found, Wolsey could perhaps have been persuaded to act upon it. But without it the Cardinal was no longer of use to the King. The next day a writ of *praemunire* brought his career to an end.

The several statutes of provisors and *praemunire* had been designed to protect the right of the King to dispose of spiritual livings within his kingdom and at the same time to preserve and protect the jurisdiction of the secular courts. They provided the severest penalties for those who were provided or appointed to English livings by the Pope, and for those who appealed to the papal curia against decisions given in the royal courts. But these statutes were never strictly enforced and Edward III himself, in whose interest they had been adopted, made a practice of selling licences to papal provisors. Richard II went so far as to accept a concordat with Boniface IX under which papal provision became once again an established custom. Certainly Henry VIII, until now an ardent champion of the papacy, had hitherto made no objection to the practice. As for Wolsey, Henry had himself desired his appointment as a papal legate, and had used his influence at Rome to obtain it. To indict him now, on the grounds that as legate he had exercised an authority prejudicial to the royal prerogative, was to ignore the notorious fact that he had acted at all times as the servant of the King. It was this that perplexed and grieved the ruined Cardinal: had I but served my God as I have served my King, he remarked as he lay dying, he would not have given me over in my grey hairs. If Wolsey was to suffer because he had recognized the supremacy of Rome, even if he had sought to use papal authority only to further the interests of the King, what was to become of those who, like Tunstal at London or Fisher at Rochester, had used their position in the Church for the advancement of learning and the cure of souls? It was a question no man liked to ask and few could answer.

At first Wolsey refused to plead in the King's Bench, not wishing to admit the jurisdiction of a lay court. But when a second bill of indictment was brought down on 20 October, he decided to answer it rather than face an act of attainder in the House of Commons. Two days later, in the hope of a royal pardon, he formally confessed his guilt and surrendered all his goods to the King. He had already given up the great seal and relinquished the office of Lord Chancellor. A few months later, he was summarily ordered to his benefice at York, where he had not been seen since his appointment as archbishop fifteen years before. His arrest at Cawood, however, cut short his slow and stately progress to the north, and he died without setting foot in his cathedral city.

The fall of Wolsey involved the whole body of the Church. If he had deserved the royal displeasure, so had they all—bishops, abbots, priests and deacons, some of whom had patiently served God as only Wolsey had served the King. As they gathered at Westminster at the beginning of November for the opening of Convocation and a new session of Parliament, they must have known what was in store for them. They had not long to wait. The Commons fell at once to enumerating their grievances against the clergy. They complained of the excessive fees charged in the ecclesiastical courts for probate of wills. It was said that estates had been compelled to pay 1000 marks and more (almost $70,000) for probate. They complained of excessive fees charged for the burial of the dead—an old grievance that recalled bitter memories of the case of Richard Hunne. They complained also of the practice of allowing one man to enjoy the revenues of a number of livings without attending to his duties as a priest in any of them. Wolsey himself, the ranking prelate in England, had been the most flagrant example of a practice that was toler-

ated at every level of the Church. He had for many years enjoyed the enormous revenues of his several livings, while devoting himself entirely to affairs of state. As in the great sees so in
many an ordinary parish, it was customary to leave the cure of
souls to an ill-paid vicar while the fruits of the living were spent
elsewhere.

In the first days of the session the Commons sent three bills
to the Lords, one concerning fines or fees to be taken by ordinaries for the probate of wills, a second concerning mortuaries
and a third concerning pluralities. The bill concerning probate
provided that after 1 April, 1530 no ordinary engaged in the
proving of wills should be permitted to charge fees in excess of
those set forth in the bill. Similar provisions were made for the
regulation of mortuary fees. The bill concerning pluralities provided that after 1 April, 1530 no ordinary having a benefice with
cure of souls worth £8 a year or more should take or enjoy any
other benefice. An exception was made for members of the
King's council, who might hold three benefices, and for the royal
chaplains, who might hold two. The bill provided further that
every ordinary should reside in his benefice unless licensed at
the pleasure of the King to reside elsewhere.[2]

On 5 November, while these bills were still before the House
of Commons, the clergy had assembled in Convocation at St.
Paul's. They proceeded at once to consider the state of the
Church. More than ten years before Wolsey had called a legatine synod at Westminster to discuss ways and means of renew-
ing spiritual discipline. On that occasion, as many of those
present must still have remembered, Fisher had spoken bitterly
of the worldly ambitions of the clergy: why should we, he had
asked, " 'exhort our flockes to eschew and shun worldly ambition, when we our selves that be byshopps, do wholely sett our
mindes to the same things we forbidd in them' "? How can we
preach " 'humilitie, sobrietie, and contempt of the world' ",
while giving ourselves up to " 'hawtines in minde, pride in

gesture, sumptuousnes in apparell, and damnable excesse in all worldly delicates' "?[3] The clergy did not need the Commons to teach them the duties of their calling. As long as Wolsey governed the Church, it is true, little progress could be made. He was preoccupied with affairs of state; furthermore, he represented in his own person many of the most shocking abuses of clerical privilege. Nor would he allow Warham to undertake the work for which he himself had so little liking. But the fall of Wolsey, however disturbing to those who saw in it a threat to the independent authority of the Church, was also an opportunity. Those in the Church who had long spoken of the need for reform were now in a position to make a new start.

The opportunity came too late. At its third session, on 12 November, the Convocation drew up a series of articles dealing with clerical morality, simony, pluralism, monastic discipline and other matters.[4] By that time, however, the bills concerning clerical reform had been adopted by the Commons and were already before the House of Lords. In the upper house the bishops and abbots were in a position to outvote the lay lords and resistance quickly developed to the bills concerning probate and mortuaries. Churchmen might recognize the need for reform, but they were suspicious that the House of Commons was less concerned with the reformation of the Church than with its revenues. Fisher at once saw which way the wind was blowing. The probate and mortuary bills were "maliciusly devised", he warned the Lords, and were intended "under coler of reformacion of abuses, to the utter ruin of the spiritualty".[5] In Convocation Fisher had been a consistent advocate of reform. He himself held one of the poorest sees in England and had more than once, it was said, refused preferment to a richer. His life was blameless. He had nothing to hide from the laity and he had nothing to lose. If he opposed the bills sent up by the Commons he opposed them because he realized that the grievances of the laity, legitimate though they might be in themselves, were being used as a pretext by those whose real purpose was to deprive the Church of its liberty : " 'our holy Mother the Churche beinge left vnto vs by the great liberallitie and dilligence of our forefathers, in most perfect & peaceable freedome, shall now by vs be brought into servile thraldome, lyke to a bound maid, or rather by litle & litle to be cleane banished and driven out of our confines and dwelling places' ". He pleaded with the Lords to take thought for the ancient " 'libertie of our mother the Church' ". He reminded them of what had happened " 'amonge the Bohemians and Germans' ", who " 'by the snares of John Husse, and after him Martin Luther' " had " 'excluded them selves from the Vnitie of *Christes* holy Church. These men now amonge vs' ", he went on, " 'seeme to reprove the life and doings of the clergie; but after such sort as they indevour to bringe them into contempt and hatred of the layetie, and so finding falte with other mens manner*s* whom they haue noe authoritie to correct, *o*mmitt and forget their owne, which is far worse & much more out of order then the other. But yf *the* truth were knowne ye shall find that they rather hunger and thirst after the riches and possessions of *th*e clergie then after amendment of their faltes and abuses. Wherfore' ", he concluded, " 'I will tell you (my lordes) playnly, what I thinke, except you resist manfully by yo*ur* authorities this violent heape of mischeefe offered by the co*m*mons, ye shall shortly see all obedience withdrawne, first from *the* clergie, and after yo*ur* selves, whervpon will insewe the vtter ruine and daunger of the Christian faith; and in place of it (that which is lykely to followe) the most wicked and tyrannicall government of the Turke; for ye shall finde that all these mischeefs amonge them ryseth throwth lack of faith.' "[6] A majority of the Lords agreed with Fisher. The bills were defeated.

The Commons took their case to the King. They sent Sir Thomas Audeley, the Speaker, with thirty of their number to York Place, to complain of the words of the Bishop of Rochester.

Fisher was sent for and asked to explain himself, whereupon he told the King that he had done no more than speak his mind in defence of the Church, which he saw daily injured and which he felt bound in his conscience to serve.[7] The King made no objection. With the lay members of both houses behind him, he could afford to ignore the opposition of a handful of the bishops. He proposed that the disputed legislation be referred to a committee of both houses. Eight members of the committee were nominated by the House of Commons, and of the eight members nominated by the House of Lords, four were laymen. The four spiritual members were outnumbered three to one by the lay members, as Henry intended they should be, and the outcome was never in doubt. The probate and mortuary bills were at once approved and became law. Parliament was prorogued on 17 December. Fisher returned to Rochester for Christmas along the familiar road through country now grown cold and bare. All the high hopes of the previous summer had turned to dust and he was alone.

Early in the New Year Cranmer, who had been at work since October in the household of the Earl of Wiltshire, finished his book on the King's marriage. His work represents something of a new departure. As long as he hoped to obtain the consent of the Holy See to a dissolution of his marriage, Henry had no desire to question the competence of the Church to decide in such a case. But now that the Holy See had refused to give its consent, he was free to develop a more radical approach. As long as the case was before the papal legates sitting at Blackfriars, the King's counsel had been satisfied to rest their case on the supposed deficiencies of the Julian bull. But as things now stood, Cranmer was prepared to go much farther. He argued that marriage within the forbidden degrees was prohibited not only by the canon law of the Church but also by natural law and the law of God. Since the Church had no right to dispense with divine law or the laws of nature, it follows that no dispensation was sufficient to remove the impediment to the marriage of the King and Queen.[8]

Henry could not hope that Clement would consent to such a proposition as this. Indeed, he no longer looked for the consent of the Holy See. What he now hoped was that he could prevail upon public opinion to sanction his view that the Church had no authority either to make or unmake his marriage. Richard Croke had already been sent to Italy to argue the King's case before the theologians of Padua, Ferrara and Bologna. Cranmer was now sent on a similar mission to the universities of France and Spain. With him went the Earl of Wiltshire, John Stokesley (soon to succeed Tunstal in the see of London) and Edward Lee (who a year later would take Wolsey's place at York). All, like Cranmer himself, were new men.

The King undertook to inform the clerks of Oxford and Cambridge of his wishes. To Cambridge he sent Gardiner and Fox with a message requiring the officers of the university to submit their opinion of his marriage under their common seal. The most learned men in Christendom, he reminded them, had declared that neither natural nor divine law permits two brothers to take the same woman to wife. They had always served him like faithful subjects, he added, and he expected them to do so now. A few weeks later he wrote in similar terms to the University of Oxford, to whom he sent the Bishop of Lincoln and Dr. Bell, who had served him as proctor at the hearing before Wolsey in 1527 and again two years later at Blackfriars.[9] Fisher seems to have taken no part in the proceedings at Cambridge and to have ignored the importunities of Gardiner and Fox just as he had ignored those of Cranmer a few months before. His influence at Cambridge must still have been considerable and there is every reason to suppose that his intervention might have been decisive. Why he chose to remain silent we do not know. In Fisher's absence, Gardiner and Fox were entertained by the Vice-Chancellor, whom they found more to their purpose. The several

doctors, bachelors of divinity and masters of arts were assembled
and the question put to them. There followed a long and acri-
monious debate. A motion favourable to the King failed to carry.
After the vote, however, a number of those who had been of the
contrary opinion were, as Gardiner himself relates, persuaded
to depart; whereupon the motion carried.[10]

There were difficulties also at Oxford. The King's message
was received early in March, but the university could not be induced to give judgment until the beginning of April. Warham,
who was Chancellor, took a more active part in the proceedings
than Fisher had done at Cambridge. Only a week after the
arrival of Longland and Bell, he sent an angry letter to the
bachelors and doctors of divinity demanding an immediate
decision. On 28 March he reproved them again for their delay,
warning them that if they failed to decide the question in a
manner satisfactory to the King they would regret their impru-
dence.[11] The warning came none too soon, for within a week
the King had sent the Duke of Suffolk to Oxford to remind the
scholars of their duty.[12] They held out no longer. On 4 April the
several faculties gave their consent to the question put to them:
"Quod ducere uxorem fratris, mortui sine liberis, cognitam a
priori viro per *carnalem copulam*, nobis christianis est de jure
divino pariter et naturali prohibitum": it is, they agreed, contrary to the laws of God and nature for a woman to marry her
late husband's brother, unless she comes to him a virgin.[13]

On the Continent Henry's agents met with equal success.
There was, it is true, resistance at Paris, and Poitiers decided for
Catherine. But with the help of Francis they were successful at
Orleans, Bourges and Toulouse. Alcala and Salamanca, sensitive
for their part to the imperial interest, declared for the Queen,
as did Naples. In Italy Richard Croke tirelessly collected as many
testimonials as he could afford. Ferrara, Padua and Bologna
were all for the King. On 21 March Clement issued a bull pro-
hibiting all spiritual persons from commenting on the marriage,

but the inhibition was largely ignored.[14] The imperial cause had few friends in France or Italy; relations between England and France were now cordial, whatever they had once been, and in Italy there was still the hope of English aid. Besides, Henry had money to spend.[15] Such, it appears, were the arguments that counted with the bachelors and doctors of divinity.

Chapter 13

Since Christmas Fisher had continued in retirement at Rochester. Aside from the normal work of his diocese, he was occupied with the preparation of new statutes for St. John's. In the intervals of his other business, however, his mind returned again and again to the events that had so radically disturbed the quiet of Christian England. He knew of course that the causes of his anxiety lay far deeper than the King's desire for a son. Knowing this, he would have done well to devote his remaining energies to persuading the bishops that their only hope and the only hope for the Church lay in a restoration of learning and a renewal of discipline. In his own diocese he had laboured for a generation to nourish and perfect, so far as he could, a community of the faithful united in charity and obedience. Had he been able to persuade others to follow his example, the Church would have been better able to give an account of itself in the present crisis. But he was not equal to the occasion. He no longer possessed the inner reserves needed for such a task. Perhaps no man could have done what had to be done. As for Warham, he was old and had no sense of the needs of the moment, and without leadership at Canterbury there was little hope that the Church would rediscover its meaning and purpose.

Fisher chose instead to meet his adversaries on their own ground. Over and over again he argued the case for the Queen. Eustace Chapuys, who had recently replaced Mendoça as imperial ambassador, wrote to Charles V on 31 December, 1529 enclosing two treatises on the marriage, one by Tunstal and one by Fisher. Tunstal had been one of the Queen's counsellors and had prepared a brief for presentation to the legates at Blackfriars in June of 1529, but he had been sent on a mission to Cambrai during the hearing and the brief had never been delivered. It was probably this brief that Chapuys now sent to Spain. Whether or not the treatise by Fisher was one that had been submitted to the legates six months before we do not know. It was probably a new version prepared during the autumn before Fisher left Rochester for the opening of Parliament. The Lords rose on 17 December and within a few days Fisher was at work on another treatise. This he sent to the Queen with the request that she have it delivered to Chapuys. On 6 February Chapuys sent word to Charles that Fisher had been revising the work he had written the autumn before and had since then completed another, a copy of which he enclosed.[1] Fisher evidently hoped that he would find support on the Continent for views that could no longer obtain a hearing in England.

Occupied as he was with these matters, before winter was over he was troubled by new anxieties. He was sent for by Warham to act jointly with the archbishop on a commission to examine one Thomas Hitton on a charge of heresy. Hitton was a priest of Maidstone. Apparently influenced by the teaching of William Tyndale, he had repudiated the established doctrines of the priesthood and the mass and had fled to the Continent to escape inquiry. Later he had returned as an agent for Tyndale and been arrested. In due course he was brought before Warham and Fisher and examined for heresy. For five days the two bishops laboured to persuade Hitton to return to the community of the faithful, but he steadfastly refused and at length, on the fifth day, they turned him over to the secular authorities. In accordance with the law, he was duly burned as a heretic at Maidstone.[2] Fisher no doubt saw Thomas Hitton as one of those who laboured in the vineyard to despoil the people—as he himself had put it in his address to the Lords—of " 'their auncient and catholyke faith' ", and who sought to exclude believers in England from " 'the Vnitie of *Christes* holy Church.' " That Hitton would have made a mute appeal to his compassion we have no reason to doubt. Before agreeing to let the law run its course, however, he may well have been reminded how on a time—as he told it—an axe that lacked a handle came to a wood, " 'and making his moane to the great trees, how that for lack of a handle to worke withall he was faine to stand ydle : he therfore desired of them to graunt him some yonge sapling in the wood to make him one; they mistrustinge no guile forth with graunted a yong small tree, wherof he shaped himself a handle, and being at last a perfect axe in all points, he fell to worke, and so labored in the wood, that in processe of time he left nether great tree nor small standinge.' "[3]

It was not long before Fisher himself was once again made to feel the sharp edge of Henry's will. A number of temporal and spiritual lords were summoned to appear at Court on Sunday, 12 June. There they found that they were required to sign a public remonstrance addressed to the Pope, urging His Holiness to recognize the justice of the King's cause and the practical necessities of his kingdom. The King of England, they were to declare, was most eminent for his virtues and reigned by undoubted right. He lacked nothing but a son born of lawful wedlock to succeed him in his inheritance. To secure the succession, His Holiness had only to pronounce the King's marriage null and void, as so many learned men had already done. But if His Holiness refused to listen to their petition and abandoned the people of England to their own devices, they would be forced to find a remedy elsewhere.[4] The petition was despatched a

month later, under date of 13 July. The Dukes of Norfolk and
Suffolk gave their names, as did the Marquis of Dorset and the
Marquis of Exeter and thirteen earls. But of the spiritual lords
only six consented: the Archbishops of Canterbury and York
and the Bishops of Chichester, Carlisle, Lincoln and St. David's.
We do not find the name of Cuthbert Tunstal, recently translated from London to the great see of Durham; nor that of Sir
Thomas More, who had succeeded Wolsey as Lord Chancellor;
nor that of the Bishop of Rochester. Whether or not these men
refused to sign the declaration we do not know; it may be that
they were spared the necessity.[5]

The answer did not arrive for more than two months, and
when it came it was not to the King's liking. Clement professed
himself unable to understand the discontent of the English lords,
unless, as he put it, they supposed that the Church was so deeply
indebted to the King of England that the dispute should be
settled in his favour regardless of the merits of the case. He reminded them of the scandal that would follow the dissolution
of such a marriage, contracted as it was with the consent of the
Holy See at the wish of Henry VII of England and Ferdinand
of Aragon, a marriage continued for so many years and blessed
with several children, one of whom was still living. He confessed that he owed much to the King, but he added that in
giving judgment he had also to consider Him by whose authority
Kings reign and princes govern. As for what they said of seeking
a remedy elsewhere, this, he replied, was a resolution worthy of
neither their good sense nor their Christian principles, and he
admonished them to think no more of such devices.[6]

Clement's answer was a brave attempt to ignore the realities
of the situation, but it did not alter the facts, nor could it
make Henry change his mind. He sent word to Rome that
he would not appear in the curia to receive judgment, either
in person or by proxy, nor would he recognize an appeal to
the curia by any of his subjects.[7] He had already, three weeks

before, published a proclamation ordaining that "no manner of person of what estate, degree, or condition soever they be of, do pursue or attempt to purchase from the court of Rome or elsewhere, nor use, put in execution, divulge, or publish anything heretofore within this year passed, purchased or to be purchased hereafter, containing matter prejudicial to the high authority, jurisdiction, and prerogative royal of this his said realm". The proclamation, which had behind it all the weight of the statutes of *praemunire*, was directed in the first instance at those who might seek authority at Rome to "interrupt and let the due execution" of the acts passed in the previous session of Parliament "for the good order and reformation" of the clergy. But, if the occasion arose, ˙ could be applied more broadly to appeals of any sort brought from England to the Holy See.[8]

Meanwhile both parties continued their efforts to win the support of the learned. The case for the King was set forth by an unknown hand in a dialogue modestly called *A Glasse of the Truthe* and printed by Thomas Berthelet. In this little tract we are introduced to a lawyer and a divine, each of whom undertakes to explain to the other how his special knowledge bears on the case. First the divine explains that the decree in *Leviticus* forbidding a woman to marry two brothers is an expression of the revealed will of God and so cannot be revoked by any human agency. Next the lawyer explains how the general principle is to be applied in particular cases. Truth is what is received for truth in a court of law. In many cases the facts are such that they cannot be determined with any certainty. What matters is what the court is entitled to presume. And the presumption, in the present case, is that the marriage of Arthur and Catherine was substantial and real and so constituted a valid impediment to the marriage of the King and Queen.[9]

The strength of the lawyer's argument was admitted on all sides. Whatever the facts might be—and it is hard to believe that

Catherine was not telling the truth—the presumption was against her. For this reason Fisher and her other advisers preferred to rest their case on the law rather than the facts. In the spring of 1530 the first full-scale defence of the Queen appeared at Alcala. Some months before, a manuscript copy had been given by Fisher to Chapuys, who had sent it to Spain in February.[10] Fisher agrees that the Levitical prohibition was intended to apply in the majority of cases. He insists, however, that there are legitimate exceptions, just as there are exceptions to the commandment, Thou shalt not kill. These exceptions are clearly set forth, he reminds the reader, in the book of *Deuteronomy*. "If brethren dwell together, and one of them die, and have no child", it is ordained that "her husband's brother shall go in unto her, and take her to him to wife, and perform the duty of an husband's brother unto her. And it shall be, *that* the first-born which she beareth shall succeed in the name of his brother *which is* dead, that his name be not put out of Israel." How then, Fisher asks, can it be unlawful for the King to have married his brother's widow and raised up a child in his brother's house?

Fisher later testified that his book on the King's marriage was printed without his consent. When he showed his manuscripts to Chapuys, however, he must have known that the imperial ambassador would place them at the disposal of the Queen and her friends. Before the end of November Chapuys was writing to Miguel Mai, the imperial agent at Rome, to ask him to see to the printing of two other works by Fisher and to the sending of copies to England. He proposed, he said, to distribute them at the opening of Parliament.[11] A few days later Fisher brought him a new work, a copy of which, at the request of the Queen, Chapuys sent to Charles on 4 December. Within two weeks there was another, and this also was sent to the imperial Court by Chapuys.[12]

It now appeared for a time as if Fisher would have a chance to argue his case openly in England. Shortly before Christmas,

Warham summoned him to his palace at Lambeth. There he found Edward Lee, John Stokesley and Edward Fox. Lee and Stokesley had recently returned from the Continent, where they had spent the previous winter gathering support for the royal cause in the universities of France and Spain. From a grateful King Lee would soon receive preferment to the see of York, which had been vacant since the death of Wolsey. Stokesley had already been installed in the see of London. Fox, fresh from his successes at Oxford and Cambridge, did not have long to wait for the death of Charles Booth and the bishopric of Hereford. Fisher had been no friend and certainly no admirer of the dead Cardinal, but, surrounded by new men such as these, he must have felt his absence with something akin to regret. His grief would have been keener still if he had known that in little more than a year Warham too would be dead and Thomas Cranmer in his place at Canterbury.

They told him that the King had decided to appoint six doctors on each side to dispute the case before two judges, who were to give judgment after hearing the evidence. Stokesley was to choose five learned persons to speak for the King; Fisher was invited to choose five who would speak for the Queen. No doubt they expected him to welcome the opportunity. But he hesitated and a letter he received from Stokesley a few days later makes it possible to guess why. I "pray you", Stokesley wrote, "to send me word by your [servant, your] pleasure and determination as well con[cerning the time] and place where we should meet [for this our] purpose, as also what persons you [shall] choose and appoint to be the said judges of our controversy"; "specially considering", he continued, "that whatsover we shall do herein, it shall rather tend to the examination and trial of the justices of both our opinions, without prejudice of any other man's sentence, than that thereby shall ensue any determination in the king's cause as your good lordship by your wisdom can consider." Wherefore, "in my opinion, ye ought the less to doubt to

prosecute and accomplish your said good intent in the same".[13]
Evidently Fisher objected to the proposal on the grounds that
the case was *sub iudice* at Rome. Clement had published a series
of bulls during the year inhibiting judgment elsewhere than at
Rome and on 23 December he was to issue a brief expressly forbidding the Archbishop of Canterbury from taking cognizance
of the suit. Fisher must have felt that if he took part in a hearing
such as this he would appear to be furthering the King's attempt
to settle the matter to his own satisfaction in England.[14] In any
case, the hearing was never held, perhaps because without Fisher
it could not have achieved its purpose.

The King, however, had already turned to new means of
accomplishing his purpose. Parliament was once again to furnish
the anvil on which to hammer out the features of a new England. Fisher had been in London during December, as we have
seen, to wait on the archbishop at Lambeth, but he had probably
returned to Rochester for Christmas. However that may be, he
left again for London on 11 January and was in his place in the
Lords when the new session opened on the 16th.[15] The King lost
no time in sounding him out. He told Fisher that Clement was
known to be at odds with the Emperor because the latter had
pressed His Holiness to convene a general council to which the
Pope would have to submit. For this reason, he added, he was
confident of success at Rome. Suspecting the truth of what
Henry had told him, Fisher sent word of it to Chapuys, who
asked the papal nuncio to explain to Fisher the actual position.
The next day the King summoned Fisher and demanded what
had passed. Fisher improvised an account of his conversation
with the nuncio, to whom he later repeated the story in case he
too should be questioned.[16]

The clergy were soon to learn what was in store for them.
Several of the bishops were notified that they were to be charged
under the statutes of *praemunire* for having submitted to the
authority of Thomas Wolsey as a legate of the Holy See. Soon

afterwards the rest of the clergy were accused of having offended against the statutes simply by exercising their traditional juris- diction in the ecclesiastical courts. The province of Canterbury was offered a pardon in return for a payment of £100,000, a sum equal to perhaps $10,000,000 in modern money. But this was not all. The King and his new principal Secretary, Thomas Cromwell, were interested in more than money. Cromwell had spent his early years in the service of Cardinal Wolsey; after Wolsey's fall he had obtained a seat in the House of Commons and soon afterwards had been introduced to the King. It was on this occasion, according to tradition, that he had advised Henry to resolve his difficulties by declaring himself supreme head of the Church of England. Now, more than a year later, Cromwell found the opportunity he had been waiting for. On 7 February, while the clergy were discussing the purchase of their pardon, several members of the King's council came before them and demanded that certain words be added to the preamble of the subsidy. The clergy were required to address the King as "Ecclesiae et cleri Anglicani . . . protector et supremum caput": protector and supreme head of the English Church and clergy.[17] Convocation hesitated. What did the strange words mean? The Earl of Rochford assured the clergy that the title was nothing but a formality, but many who were present that day at St. Paul's knew the King too well to believe that. In the upper house, Fisher urged the Convocation to "consider wel what in- conueniencis wold ensue by this graun [t of] supremacey to the *kynge* thus absolutely *and* simpliciter, if the *kynge* chainged his [mynde] *and* wolde practise the said supremacey ouer the *Bushopes and* clargi of his realme."[18] To satisfy Fisher and others who were unwilling to agree to the title as it stood, the King made a modest proposal. He would consent to take his place in the Church *after God* : "protector et supremum caput post Deum."[19] This offer provoked further discussion, during which the clergy were told that the King intended the royal supremacy to extend no farther than the law of Christ allowed. The Convocation seemed satisfied. Whereupon Fisher, "beinge angri", we are told, "with there so soden *and* lighte persuasion, *and* withal veri lothe [that the] graunt shuld thus passe absolutly, *and* not beinge able to stai yt otherw[ise, he] counselled the conuocacion that, seinge the kynge had no furder meaninge by his [requeste] then 'Quantum per legem dei licet,' *and* that he intendid not to meddel by uertue there[of] with any spiritual lawes or spiritual iurisdiccion anny further then his predeces[sors] had done before hym, 'If you wil neads,' quoth he, 'graunt hym this his request, yet, for [decla]racion of your ful *and* hole meaninge to the kynge *and* his successors *and* there posterity, [expresse] these condicional woords in your graunte, 'Quantum per legem Dei licet.' "[20] On 11 February, the preamble, with this amendment, was put to a vote by the Archbishop of Canterbury. There was silence on both sides. Whereupon Warham, anxious as always to avoid the anger of the King, announced that silence meant consent. " 'Itaque tacemus omnes' ", someone replied : so are we all silent.[21]

It is hard to see what Fisher hoped to gain by his amendment. Chapuys saw clearly enough that it would prove little more than a formality. No-one from now on, he told Charles, would be able to dispute the royal supremacy.[22] Fisher probably knew this as well as Chapuys. No doubt he realized that Convocation would consent to the title demanded by the King, and thought it best to save something to sustain the dignity, if not the liberty, of the Church. It was a mistake. When the amended title was put to a vote, he could no longer raise his voice against it. Had he allowed the title to come to a vote in its original form, and voted against it, the King would not have been able to say that the Canterbury Convocation had accepted the title without a single dissenting voice and that the Bishop of Rochester had himself drawn up the instrument by which it was conveyed. For that is what happened. The northern province, which was also implicated in Wolsey's guilt, was assessed £18,840 0s. 10d. as the price of a royal pardon for offences against the statutes of *praemunire*. It met in Convocation at York on 12 January, but discussion of the grant was prolonged for many months. On 6 May Cuthbert Tunstal wrote to the King in the name of his province. He said that he and his clergy were willing to acknowledge the royal supremacy in temporal things but not in things spiritual. He suggested that the title be further amended to include the words *in temporalibus*. This would have left the independence of the Church still essentially intact, and for this very reason it was not acceptable to the King. In his reply he chided Tunstal for being so nice where the Bishops of Rochester, London and St. Asaph had made no objection. There is no form of words, he explained, that cannot be twisted by a subtle wit. Would the Bishop deny a man the right to say, this land is mine, simply because it is written in the Scriptures that the earth is the Lord's? The King can be, as he is, the supreme head of the Church without presuming to exercise the functions of a priest. This is what is meant by saying that the royal supremacy extends *quantum per legem Dei licet*: as far as the law of Christ allows. The King's answer can hardly have deceived Tunstal, but it satisfied his clergy. The Convocation of York granted the title on 18 May.[23] So it was that, unknown to himself, Fisher became a witness to the King's proposition that the liberty of the Church consists in the saying of mass and the burial of the dead.

His adversaries showed him little gratitude. A week after the King's amended title had been approved by the Canterbury Convocation, a man came to Fisher's house in Lambeth and found his way to the kitchen. Once there, he slipped a powder into a vessel of yeast while the cook was out of the room fetching him a drink. The yeast was made into a gruel that was given to most of the household and to several beggars who came to the gate. At least two persons died of the effects of the poison. Fisher himself was spared only because he had fasted that day. The stranger, a man named Richard Rose of Rochester, was apprehended and taken into custody. Suspicion pointed at once to those of the King's friends who stood to gain most from Fisher's death. Chapuys was ready enough to blame Anne Boleyn and her family, though the accused himself—so far as we know—made no attempt to implicate anyone of importance. Perhaps the authorities did not encourage him to do so. Their main concern was to avoid a scandal by making Rose play the part of a scape-goat. A new bill was hurriedly drafted and adopted by both houses of Parliament. It provided that poisoning should be considered high treason, in this and all future cases. In due course Richard Rose was boiled to death in a cauldron at Smith-field.[24]

Fisher decided to return to Rochester without waiting for the session to end. He was tired and ill, weighed down with a sense of frustration and defeat. When a gunshot pierced his house, close to the place where he was accustomed to sit, he made up his mind. " 'Let us trusse vp our geere and be gone from hence' ", he said, " 'for here is no place for vs to tarrie any longer.' "[25] He left for Rochester heavy with infirmity and despair.

Chapter 14

While Fisher was at Rochester the tide of events pressed on in London. On 30 March Sir Thomas More, the Lord Chancellor, laid before Parliament the testimony gathered the year before at Oxford and Cambridge and the several foreign universities. Stokesley and Longland addressed both houses and explained that since, in the opinion of the learned divines consulted by the

King, the marriage of Henry and Catherine was contrary to divine and natural as well as canon law, the Pope had no authority to remove the impediment to their union. Outside the houses of Parliament their opinion was printed and circulated as widely as possible.[1] A few weeks later the clergy assembled in Convocation at York ended their resistance and, as we have seen, conceded the King to be the supreme head of the Church of England, saving no more for their consciences than the Convocation of Canterbury had done, the empty phrase *quantum per Christi legem licet*. They agreed further, as the price of a royal pardon for their offences against the statutes of *praemunire*, to pay the fine of £18,840 0s. 10d. demanded by the King, an enormous sum for the small northern province of the Church.

During the rest of the spring and summer Fisher remained in his diocese.[2] Still, however, he kept in touch with events at Court. He must have seen the testimony of the universities soon after it was printed, for he composed a reply that was circulating at Rome before the end of July.[3] He had probably given a rough draft to the papal nuncio, who sent it to the Holy See. In any case, he continued to work on his reply, revising it repeatedly, as was his habit, to take account of each fresh argument advanced by the King's party. Summer had turned into autumn before a copy of the finished book was taken at last to Chapuys, who sent it at once to Charles V.[4] Fisher's method was to build up a case for regarding the rule in *Leviticus* against marriage with a brother's widow as a judicial precept deriving its authority not from natural or divine law but from the canon law of the Church. This meant that the inhibition could be dispensed with by the Pope wherever there was good cause on other grounds for such a marriage. And since in the present case the circumstances were exactly similar to those described in *Deuteronomy* as grounds for just such a marriage as that of the King and Queen, there was every reason to conclude that the Julian dispensation was, in fact and in law, sufficient to remove the original impediment.

His work brought Fisher admiration on the Continent but it failed to bring him the gratitude of the Queen. Compelled now to live at the More, where she was separated from the King, she continued to complain bitterly of the advisers she was allowed. The Archbishop of Canterbury would say nothing to her but *ira principis mors est*: the wrath of the King is death; the Bishop of Durham confessed that he could not advise her to resist because his first duty as a subject was to obey and serve the King; and as for the Bishop of Rochester, all he could do, she said, was to tell her to keep up her courage—and of what use was that?[5] The Queen, naturally enough, could see the cause only as a personal affair involving her marriage to the King and the injustice done to her love and devotion. She was impatient of anyone who, like Fisher, saw the issues in a larger perspective. Fisher would have been glad enough to advise Catherine to submit if he had not been persuaded that her submission would injure the Church. It was not in the first instance the sorrows of the Queen that moved Fisher, but his fears for the liberty of the Church— and for this Catherine could never forgive him.

He deserved better. That he was, whatever his motives, the ablest spokesman for the Queen, the Lady Anne, more perspicuous than Catherine, knew well enough. She was, indeed, very much afraid of him, and when the writs were issued in October for a new session of Parliament, she sent Fisher a message advising him not to take his place for fear of sickness.[6] Such a reminder of the bishop's narrow escape the previous spring must have been disconcerting, but there is no indication that Fisher paid any attention to it. He was determined to attend. For the present he continued in his diocese, devoting what time he could spare to the Queen's cause. Chapuys sent him a copy of a treatise prepared at Paris by a Spanish doctor-at-law; Fisher thought well of it and urged that it be printed, suggesting also that the author be asked to answer the testimony of the universities.[7] This had now been reissued in English and Fisher himself prepared a new reply, which he gave to Chapuys to be sent to Rome.[8]

On 15 January Parliament reassembled. All the spiritual lords were summoned to attend except the two who had opposed the royal supremacy the winter before: Cuthbert Tunstal of Durham and John Fisher of Rochester. Tunstal remained in the north, but Fisher ignored the slight and took his place as usual. When Henry heard of this he sent for the bishop to be brought before him. Fearing the King's displeasure, Fisher seized an opportunity to make his reverence when the King was on his way to mass. It appears that Henry, magnanimous for the moment, received him well. Fisher was not deceived, however, by the royal smile; he knew too well how he stood with the King. For some time he had been closely watched and he could no longer afford to be seen with the imperial ambassador in public or to receive letters from him except in cipher.[9] He had declared himself openly and now he could do nothing but wait for the King's men to make the next move.

They did not delay for long. The council had decided to press their advantage along two lines at once: they would see that the King possessed the means of persuading the Holy See to submit to his wishes; failing that, they would compel the Church of England to surrender to the King. In either case they would gain their object.

They sought first to discover a means of influencing the Pope. The means lay ready to hand. Since the second year of the reign of Henry VII, over £160,000 (equal to about $160,000,000 in modern money) had been paid into the papal treasury in the form of annates or first-fruits charged on the revenues of English sees. In 1529, Wolsey had been obliged to pay 16,000 ducats before being invested in the see of Winchester. Henry knew he could count on the bishops to dislike such a custom and he no doubt hoped that self-interest would impel them to acquiesce in a proposal that promised to relieve them of so heavy a burden. A bill to discontinue the payment of annates was introduced early in the session and passed by both houses. It provided that no bishop or archbishop, on being invested in his see, should pay more than 5% of the income of the see for the drawing of his bulls; providing further that any bishop or archbishop denied his bulls at Rome for refusal to pay first-fruits might be invested by any two other bishops appointed by the King for the purpose. Finally, the King was authorized to determine, at any time before Easter of the following year, whether or not the act or any part of it was to come into force. In the event, none of the bishops supported the bill, but the lay lords gave it the necessary majority in the upper house.[10] Whether or not the spiritual lords realized that the purpose of the act was not to relieve them of an onerous obligation but to provide the King with an effective means of influencing the decisions of the curia, we do not know; in any case, their opposition was ineffective and within two years payment of first-fruits was resumed under a new act that made the crown the beneficiary instead of the Holy See.

The council hoped that the Annates Act would provide incentive enough to induce Clement, faced with the imminent loss of his revenues from the English Church, to yield to the wishes of the King. A copy of the bill was promptly sent to Rome, where the English agents were told to explain that Henry would continue to stand fast for the papacy against the importunities of his subjects, if only the Pope and College of Cardinals showed themselves deserving of his support.[11] If Clement should prove obstinate, however, the council had prepared an alternative: the King would assert his supremacy in the Church of England and compel the English clergy to give him the seal of approval denied him at Rome.

To bring this about, it was essential for Henry to attract and hold the support of a majority in the House of Commons. This he could do easily enough, as he had discovered two years before during debate on the probate and mortuary bills, by playing on popular dislike of clerical privileges. Cromwell set about the task with characteristic skill and thoroughness. First he prepared an address setting forth the various grievances of the laity. There are to begin with the familiar complaints of excessive fees and dilatory service. But there is something new as well: the laity are made to question the competence of Convocation to pass laws to which the King's subjects have had no opportunity of giving their consent in Parliament. They are made to complain that "where the prelates and spirituall Ordynaries of this your most excellent Realme of Englonde and the clergie of the same haue in the conuocacions heretofore made and caused to be made and also daylie do make dyuers and manye *Facyons of* lawes constytucions and ordenaunces without your knowlege or most royall assente and without the assent and consent of any your lay Subiectes vnto the whiche lawes your saide Subiectes haue not onelie heretofore and daylie be [boundene] *constraynyd to obbeye* aswell in their bodies goodes and possessions But also ben compelled daylie to incurre into the censures of the same and ben contynuallie put to importable charges and expenses ayenst all equytee right and good conscience."[12] These words go to the very heart of the matter. The canons of the Church were made, as they had always been made, with the consent of the spiritual persons represented in Convocation, just as the statutes of the realm were made with the consent of the spiritual and temporal persons represented in Parliament. Cromwell's plan was to deprive the Church of its independence by pretending that only the King's laws were made with the consent of the people. In this way the King could augment his own authority while at the same time posing as a defender of the liberties of his subjects.

The address prepared by Cromwell was presented in the House of Commons in the form of a Supplication against the Ordinaries. The Supplication was adopted in the lower house and submitted to the King; on 12 April it was brought before Convocation by the Archbishop of Canterbury. At first the clergy seem to have been disposed to stand their ground. An answer was prepared, in part at least by Stephen Gardiner, now Bishop of Winchester. Gardiner had been the most effective advocate of English interests at Rome, but for all that he was unwilling to countenance secular authority in the Church, a fact that was soon to cost him the see of Canterbury and his hopes of the primacy. In their first answer the ordinaries pointed out that their right to make law in Convocation was established by Scripture; if the laws of the Church and those of the State disagreed in any particular, they added, it could only be because one or the other was contrary to the laws of God as set forth in the Scriptures, to which alone they as ordinaries were prepared to submit. As for submitting their ordinances to the King for his approval and consent (as the Commons in their Supplication had been encouraged to suggest), the clergy made bold to answer that they could not "submytt thexecucon of owr charges and dewtie certaynly prescribed by god, to your highnes assent", for they might not "in suche sorte restrayne the doyng of owr Office, in the fedyng and rulyng of Christes people your graces Subiectes." Nevertheless, they promised that if the King would show them his "mynde and opynyon" they would "most gladly here and folowe" it, if, as they put it, "it shall please god to inspire vs so to do".[13] It was their last flourish. Their reply was sent on the 19th to the King, who gave it to Sir Thomas Audeley, Speaker of the House of Commons, with the dry comment, "We think this answer will smally please you." Certainly it did not please the King. The Duke of Norfolk told Stokesley that Convocation had better look to itself and return the King a more prudent answer.

This it did. At one stroke the clergy abandoned the resistance so bravely begun a few days earlier. They protested still that the Church had always possessed the authority to make spiritual ordinances for the cure of souls without the consent of "any secular prynce", as the King himself had freely acknowledged in his reply to Martin Luther. Notwithstanding these high words, however, they professed themselves willing to refrain, for the natural life of the King, from enacting any new ordinance without royal assent. As for ordinances already in effect, these they consented to submit to the King, to be approved or, if judged prejudicial to the King's lay subjects, to be annulled. For themselves they saved nothing but the right to make and keep ordinances concerning the "mayntenance of the faith" and the "reformatyon and correctyon of synne, after the commandmentes off almyghty god accordyng vnto soche lawes, of the churche, and laudabyll customys, as hath been hertofore made and hitherto receyvid and vsid" within the realm of England.[14]

Henry was still dissatisfied and on 10 May he summarily sent Fox to the Convocation with three articles for the clergy to subscribe. The articles did not differ in any important respect from the second answer of the clergy, but they stripped away the decencies with which the clergy had tried to clothe their weakness. There were to be no saving graces. The supremacy of the State was to be asserted in all its nakedness. Convocation must promise, first, "that no constitution or ordinance should be thereafter by the clergy enacted, promulged, or put in execution, unless the King's Highness did approve the same by his high authority and royal assent". It must agree, in the second place, that "whereas divers of the constitutions provincial, which had been heretofore enacted, were thought not only much prejudicial to the King's prerogative, but also much onerous to his Highness subjects", the same should be submitted to the examination and judgment of a committee of 32 persons, sixteen from the commons and lay lords and sixteen from the clergy, all to be appointed by the King. Lastly, Convocation must consent to the annulment of such of its ordinances as were judged to be prejudicial to the King or his subjects, the remainder to "stand in full strength and power, the King's Highness royal assent given to the same."[15]

When these articles were brought before the Convocation, Fisher was lying ill at his house in Lambeth Marsh across the river. He had taken his place in January and had, we know, attended Convocation in March and April, when he sat with Stokesley of London, Lee of York, Gardiner of Winchester and Voysey of Exeter on a commission appointed to deal with charges of heresy brought against Hugh Latimer. Latimer had been summoned before the commission on 11 March. He had refused to recant and had been pronounced contumacious and committed to the custody of the Archbishop of Canterbury in Lambeth Palace. Ten days later he had confessed that on occasion he had spoken too freely, whereby "the people that were infirm hath taken occasion of ill", but it was late in April, after a month in which he had "better seen his own acts, and searched them more deeply", before he was brought to acknowledge that he had "not erred only in discretion, but also in doctrine".[16] Presumably Fisher continued to attend these hearings until they came to an end on 21 April. If so, he must have been present in Convocation while the clergy were preparing their first answer to the Supplication of the Commons. It may be that he was by now exhausted by the anxious days of deliberation in the upper house. Or it may be that his spirit was crushed by the implacable hostility of the council and the inability of the clergy to summon an effective resistance. Now an old man by the standards of the time, he was no longer able to endure the agony of isolation and defeat. He had suffered in the same way the year before when Convocation was called upon to acknowledge the supremacy of the King. Now once again he became ill and was forced to withdraw from his seat.

Apparently he was missed, for when the King's articles were brought to Convocation, it was agreed that a delegation from both houses should wait on him to ask his advice. What advice he gave we do not know. Convocation had by now gone too far to turn back; it had already yielded the ground on which it might have made a stand. Nor was the King disposed to accept a compromise of any sort. On 11 May, while the Convocation was still considering the three articles delivered by Fox the day before, the King sent for twelve commoners and eight lay peers and announced to them that he had only just discovered that the bishops were, as he put it, but half his subjects, since when they entered upon their sees they swore an oath to the Pope as well as to the King. This was nothing new to the lay lords; nor was it new to the King. But his words were significant. That churchmen had been but half the King's men, attending as they did to the spiritual concerns of the Church as well as the temporal interests of the State, was neither more nor less than the truth. Nor was it in any way remarkable. What was remarkable was the evident intention of the King to compel the clergy to recognize the spiritual jurisdiction of the crown. His meaning was not lost on the clergy. Two days later the articles were put to a vote and passed. In the lower house of Convocation 26 votes were cast against them, including eight proxies voted against the first article and seven against the other two. In the upper house there were only four opposed—Standish of St. Asaph, Longland of Lincoln, Stokesley of London and Clerk of Bath and Wells—and of these Standish, Longland and Stokesley were willing to consent provided the King formally undertook to confirm any ordinance not contrary to the will of God. Fisher remained ill at Lambeth and did not vote.[17]

In their answer to the King, the clergy made a last effort to save something of their integrity. They restricted their grant to the life of the reigning King (which they heartily desired Almighty God long to preserve) and they submitted themselves and the laws of the Church, not to the committee of 32 but, as they put it, "to thexamination and iudgement of your grace only". They reserved to themselves "al suche immunities &

liberties of this churche of Ingland, as hath ben graunted vnto
the same by the goodness and benignite of your hieghnes and of
others your moost noble progenitors" and they required the
King to confirm all canons "as do stand with the lawes of almightie god and holy churche and of your Realme hertofore
made".[18] The King would have none of such conditions. On the
15th Convocation was induced, after further consultation, to
make an unconditional submission. The clergy humbly promised that they would "never from hensforth enact put in vre
promulge or execute any new canons or constitucion", unless
the King "shall licence vs to assembyll our conuocation and to
make promulge and execute soche constitucions and ordinaunces
as shalbe made in the same and therto geue your Royall assent
and auctoritie." Existing canons were, as the King desired, to be
submitted to the examination and judgment of 32 persons
chosen by the crown, to be approved or, if found to be contrary
to the laws of God or the realm, to be annulled.[19] The next day
the Archbishop of Canterbury presented the submission of the
clergy to the King in his palace garden, attended by the Bishops
of St. Asaph, Lincoln and Bath and Wells, all of whom had
initially opposed it.

It was a bitter moment for them, as it was for Fisher. Deprived of the right to assemble or to govern themselves, churchmen were now to be, as Chapuys remarked, of less account than
shoemakers.[20] For Gardiner, already on his way to his seat at
Winchester, the submission meant the permanent loss of royal
favour. He sent to the King asking to be forgiven for his part in
resisting the council's demands, pleading that he had said only
what he had believed to be true and what had been held to be
true by learned men in all ages.[21] For More it meant the end of
his career in the service of the King: he retired as Lord Chancellor the same day. For Warham, who as Archbishop of Canterbury had presided over the several sessions at St. Paul's, the
submission was the last of many humiliations. Until now all too

JOHN FISHER OF ROCHESTER

willing to bend his conscience to the King's will, on the principle Catherine had complained of—*ira principis mors est*—he
found at last courage enough for one gesture of resistance.
Some weeks earlier he had drawn up a statement in which he
announced that he would not admit or recognize any law made
in the present Parliament in derogation of the Holy See or the
see of Canterbury.[22] Parliament was prorogued as soon as the
submission was completed and did not sit again until the following winter. Warham died in August and so the statement, which
he had intended to read out from his place in the House of Lords,
was never published. Before he died, however, he had one last
opportunity to prove himself. Charged with having consecrated
Henry Standish fourteen years before in the see of St. Asaph
before Standish had exhibited his bulls to the King, he answered
tartly that if an archbishop could not consecrate a bishop without the consent of the King, the Church was nothing but a jewel
in the crown of the prince. The liberty denied by the King, he
added, was one that St. Thomas Becket died to establish and
one that his successor at Canterbury was determined to preserve.[23] But it was too late. Warham was over eighty and had
enjoyed the primacy for nearly thirty years. During all that time
he had governed his see and his province without giving any
sign that he understood that the Church existed to nourish the
spiritual aspirations of the people. Now that he saw the fruits of
his handiwork, he no longer had time to do the things he had
left undone for so long.

As for Fisher, he had by now recovered from the sickness that
had seized him in April. His mind was still occupied with the
problems of the last session, and apparently he still hoped to find
a means of resisting the demands of the King. It was probably
during these weeks that he began work on a defence of the
clergy.[24] In June he preached a sermon in favour of the Queen
that brought him once again to the attention of the authorities.
Chapuys reported that he was likely to be arrested, but in the

event he was not disturbed.[25] Others were less fortunate. On Easter Sunday William Peto, provincial of the Friars Minor, preached before the King at Greenwich, declaring that he was deceived in his lust by the flattery of courtiers. Next week, in Peto's absence, the King caused one of his own chaplains, Richard Curwen, to preach in the same place. Curwen told his hearers of the King's scruples and explained that all those who knew and understood the law were of the opinion that the marriage of the King and Queen was unlawful. At this another friar, William Elstowe, rose in his place and told Curwen he was a liar. Peto and Elstowe were both arrested.[26] A month later a sermon was preached at St. Paul's setting forth the reasons for the proceedings against the Queen, but before the preacher could finish he was interrupted by a woman who cried shame on the King for his sins against the sacrament of marriage. She too was arrested.[27] In July a priest was apprehended in a felony. He had filed down the edges of a number of new angelots and sold the filings to a goldsmith. He was tried and convicted and, without being degraded from the priesthood, dragged through the streets of London and hanged at Tyburn. Such a thing, Carlo Capello reported to the Signory at Venice, had never happened in England before.[28] Six weeks later, on 28 August, William Warham died at the age of 82 and Henry sent for Thomas Cranmer, a man who had shown himself amenable to royal policy, to take his place. On 1 September the Lady Anne was created Marchioness of Pembroke with a settlement of £1000 in land and a present of royal jewels taken from the Queen. Secure in the knowledge that in the see of Canterbury there was now to be a man who would be willing to give judgment in favour of the King, Anne was prepared at last to be known as the royal mistress.[29] In a few weeks she was with child and before the end of January the King had secretly married her.

Chapter 15

Fisher had returned to Rochester for the summer and by September he had recovered something of his strength and spirits. One night while he was staying at his manor of Halling, near Rochester, a company of thieves broke into his house and carried off his plate. Next morning his servants, discovering the loss, set out in pursuit with such haste that part of the plate, left behind by the thieves in a wood near by, was recovered. They were afraid, however, to tell the bishop what had happened, but he noticed their anxiety and refused to eat his dinner until they told him what it was that troubled them. When he had heard, he urged them to be merry and to go to dinner and afterwards to look better to the rest than they had done before.[1] He had feared worse.

For events were preparing that he knew would cost him dearly. Cranmer, who had been on the Continent when Warham died, was summoned to return in November and reached England the following January. To hasten the expedition of his bulls from Rome—for despite the act of the previous year the payment of annates had not yet been suspended—the King lent him out of his own pocket the money he needed. Clement was made to understand that if the bulls were not forthcoming the King could hardly be expected to look with favour on the continued payment of annates, contrary to the will and desire of both houses of Parliament.[2] It was customary for the Holy See to confirm persons nominated by the King to a benefice in the English Church, and Clement no doubt felt that he could not

afford to displease Henry without good cause. He had so far refused to satisfy the King in the matter of his marriage and,
indeed, in a few months was to give final judgment in favour of
the Queen. In expediting Cranmer's bulls he was probably thinking less of the annates than of his hold on the Church of England. Apparently it did not occur to him that with Cranmer in
the see of Canterbury, Henry would be able to complete the
separation from Rome without fear of effective opposition
within the English Church.[3]

In any case the bulls arrived and Cranmer was consecrated in
the Chapter House at Westminster on 30 March. Like all his
predecessors, he took an oath to the Pope as well as to the King,
binding himself to be faithful and obedient to the Holy Roman
Church and to further and defend the authority and privileges
of the Holy See.[4] In his oath to the King he then renounced any
"clauses, words, sentences, and grants, which I have of the
pope's holiness in his bulls of the archbishoprick of Canterbury,
that in any manner was, is, or may be hurtful, or prejudicial to
your highness, your heirs, successors, estate, or dignity royal :
knowledging myself to take and hold the said archbishoprick
immediately, and only, of your highness, and of none other.
Most lowly beseeching the same for the restitution of the tem-
poralities of the said archbishoprick : promising to be faithful,
true, and obedient subject to your said highness, your heirs and
successors, during my life. So help me God and the holy evange-
lists !"[5] In case there was any doubt as to the meaning of these
words, Cranmer read out a protestation, declaring that his oath
of canonical obedience to the Pope would not oblige him to any
course of action that was or might be hurtful to the King of
England or to the laws or prerogatives of his realm. Clearly the
King was determined that, unlike the rest of the bishops of
whom he had spoken so bitterly the year before, Cranmer should
be more than half his subject.

Parliament was already in session and Convocation had

assembled on 26 March. Fisher once more took his place in the upper house. At the second sitting John Stokesley, who presided, read out the decisions of the several universities in the matter of the King's marriage. He then put two questions. The first was addressed to the theologians: "An ducere liceret uxorem cognitam a fratre decedente sine prole, et an sit prohibitio juris divini indispensabilis a papa". They were to decide whether or not it was lawful for a man to marry a woman who had been carnally known by his brother and, if not, whether or not it was lawful for the Pope to dispense with the impediment in such a case. Stokesley himself spoke for the negative, as did Longland. Henry Standish, who had defended the Queen at the Blackfriars hearing four years before, now took the King's part. Thirty-six abbots and priors followed suit on the same day. On the 29th, six more added their voice. According to Chapuys, no-one spoke for the affirmative but the Bishop of Rochester.[6] His words had little effect, for the question was answered in the negative by an overwhelming majority. Of the theologians who were present, 56 voted in the King's favour, sixteen against. There were in addition 197 proxies voted for the King and three against, making the aggregate vote in his favour 253 to nineteen. Those who opposed him were the Bishops of Rochester and Llandaff (a Spaniard), the Abbots of Winchcombe and Reading, the Priors of Ely, Walsingham and St. George's, Canterbury, and twelve others including Nicholas Wilson, who was later to go to the Tower with Fisher and More.

The second question was addressed to the canonists: "An carnalis copula inter illustrissimum principem Arthurum et serenissimam dominam Catharinam reginam, ex propositis, exhibitis, deductis, et allegatis sit sufficienter probata." This was a question of fact: the assembled churchmen were to decide whether or not Arthur and Catherine had ever been man and wife in fact as well as in name. On 3 April the question was answered in the affirmative by 41 of the canonists. Three proxies were voted in favour as well, making a total of 44. It was opposed by only six, including John Clerk, Bishop of Bath and Wells.[7]

Convocation had done its part to serve the King. It now remained for Parliament to complete the work of previous sessions. The statutes of *praemunire* had made it unlawful for any of the King's subjects to bring an appeal from the *curiae regis* to the papal curia or any other foreign court. The purpose of these acts was to protect the jurisdiction of the King's Courts. Cromwell was now determined to extend the effective jurisdiction of the King by inhibiting appeals to Rome from any English court, secular or ecclesiastical. Having secured control of the English Church, he would provide that no appeal should lie from the ecclesiastical courts to the high court at Rome. His immediate purpose was to prevent an appeal by the Queen from the judgment that Cranmer was about to pronounce on the King's marriage. The ultimate effect, however, was to create a new concept of kingship. Henceforward Englishmen would have no right of appeal, on grounds of conscience, against the laws of the realm. Hitherto the liberty of individual subjects had been guarded by the Church, which for generations had had the undoubted right to assert and maintain the imperatives of right and wrong. From now on, good and evil were to have little to do, except in name, with the nature and being of God, as understood by the Church; they were to become instead a matter of the national interest, as defined by the laws of the realm. The act in restraint of appeals, adopted by the two houses of Parliament in April, in effect created a new England. "Where by divers sundry old authentick Histories and Chronicles", the preamble began, "it is manifestly declared and expressed, that this Realm of *England* is an Empire, and so hath been accepted in the World, governed by One supreme Head and King, having the Dignity and Royal Estate of the Imperial Crown of the same; unto whom a Body politick, compact of all Sorts and Degrees of People, divided in Terms, and by Names of Spiritualty and Temporalty, ben bounden and owen to bear, next to God, a natural and humble Obedience; he being also institute and furnished, by the Goodness and Sufferance of Almighty God, with plenary whole and entire Power Pre-eminence Authority Prerogative and Jurisdiction, to render and yield Justice and final Determination to all Manner of Folk Resiants or Subjects with this his Realm, in all Causes Matters Debates and Contentions, happening to occur insurge or begin within the Limits thereof, without Restraint or Provocation to any foreign Princes or Potentates of the World".[8] Henry preferred, wherever possible, to invest his innovations with all the dignity of tradition and ancient custom. But despite the language of history and precedent in which it was clothed, the bill marked a radical departure from established usage. Though the fact was not fully recognized for more than a hundred years, Leviathan was fashioned on the day when this great act became law.

The stage was now set for the climax of the drama. Fisher, however, was not to witness the extraordinary events that led up to the coronation of the new Queen on 1 June. On Palm Sunday, 6 April, he was seized and placed in the custody of the Bishop of Winchester, where he remained for nearly two months. It was given out as a pretext for his arrest that he had let it be known at Court that Lord Rochford, the Lady Anne's brother, had been sent to France to offer a bribe to the Pope through the good offices of the Cardinal of Lorraine. Henry's real reason for wishing to silence Fisher was his anxiety as to the outcome of the crucial hearing that Cranmer was about to open at Dunstable. Anne was now four months pregnant and her coronation could not be long delayed. Throughout the hearing Fisher was kept in the custody of the Bishop of Winchester, though he was apparently allowed to occupy his own quarters at Lambeth.[9]

The proceedings began at once. On 11 April Cranmer wrote to the King asking that he submit his cause to the judgment of the Church of England. His letter did not satisfy the King, who returned it with a number of amendments intended to show

beyond doubt that the archbishop was the creature of the King
he was to judge. Cranmer was made "most humbly to beseech
your most noble grace, that where the office and duty of the
archbishop of Canterbury, by your and your progenitors' sufferance and grants, is to direct, order, judge, and determine causes
spiritual in this your grace's realm; and because I would be right
loth, and also it shall not become me, forasmuch as your grace
is my prince and sovereign, to enterprise any part of my office in
the said weighty cause touching your highness, without your
grace's favour and licence obtained in that behalf: it may please,
therefore, your most excellent majesty . . . to license me, according to mine office and duty, to proceed to the examination, final
determination, and judgment in the said great cause touching
your highness: eftsoons, as prostrate at the feet of your majesty"
—this was one of the phrases inserted by the King—"beseeching
the same to pardon me of these my bold and rude letters, and
the same to accept and take in good sense and part as I do mean;
which, calling our Lord to record, is only for the zeal that I
have to the causes aforesaid, and for none other intent and purpose."[10] The King was graciously pleased to consent. Now at
last, after almost four years of waiting, he was in a position to
decide his own cause in his own favour while acting in the name
of the Archbishop of Canterbury and the Church of England.
He did not mince his words: "albeit we, being your king and
sovereign do recognise no superior in earth, but only God, and
not being subject to the laws of any other earthly creature; yet,
because ye be under us, by God's calling and ours, the most principal minister of our spiritual jurisdiction, within this our realm
. . . [we] will not therefore refuse . . . your humble request,
offer, and towardness; that is, to mean to make an end, according to the will and pleasure of Almighty God, in our said great
cause of matrimony". Wherefore he consented that the archbishop should proceed to judgment—"not doubting", he added
with unconscious irony, "but that ye will have God and the

justice of the said cause only before your eyes, and not to regard
any earthly or worldly affection therein. For assuredly, the thing
that we most covet in this world is to proceed, in all our acts
and doings, as may be most acceptable to the pleasure of
Almighty God, our Creator, and"—it was almost an after-
thought—"to the wealth, honour of us, our succession and pos-
terity, and the surety of our realm, and subjects within the
same."[11]

Cranmer opened his court on 10 May in the priory at Dunstable. Catherine, who was living nearby at Ampthill, was summoned to appear, but she refused. Chapuys had told her that if
she recognized Cranmer's court she might jeopardize the success
of her appeal at Rome, and she took his advice. She was pronounced contumacious and the hearing was pressed forward
with all possible haste. On 13 May the Convocation of York
assented to the two resolutions already adopted by the southern
province. The theologians at York voted 27 to two in the King's
favour on the question put to them as to the right of the Pope to
dispense with the impediment to his marriage. The canonists
voted 44 to two in his favour on the question of fact.[12] Four days
later the resolutions of the two Convocations, along with the
testimony of the universities and the evidence submitted at the
Blackfriars hearing, were laid before the archbishop. He was
now in a position to announce his decision, and he sent word to
the King that he would give judgment the following Friday,
"at which time", as he put it, "I trust so to endeavour myself
further in this behalf, as shall become me to do, to the pleasure
of Almighty God, and the mere truth of the matter."[13] Whether
or not his sentence was pleasing to God we do not know, but
there is no doubt that it pleased the King exceedingly. The court
found, after a judicious examination of all the available evidence,
that the marriage of Henry and Catherine was contrary to the
will of God and wanted the sanction of both natural and positive
law; whereupon the archbishop gave sentence and declared that

it was unlawful for the King and Queen to continue living together as man and wife.[14] Cranmer at once sent word of the sentence to the King, asking at the same time for instructions as to the confirmation of his marriage with the Lady Anne, which had taken place four months before. That the first marriage would be annulled and the second confirmed was, of course, a foregone conclusion. The coronation was already arranged and, as Cranmer reminded the King, it was "so instant and so near at hand that the matter requireth good expedition to be had in the same."[15] Five days later the marriage of Henry and Anne was duly confirmed at Lambeth. The very next day Anne, who had been waiting at Greenwich for the decision in her favour, proceeded in triumph up the river to the Tower of London. On the Saturday following she was brought in state from the Tower to Westminster Hall. It was a magnificent spectacle: "she sitting in her hair upon a horse litter, richly apparelled, and four knights of the five ports bearing a canopy over her head. And after her came four rich chariots, one of them empty, and three other furnished with divers ancient old ladies; and after them came a great train of other ladies and gentlewomen: which said progress, from the beginning to the ending, extended half a mile in length by estimation, or thereabout. To whom also, as she came along the city, was shewed many costly pageants, with divers other encomies spoken of children to her." At Westminster Hall she attended a banquet given in her honour, after which she left by barge for York Place, where the King awaited her. The next day, Sunday 1 June, she was crowned in Westminster Abbey. Cranmer tells the story in his own words: "In the morning there assemble[d] with me at Westminster church the bishop of York, the bishop of London, the bishop of Winchester, the bishop of Bath, and the bishop of St Asse [Asaph]; the abbot of Westminster, with ten or twelve more abbots; which all revestred ourselves in our pontificalibus, and so furnished, with our crosses and crosiers, proceeded out of the abbey in a procession unto Westminster-hall, where we received the queen apparelled in a robe of purple velvet, and all the ladies and gentlewomen in robes and gowns of scarlet, according to the manner used before time in such business: and so her grace sustained of each side with two bishops, the bishop of London and the bishop of Winchester, came forth in procession unto the church of Westminster, she in her hair, my lord of Suffolk bearing before her the crown, and two other lords bearing also before her a sceptre and a white rod, and so entred up into the high altar, where divers ceremonies used about her, I did set the crown on her head, and then was sung *Te Deum*, &c. And after that was sung a solemn mass: all which while her grace sat crowned upon a scaffold, which was made between the high altar and the choir in Westminster church; which mass and ceremonies done and finished, all the assembly of noblemen brought her into Westminster-hall again, where was kept a great solemn feast all that day".[16]

England had a new Queen. And it was a new England too that awoke that day to the pageantry of a coronation. Not everyone welcomed the great event. Catherine continued in seclusion at Ampthill, degraded now to the title and standing of Princess Dowager and widow of the late Prince Arthur. Many of the people who filled the streets of London, and who remembered the fond woman who had been their Queen for more than twenty years, were hostile and suspicious. Sir Thomas More, living in retirement now at Chelsea, was sent £20 by Tunstal and Gardiner with which to buy a gown for the occasion. He accepted the money but declined their invitation. As for Fisher, he continued still in the custody of the Bishop of Winchester. It was a new breed of men who had seized the tide that leads on to fame and fortune.

Fisher was released at last two weeks after the coronation.[17] Much had changed in the ten weeks of his confinement. The new England was increasingly hostile to everything he most valued. For the moment he was no doubt heartened by the news from Rome. On 11 July Clement published a statement denouncing the proceedings at Dunstable and calling upon the King to put away the Lady Anne before the last day of September, on pain of excommunication.[18] But the King, anticipating the action about to be taken at Rome, had already appealed from the curia to a general council. And since there was no likelihood that such a council would be convened in the near future, his appeal was nicely calculated to delay the execution of any sentence that might be pronounced against him by the Pope. Meanwhile the King's council issued a proclamation declaring that any person who did or moved any act to the let or derogation of the new Queen or who addressed the late Queen as other than Princess Dowager, would be liable to the penalties provided by the statutes of *praemunire*.[19] And on 9 July, having derived what advantage he could from delay, the King ratified the act concerning annates sent to him by the two houses the previous year.

Cromwell lost no time in making the presence of the King felt in every corner of England. Before the end of July he sent him a report concerning certain friars who had been in the service of the late Queen and who, as he put it, "being subtillie conueyed from thens were first espied at Ware by suche espialles as I leyed for that purpose", and having been "from thens dogged to London, and there (notwithstonding many wyles and cauteles by them invented to escape) were taken and deteyned till my cummyng home". Cromwell could find nothing amiss on examination of the friars, but he suspected nevertheless that at least one of them was "a veray sedycious person, and so commytted them vnto warde where they now do remayne till your gracious pleasure knowen". He had no doubt, he said, that they would "confesse sum grete matier" if they were examined "as they ought to be that is to sey by paynes".[20] Cromwell also had agents abroad. In August he received a report from Antwerp that implicated Fisher. From George Gee, an Englishman living in

Antwerp, the agent had learned that the author of a book on the King's marriage then circulating on the Continent was none other than the Bishop of Rochester. The book was presumably Fisher's *De causa matrimonii*, a copy of which had been sent by Chapuys, at the Queen's request, to the imperial Court in February of 1530. Apparently, however, the copy sent out by Chapuys never came into the hands of the printer, for the agent reported that the book had been set up from a manuscript brought secretly from England for that purpose by Friar Peto, the Minorite who had scandalized the Court with the sermon he had preached before the King at Greenwich the year before.[21] In any case, Cromwell was now aware that Fisher was or had been actively engaged abroad in opposition to the policy of the council.

For the moment, however, the Secretary was not seriously concerned. His policy had been vindicated. The King had established his supremacy in both Church and State. He had deprived the Holy See of its authority in England and disrupted the unity of Catholic Christendom, without an effective answer from either the Most Christian King or His Imperial Majesty. The liberty and substance of the English Church were his for the taking. Above all, the new Queen was great with child and was promised a son by her physicians. Given a son, the King could be sure of the hearts of his people.

This blessing, however, he was to be denied. On 7 September Queen Anne gave birth not to a son but to a daughter. Three days later the child was christened at Greenwich by the Bishop of London. She was carried to the font by the Duchess of Norfolk, flanked by the Dukes of Norfolk and Suffolk. The Duchess of Norfolk and the Marchioness of Dorset were her godmothers; her godfather was the Archbishop of Canterbury.[22] But all the pageantry of a royal baptism could not conceal the disappointment of the King. That the Princess Elizabeth would one day be acclaimed as Queen and that her reign would see the first bright flowering of the English spirit, her father could neither hope nor expect. To him the birth of a daughter was a bitter misfortune. At one stroke it put the succession in doubt and gave new hope to those who looked to the Princess Mary for their eventual succour. His anxieties were, it must be admitted, real enough. Chapuys had more than once advised Charles V to take advantage of the unpopularity of the Lady Anne and of the policies that had made her Queen. For him the expansion of imperial influence was, of course, an end in itself. Others looked to the Empire as the only hope of deliverance from the growing tyranny of the State. If, they reasoned, the Church was to be deprived of its accustomed liberties, if the clergy were to be left without the freedom and authority proper to their calling, was it not best that the faithful should put on the sword? Not long after the birth of the Princess Elizabeth, Chapuys received such a message from the Bishop of Rochester. The English Church, he told Chapuys, lay helpless at the feet of the King. If the Emperor would come to her aid, he would be doing a work as agreeable to God as making war against the Turk. Chapuys himself suggested that Charles encourage a marriage between the Princess Mary and Reginald Pole, in the hope of restoring a legitimate Catholic succession. Pole, a grandson of the Duke of Clarence, had perhaps as good a claim to the throne as Henry himself; he had left England to escape the consequences of Henry's proceedings against the Church and was now in Italy, working on a defence of the papal supremacy. He was made a cardinal in 1536 and at the end of his life was elevated by Mary to the see of Canterbury. This was the prospect to which Fisher raised his eyes in the autumn of 1533 when, helpless and alone, he waited for the hour of trial.[23]

Chapter 16

It was not long in coming. Mary had been deprived of her title and household soon after the birth of her younger sister. Towards the end of November worse news followed. The council was examining a young woman called Elizabeth Barton and intended to bring charges of treason against her and her accomplices. Elizabeth Barton came from the village of Courthope Street in Kent. As early as 1526 she had begun to have visions in which the Lady of Courthope Street appeared and spoke to her. She entered the nunnery of St. Sepulchre, near Canterbury, where her visions were encouraged by her confessor. After a time she began to make prophecies concerning the King and Queen. These became more and more provocative. Eventually she prophesied that if the King took the Lady Anne to wife he would lose his crown within a month. Word of this reached the Court and the nun was sent for by the King. Examined by Cranmer in July and again in November, she disclosed that she had revealed her prophecies to a number of persons, including Dr. Edward Bocking (a monk of Canterbury and her confessor), Hugh Rich (a Friar Observant of Richmond), Richard Risby (warden of the Observants at Canterbury) and several others, including the Bishop of Rochester. She testified further that Fisher had wept for joy when he heard what she had to say. Fisher had heard of the nun from Rich and had sent for her at his suggestion. When Rich was asked whether or not he had discussed the nun and her prophecies with More as well, he answered, according to the record of the interrogation, "that he hath showed other revelations to Sir Thos. More, but none concerning the King, for he would not hear them." Cromwell, however, deleted Rich's answer from the record and More, despite his complete innocence, found himself, like Fisher, implicated in the affair. Risby had also tried, without success, to tell More of the nun's prophecies concerning the King; when he came to Rochester with the news, however, he found Fisher more inclined to listen. Dr. Bocking came to Rochester with the same story and even told Fisher that he could show him a "great book" of the nun's revelations.[1] On 23 November Elizabeth Barton was taken to St. Paul's, where she was placed on a scaffold with Bocking, Rich, Risby and five others: John Dering (a monk of Canterbury), two secular priests, Henry Gold (parson of Aldermary in London) and Richard Master (parson of Aldington in Kent), and two laymen, Thomas Gold and Edward Thwaites. The nun and her accomplices were denounced by the Bishop of Bangor, who accused them of attempting to incite the people to rebellion by prophesying the death of the King.[2] In the credulity of the nun and her accomplices Cromwell saw the opportunity he had been looking for. Anyone who had listened to the prophecies concerning the King could be regarded as an accessory and charged with misprision of treason, the penalty for which was loss of liberty and property.

Writs were issued for a new session of Parliament, to open on 15 January. Meanwhile, Cromwell saw to the preparation of a book of nine articles setting forth the position of the King. No person, it declared, may be cited to appear in any court outside the jurisdiction in which his offence is alleged to have been committed. In any case, if such a person is cited to appear at Rome he has the right to appeal from the papal curia to a general council of the Church. And while such an appeal is pending, nothing may be done at Rome to injure the appellant, either by way of excommunication or by any other means.[3] Publication of these articles aroused concern in some quarters. Cuthbert

Tunstal wrote to the King to warn him that his policy would permanently disrupt the unity of Christian Church. Henry's answer could have left Tunstal in little doubt as to his intentions. To separate from Rome, the King wrote, is not to leave the body of Christ, which is the true community of the faithful. To forsake the Pope is to follow Christ. The King of England acknowledged no superior but God and he saw no reason to be ashamed of that.[4] What Henry meant by obedience to God was explained soon afterwards in a *Litel Treatise ageynste the mutterynge of some papistis in corners* printed for the council by Thomas Berthelet. "According as the holy Apostle Paule saith", the argument ran, "Let every soul be subject unto the high powers, for the powers that be are ordained of God. So that he that resisteth the high powers, resisteth the ordinance of God. And they that resist seek their own damnation. Look how straitly the Apostle bindeth us to the obedience of our prince: for in the same chapter he nameth none other powers but only of princes."[5] Edward Fox was ready with a similar argument. The royal almoner, who was soon now to be rewarded with the see of Hereford, prepared a short defence of the royal supremacy that was printed by Berthelet early in the New Year. His arguments were not new; they had already been made familiar by William Tyndale in his *Obedience of a Christen man*, a book that had delighted Henry when it first appeared five years before. This was, as Henry so aptly remarked, a book fit for Kings, for it identified the will of God with the will of the prince and made civil disobedience a sin worthy of damnation. Nor was Henry the first to realize what could be done with such ideas. Lewis IV of Bavaria had made good use of them two hundred years before and had taken pains to find a place at his Court for such advocates of secular authority as William of Ockham, Marsiglio of Padua and John of Jandun. Their work had never been altogether forgotten and Cromwell now seized the occasion to have an English translation of Marsiglio prepared and printed by Berthelet.[6]

This was the setting when Parliament assembled in January. In the upper house, where—if anywhere—resistance to the King might have been expected, there were now 51 lay lords, two more than the combined number of the clergy. And of the nineteen bishops, 28 abbots and two priors on the roll, fewer than half were in their places. Fisher probably received the customary summons, but in any event he was ill again and unable to attend.[7] On 21 February a bill of attainder was brought in. It named Elizabeth Barton and her accomplices as guilty of high treason for having under colour of pretended revelations conspired to discredit the marriage of the King and Queen and the legitimacy of their issue. Fisher and More were both named in the bill as accessories after the fact and therefore liable to the penalties of misprision of treason. If the bill was passed both knew they would go to the Tower.

Fisher learned early in January that his name was to be included in the bill. Cromwell sent him word of it by his brother Robert, advising him to confess his guilt and apply to the King for a pardon. Apparently Cromwell hoped he could deceive Fisher into admitting more than the council would otherwise be able to prove. If so, he was disappointed, for on the 18th Fisher sent a reply explaining his part in the affair of the nun and asserting his innocence of any malicious intent. His letter has not survived, but its contents can be inferred from Cromwell's answer. You say, Cromwell wrote, that you are ready "so to declare yourself, whatsoever hath been said of you, that ye have not deserved such heavy words, or terrible threats, as hath been sent from me unto you by your brother; how ye can declare yourself affore God and the world, when need shall require, I cannot tell; but I think verily that your declaration made by these letters, is far insufficient to prove that ye have deserved no heavy words in this behalf." By his brother Robert he had sent

Fisher nothing but good advice, saying "that I thought it expedient for you to write unto his highness, and to recognise your offences, and desire his pardon, which his grace would not deny you now in your age and sickness". Instead, he went on, you have denied your fault, arguing that you were persuaded by the reputation of the nun and by the testimony of her confessor and the late Archbishop of Canterbury to believe in her. But you made no real effort to try her, contenting yourself with asking her how many Magdalens were in the company of the blessed. After scoring with this pitiless jest at Fisher's expense, Cromwell thrust an ugly question at him. "I appeal [to] your conscience, and instantly desire you to answer. Whether if she had shewed you as many revelations for the confirmation of the king's grace's marriage, which he now enjoyeth, as she did to the contrary, ye would have given as much credence to her as ye have done". You say, he added, that you did not repeat her prophecies to the King because she told you that she herself had revealed them to him. Supposing this was true (as it was), what right, he asked, had you to believe it? You can do nothing now, he concluded, but admit your fault and pray to the King for mercy.[8]

It was a letter of unmatched brutality. Clearly, Cromwell meant, if he could, to use a trifling indiscretion to bring the old man to his knees. For the moment Fisher was too weary to resist. Before the relentless savagery of Cromwell's words his strength failed and he asked for pity: "after my right humble commendations", he replied, "I beseiche you to haue some pytye of me, consideryng the case and condition that I ame in. And I dout not but yf ye myght see in what plyte that I ame ye wulde haue some pyte uppon me. For in godfaythe now almoste this six weekys I haue hadde a grevous cowighe with a fever in the bigynnynge thereof as dyvers other heare in this countre hathe hadde and dyvers haue dyed thereof. And now the mattyer is fallen downe in to my leggis and feit with suche swellinge and aiche that I maye nother ryde nor goo. For the whiche I beseiche you eftsonys to haue some pyte uppon me and to spare me for a season to thene the swellinge and aiche of my leggis and feit maye swaige and abait. And then by the grace of our lorde I shall with all speide obeye your commaundement. Thus fare ye weall."⁹ But Fisher never did obey his commandment. In a day or two he took heart and wrote to Cromwell again. This time he took his stand proudly on what he had already said and done and urged the Secretary to trouble him no further with his letters. "Aftir my right humble commendations I most intierly beseche you that I no farther be moved to mak awnswere vnto your letters", he began, "for I se that myn awnswere most rather growe in to a greate booke or els be insufficient so that ye shall still therby tak occasion to be offendid and I nothing proffitt. For I perceyve that every thinge that I writte is ascrybed either to craft or to willfulness or to affection or to unkyndnes agaynst my soveraigne, so that my writinge rather provokithe you to displeasur then it forderithe me in any poynt concernyng your favour whiche I most affectually coveyte. Nothinge I redd in all your longe letters that I tak any comfort of but the oonely subscription wher in it pleaside you to call you my Frende whiche vndoutydly was a wurde of moche consolation vnto me. And therefor I beseiche you so to contynew and so to shew your self vnto me at this tyme. In ij poyntes of my writinge me thought ye were most offendide and boithe concernyd the kinges grace. That oone was where I excusyd my self by the displeasur that his highnes toke with me when I spake oons or twyse vntill hyme of lyk matters. That other was where I towchide his great mattier. And as to the Furst"—apparently Fisher had told Cromwell that he had hesitated to inform the King of the nun's prophecies for fear of arousing his anger— "me thinke it veary herde that I myght not signyfye vnto you suche thinges secreatly as myght be most affectuall for myn excuse. And as to the seconde my study and purpose was specially to declyne that I shulde not be straytede to offende his grace in that behalf for thene I most nedis declare my conscyence the whiche as thane I wrote I wulde be loithe to doo any more largely than I haue done. Not that I condeme eny other menys conscyence there conscyence maye save theme and myne most save me. Wherefor good master Cromewell I beseiche you for the love of god be contentid with this myne awnswere. And to give creadence vnto my brother in suche thingis as he hathe to saye vnto you. Thus fare ye weale."[10]

Unable to prevail upon Fisher to implicate himself more deeply in the affair, Cromwell had no alternative but to put Fisher's name into the bill of attainder as an accessory. And this he did. Meanwhile, however, there was other legislation before the two houses. An act concerning heresy provided *inter alia* that henceforth denial of the supremacy of the Pope should not be adjudged heresy or be punishable as such. A second act concerning annates confirmed the act of 1532, which had authorized the King to suspend the payment at Rome of the first-fruits of English sees. The new act went farther than the old in asserting the authority of the King. The act of 1532 had provided that a bishop denied his bulls at Rome for refusal to pay the first-fruits could be invested by any two other bishops appointed by the King for the purpose. It left untouched the right of the Holy See to make appointments to English sees and to receive an oath of canonical obedience from the bishop-elect, provided that the King consented to the appointment and received the customary oath of allegiance. The new act went much farther. It provided that bishops were henceforth to be nominated by the King and elected by their chapters; when elected, the bishop was to take one oath only and that an oath of allegiance to the King.[11] Later in the year the suspended levy on first-fruits was restored; henceforward bishops-elect were to pay the same tax as before, only now it was to be paid into the royal exchequer.

On 21 February the bill of attainder was brought before the

Lords. More had already written to Cromwell to clear himself of any suspicion that he was the author of an answer to the book of nine articles issued by the council the previous Christmas. He now wrote again, expressing surprise that his name had been included, since he had refused even to listen to the prophecies of the nun concerning the King. He asked for a copy of the bill, so that he could correct any untruths it might contain.[12] Fisher, who was still at Rochester, learned of the bill soon after it was brought in, and on 27 February he wrote to the King. It was a very different letter from what Cromwell had expected. "To the kynge his moost graciouse highnes", it began. "Please it your moost graciouse highenes benignely to heare this my moost humble sute, which I haue to make vnto your grace att this tyme, and to pardone me that I come nott myself vnto your grace for the same, for in good faith I haue hadde so meny periculouse diseases oone after an other which beganne with me before advent, and so by long continuaunce hath now brought my bodie in that weakenesse that withowten perill of destruction of the same, which I darr saye your grace for your soveraigne goodness wold not, I maye not as yett take any travayling vpon me. And soo I wrote to maister Cromwell your moost trustie Counsaillor, besechyng him to obtayne your graciouse licence for me to be absent from this parliament for that same cause, and he putt me in comforthe soo to doo.

"Now thus it is moost graciouse Soueraigne Lorde, that in your moost highe Courte of Parliament is put in a bill agaynest me concernyng the Nunne of Canterburye and intendyng my condempnation for not reuelyng of such wordes as she hadde vnto me towching your highnes. Wherin I moost humblie besech youre grace that withowten youre displeasor I maye shew vnto yow the consideration that moved me soo to doo, which when youre moost excellente wisdome hath deaplye considered I trust assuredly that your charitable goodnes will not impute any blame to me therfore.

"A trowth it is, this Nunne was [with] me thries in commyng from London by Rochester, as I wrote to Maister Cromewell, and shewed vnto hym the occasions of hir commyng, and of my sendynges vntill hir agayne.

"The fyrst tyme she came vnto my howse vnsent for of my partye, and than she told me that she hadde bene with your grace, and that she hadde shewed vnto yow a Reuelation which she hadde from allmyghty god, youre grace I trust will not be displeased with this my rehearsall thereof. She said that if your grace went forth with the purpose that ye entended, ye shold not be Kynge of Englaunde vij monethes after.

"I conceaved not by theis wordes, I take it vpon my sowle, that any malice or euill was entended or ment vnto your highenes by any mortall man, butt oonly that thei were the threattes of god, as she than did afferme.

"And thoughe thai were feaned [feigned], that (as I wold be saved) was to me vnknowen. I neuer counsailled hir vnto that feanynge, ner was pryvaye therevnto, ner to any such purposes, as it now is sayd, thei went abowte.

"Neuerthelesse if she hadde told me this Reuelation and hadde not alsoo tolde me, that she hadde reported the same vnto youre grace I hadde bene verylie farre to blame, and worthy extreame punysshement, for not disclosyng the same vnto youre highenes, or elles to some of your Counsaill.

"Butt sithen she did assure me therwith that she hadde playnelye told vnto your grace the same thynge, I thought dowtlesse that your grace wold haue suspected me that I hadde commyn to renewe hir tale agayne vnto yow, rather for the confermyng of myn opinion, than for any other cause.

"I beseche your highnes to take no displeasor with me for this that I will saye. It stykketh yet moost graciouse Soveraigne Lorde in my hart to my no litle hevynesse youre greviouse letters, and after that your moch fearfull wordes that your grace hadde vnto me for shewyng vnto yow my mynde and opinion in

165

the same matter, notwithstandyng that your highenes hadde soo often and soo straytly commaunded me to serch for the same before, and for this cause I was right loth to haue commyn vnto your grace agayne with such a tale pertaynyng to that matter.

"Meny other considerations I hadde, but this was the very cause why that I came not vnto your grace. For in good faithe I dradde lest I shold therby haue provoked your grace to farther displeasor agaynst me.

"My lorde of Canterbury also which was your greate Counsaillor [Warham] tolde me that she hadde bene with your grace, and hadde shewed yow this same matter, and of hym (as I will answere bifore god) I learned greatter thynges of hir pretensed visions than she tolde me hirself. And at that same tyme I shewede vnto hym, that she hadde bene with me, and told me as I haue writen before.

"I trust now that your excellent wisdome and learnynge seeth there is in me noo defawte, for not reuelynge of her wordes vnto your grace, when she hirself did affirme vnto me that she hadde soo done, and my Lorde of Canterbury that then was confermed also the same.

"Wherfore moost graciouse Soveraigne Lorde in my most humblie wise, I besech your highnes to dismisse me of this trooble, wherby I shall the more quietly serve god, and the more effectually pray for your grace.

"This if there were a right greate offense in me shold be to your merite to pardon, butt moch rather takyng the case, as it is, I trust veryly ye will soo doo.

"Now my bodye is moch weakened with meny diseases and infirmities, and my sowle is moch inquieted by this trooble so that my harte is more withdrawen from god, and fro the devotion of prayer than I wold. And veryly I thynke that my lyve maye not long continewe. Wherfor eftsoones I besech your moost graciouse highnes, that by your charytable goodnes I maye be delyuered of this besynesse, and onely to prepare my sowle to god, and to make itt ready agaynest the commyng of death, and nomoore to come abroode in the worlde. This mooste graciouse Soveraigne Lorde I besech your highnes by all the singuler and excellent endewmentes of your most noble bodie and sowle, and for the love of Christ Jesu that soo dearly with his moost preciouse bloode redeamed your sowl and myn, and duryng my lyve I shall not cease (as I am bownden) and yet now the more entearly to make my prayer to god for the preservation of your moost Royall maiestie."[13]

More had an even stronger case than Fisher. When the bill of attainder was first brought in, he had sent to Cromwell for a copy. A few days later he wrote at length to explain his part in the affair. Eight or nine years before, he told the Secretary, the King had asked him to examine Elizabeth Barton. At that time he found in her nothing remarkable, though he did not make bold to deny a miracle. Several years later, More continued, Father Risby spent a night at his house in Chelsea, and after supper fell to conversation about the nun. He offered to tell More of her prophecies concerning the King, but he refused to hear them. A few months after that Father Rich visited him at Chelsea and again More refused to listen to the nun's revelations. After this, being one day with the monks of Sion, More saw the nun and spoke with her. Once again, however, he refused to hear anything of the King or any other man.[14] More's prudence proved equal to the occasion. It was plainly impossible to implicate him in the proceedings against Elizabeth Barton and her accomplices. To avoid opposition in the House of Lords, the council consented to take his name out of the bill.

Fisher's name was, however, allowed to stand. Too ill to make the journey to Westminster to speak in his own defence from his place in the House of Lords, he addressed a letter to the peers from his palace at Rochester. "My lordes after my most humblie commendations vnto all your good Lordeshippes that sitt in this moost highe Courte of Parliamente, I besech yow in

like maner to heare and to tendre this my sute which by necessitie now I am dryven to make vnto all your Lordeshippes in
writyng bicause that I maye not by the Reason of my disease and
weakenes att this tyme be present my self before yow, withowten
perill of destruction of my bodie, as heretofore I haue writen to
maister Cromewell, which gave me comforte to obtayne of the
kynge his grace respite for myn absense to then I be recovered.
If I might haue bene present my self I dowte not, but the greate
weakenes of my bodie with other manyfold infirmities, wold
haue moved yow moch rather to haue pitie of my cause and
matter whereby I am putt vnto this greviouse trooble.

"So it is my good Lordes, that I am enformed of a certayne
bill that is putt into this highe courte against me and other
concernyng the matter of the Nunne of Canterburye, which
thynge is to me no litle hevynesse and most speciallie in this
pitiouse condition that I am in. Neuertheless I trust in your
honors, wisdames, and consciences, that ye will nat in this highe
courte, suffer any acte or condempnation to passe agaynest me
to then my cause may be well and duely herd. And therof in my
most humblie wise, I besech all yow my lordes in the waye of
Charitie, and for the love of Christe. And for the meane ceason
it maye please you to consider that I sought not for this womans
commynge vnto me nor thought in hir any maner of deceatte.
She was the parson that by meny probable and liklye coniectures
I than reputed to be right honeste religiouse and very good and
vertuouse. I verilye supposed that such feanyng and craftye com-
passynge of any gyle or fraude hadd bene farr from hir. And
whatt defaute was this in me soo to thynke when I hadde soo
meny probable testimonies of hir vertue.

"First the brute of the countree which generallie called hir the
hooly mayde.

"Secounde hir entresse into Religion vpon certayn visions
which was comonly saide that she hadde.

"Thirdde for the good religion and Learnyng that was

thought to be in hir goostly father [Edward Bocking], and in other vertuouse and well learned preistes, that then testified of hir holynesse as it was commonly reported.

"Finallie my Lorde of Canterburie that then was hir ordinarie, and a man reputed of highe wisdame and learnyng, told me that she hadde meny greate visions. And of hym I learned greatter thynges then ever I herd of the Nunne hirself.

"Your wisedames I dowte nott here seeth playnely that in me there was no defawte to beleve this woman to be honeste religiouse and of good credence.

"For sithen I am bownden by the law of god to beleve the best of every parson vnto then the countrarye be proved, moch rather I aught so to beleve of this woman that hadde then so meny probable testimonies for hir goodnes and vertue. Butt here itt wilbe said, that she told me such wordes as was to the perill of the prynce, and of the Realme. Surely I am right sorye to make any rehearsall of hir wordes, butt oonly that necessitie soo compelleth me now to doo. The wordes that she told me concernyng the perill of the kynge his hieghnesse was theis.

"She said, that she hadde a Reuelation from god that if the kynge went forth with the purpose that he entended, he shold not be kynge of Englaunde, vij monethes after, and she told me also that she thanne hadde bene with the kynge, and shewed vntill his grace the same Reuelation.

"Thoughe this were foorgied by hir, or by any other what Defawte is in me, that knew noo thyng of that foorgyng. If I hadd gevyn hir any counsaill to the foorgyng of this Reuelation or had hadde any knowleage that it was feaned, I hadde bene worthie greate blame and punysshement. Butt where I nouther gave hir any counsaill to this matter ner knew of any foorgynge or feanyng therof, I trust in your greate wisdames that ye will not thynke any defawte in me towchyng this poynte.

"And as I will answere before the Throone of Christ I knew not of any malice or evill that was entended by her, or by any other earthly creature vnto the kynges hieghnesse, naither hir wordes did so sownde that by any temporall or worldly power such thynge was intended, but oonly by the power of god, of whome as she than said, she hadde this Reuelation to shew vnto the kynge.

"Butt here itt will be said, that I shold haue shewed the wordes, vnto the kynge his highenesse, verily if I hadde not vndowtedly thought, that she hadde shewed the same wordes vnto his grace, my duetie hadde bene soo to haue done. But when she hirself, which pretended to haue hadde from god this Reuelation hadde shewed the same, I saw noo necessitie, why that I shold renewe it agayne vnto his grace. For hir esteamed honestie qualified, as I said before, with soo meny probable testimonies affirmyng vnto me that she hadde tolde the same vnto the kynge, made me right assuredly to thynke that she hadde soo shewed the same wordes vnto his grace.

"And not oonly hir owne saying thus persuaded me but hir prioresse wordes confermed the same, and ther servaundes also reported vnto my servaundes that she hadde than bene with the kynge. And yett besides all theis, I knew it, not long after by some other that soo itt was in deade. I thought therfor that it was not for me to rehearse the Nunnes wordes vnto the kynge agayne, when his grace knew them all readie, and she hirself hadde told theim hym before. And surely dyverse other causes dissuaded me soo to do, which are not here oppenly to be rehearsed. Neuertheless when thei shalbe herd, I dowt nott but thei all togeder will clearely excuse me as concernyng this matter.

"My sute therfor vnto all yow myn honorable Lordes att this tyme is, that noon acte of condempnation concernyng this matter be sufferde to passe agaynst me in this highe Courte before that I be herde orelles some other for me, how that I can declare my self to be giltles herin.

"And this I moost humblie besech yow all of your charitable

goodnesses, and also that if peraventure in the meane tyme ther shalbe thought any negligence in me, for not reueling of this matter vnto the kynge his highenesse, ye for the punysshement therof which is now past, ordayne no new lawe, but latt me staunde vnto the lawes which hath bene heretofore made, vnto the which I must and will obeye, besechynge allwaye the kynge his moost noble grace, that the same his lawes maye be ministerd vnto me with favor and equitie, and not with the strayttest rigor. Me neadeth not here to aduertise your moost highe wisdames to loke vpp to god, and vpon your owne sowles in ordaynyng such lawes, for the punysshement of negligences, or of other deades which are all ready past, ner yet to loke vpon your own perilles, which maye happen to yow in lyke cases. For ther sitteth not oone Lorde here, but the same or other like maye chaunce vntill hymself, that now is imputed to me.

"And therfore eftsoones I besech all your benigne charities to tendre this my moost humblie sute, as ye wold be tendred if ye were in the same daungiour your selfes, and this to do for the Reuerence of Christ for the discharge of your owne sowles, and for the honour of this moost highe Courte, and finallie for your own Sureties and other that hereafter shall succede yow. For I verily trust in allmyghtie god that by the succour of his grace, and your charitable supportacions I shall soo declare my self, that every noble man that sitteth here shall of good reason be therwith satisfied.

"Thus our lorde haue yow all, this moost honorable Courte in his protection. Amen."[15]

It was a forceful appeal. If the subject had no right to be tried in the King's courts according to the laws and usages established by custom, there would be no security for any man. The council could deprive anyone of his life or liberty, without troubling to obtain a conviction in the ordinary way, by the simple expedient of bringing in a bill of attainder. Fisher was willing enough to stand trial according to the law; he asked only that the Lords refuse to convict him by the arbitrary process of attainder. His appeal had little effect. The bill was given second reading in the House of Lords on 26 February and on 6 March it was given third reading. On this occasion a rider was attached praying that Sir Thomas More and the others named in the bill—except Fisher—be allowed to appear in the Star Chamber to speak for themselves. Fisher was to be denied this privilege, though he had asked to be heard in his own defence, because he was held to have declared his mind in the letter he had already sent to the Lords. In the event, none of the accused was given a hearing. Instead, More's name was removed from the bill, which in this form was given fourth reading and passed by the Lords on 12 March. Five days later it was passed by the House of Commons and on the 30th it received the royal assent.[16] Fisher was not, however, required to pay the full penalties of the law. He was allowed instead to compound for his offence by paying a fine of £300—a sum about equal to his yearly income from the see of Rochester and equivalent to at least $30,000 in modern money.

Meanwhile, an act for the submission of the clergy had been adopted by both houses. Two years before, the clergy assembled in Convocation had undertaken never to "enact put in ure promulge or execute any new canons or constitucion" without royal licence and authority. This undertaking was now incorporated in a new act, giving statutory authority to what until then had been only a resolution of the ecclesiastical provinces of Canterbury and York. The council was careful to amplify and enlarge on the scope of the submission. Where in Convocation the clergy had been required to promise that they would never "enact put in ure promulge or execute any new canons" without the consent of the King, they were compelled by the act to relinquish the right to "presume to attempt alledge claim or put in ure any Constitutions or Ordinance, Provincial or Synodal, or any other Canons, nor shall enact promulge or execute any such Canons Constitutions or Ordinances Provincial, by whatsoever

Name or Names they may be called, in their Convocations in
Time coming . . . unless the same Clergy may have the King's
most Royal Assent and Licence".[17]

The session was now in its last days. Before the two houses
were permitted to rise, however, they were required to consider
and approve a still more important piece of legislation. This was
the Act of Succession, which was given a first reading on 20
March and hurried through second and third readings in the
course of the next three days. The act in restraint of appeals, the
acts concerning heresy and annates and the act for the submission of the clergy had already made the King, in fact as well as
in name, supreme in both Church and State. The new act took
away nothing from the Church it had not already lost. Its purpose was to secure the succession on the issue of the King by
Queen Anne. This, however, involved the whole question of the
legitimacy of the Princess Mary. To establish the title of the
King's issue by Queen Anne, it was necessary to declare the
Princess Mary illegitimate; and to do this it was essential to
declare that the Lady Catherine, who was still living, was not
and had never been Henry's lawful wife. That the King in Parliament was competent to determine such questions, insofar as
they affected the succession itself, no-one had any wish to deny.
Even Fisher, who had for years stubbornly defended the liberties
of the Church against both King and council, was prepared to
acknowledge that the King and Parliament had the right to
settle the succession on any person they might choose. This was
a matter within the competence of the two houses and had nothing to do with the lawful authority of the Church.

But the act now brought before the Lords did more than establish the succession. In the preamble it set forth the reasons for
the enactment: the impediment to the marriage of Henry and
Catherine and the insufficiency of the Julian dispensation; the
right of the King, regardless of the pretended jurisdiction of the
Bishop of Rome, to invest the Archbishop of Canterbury with

the authority to hear and determine his cause; the sentence pronounced by the archbishop with the assent and approval of the clergy assembled in Convocation, separating the King from the Lady Catherine and confirming his marriage to Queen Anne. Furthermore, the act provided that an oath be tendered to all the King's subjects, by which they would be required, as a test of their allegiance, to subscribe to the whole content and effect of the law. This meant that any man or woman could be required, on his or her oath, to acknowledge the supremacy of the King in the Church of England and the validity of the sentence pronounced at Dunstable in his favour by the Archbishop of Canterbury. Hitherto Fisher had been free to oppose bills brought before the Lords and to dissent from resolutions adopted by Convocation, provided he did not disobey the law. This right was now to be taken away. He was no longer to be allowed even the prerogative of silence. He was to be made to rise and declare before God and the people that the authority of the Holy See in the Church of Christ had been usurped from Kings, that the King of England was supreme within his own dominions in spiritual as well as temporal matters and that the succession as by law established was consistent not only with political necessities but also with the will of Almighty God.

While the Act of Succession was before the upper house, Clement at last decided to act. Catherine's appeal, delivered to the Holy See five years before during the legatine hearing at Blackfriars, was brought into the consistory, where it was upheld by a majority of the cardinals on 23 March, the very day on which the act that was to complete the break between England and Rome was given third reading in the House of Lords. In France a final effort was made to save appearances. Francis sent the Bishop of Paris to England in an attempt to negotiate a compromise whereby Henry would submit to papal jurisdiction provided he was assured in advance of a judgment in his favour. But it was too late. Both sides had gone too far to withdraw. Clement published a bull pronouncing Henry and Catherine to be man and wife and confirming the legitimacy of the Princess Mary.[18] A week later the Canterbury Convocation voted on a question placed before it at the command of the King: "Whether the Roman pontiff has any greater jurisdiction bestowed on him by God in the Holy Scriptures in this realm of England, than any other foreign bishop?" Almost to a man, the assembled clergy cast their votes for the negative. Two months later, on 2 June, the York Convocation approved, without a single dissenting voice, a similar resolution declaring that "the Bishop of Rome has not, in Scripture, any greater jurisdiction in the kingdom of England than any other foreign bishop."[19] On 31 March, the very day on which the clergy of the southern province repudiated the authority of the Holy See, the King was pleased to give his assent to the Act of Succession.

This great act declared in the preamble that it was the desire and intent of the King to preserve his people from the several mischiefs of a disputed succession, which in the past had provided the occasion for the Bishops of Rome, "contrary to the great and inviolable Grants of Jurisdictions given by God immediately to Emperors Kings and Princes, in Succession to their Heirs", to "invest who should please them, to inherit in other Men's Kingdoms and Dominions". Which thing "we your most humble Subjects, both Spiritual and Temporal", it went on, "do utterly abhor and detest"; wherefore it is enacted that "the Marriage heretofore solemnized between your Highness and the Lady *Katherine*, being before the lawful Wife to Prince *Arthur*, your elder Brother, which by him was carnally known, as doth duly appear by sufficient Proof in a lawful Process had and made before *Thomas*, by the Sufferance of God, now Archbishop of *Canterbury*, and Metropolitan and Primate of all this Realm, shall be, by Authority of this present Parliament, definitively clearly and absolutely declared deemed and adjudged to be against the Laws of Almighty God, and also accepted reputed and taken of no Value nor Effect, but utterly void and adnihiled, and the Separation thereof, made by the said Archbishop, shall be good and effectual to all Intents and Purposes". It was further enacted that "the said Lady *Katherine* shall be from henceforth called and reputed only Dowager to Prince *Arthur*, and not Queen of this Realm; and that the lawful Matrimony had and solemnized between your Highness and your most dear and entirely beloved Wife Queen *Anne*, shall be established and taken for undoubtful true sincere and perfect ever hereafter, according to the just Judgement of the said *Thomas* . . . whose Grounds of Judgement have been confirmed, as well by the whole Clergy of this Realm in both the Convocations, and by both the Universities thereof, as by the Universities of *Bonony*, *Padua*, *Paris*, *Orleans*, *Toulouse*, *Angiewe* [Anjou], and divers others, and also by the private Writings of many right excellent well learned men"; all of which "we your said Subjects, both Spiritual and Temporal, do purely plainly constantly and firmly accept approve and ratify for good, and consonant to the Laws of Almighty God, without Error or Default; most humbly beseeching your Majesty, that it may be so established for ever by your most gracious and Royal Assent." Pursuant to the considerations set forth in the preamble, the succession to the crown is settled on the King's issue by Queen Anne and in default of such issue on the King's right heirs forever.[20]

The act provided that all the King's subjects who were of full age were to be required to take an oath on the act; any who refused were to suffer the penalties of misprision of treason. This meant that anyone who was unable in good conscience to take the oath must forfeit all he possessed to the crown and suffer himself to be imprisoned at the pleasure of the King. The form of the oath to be taken was not set forth in the act, but was established by letters patent. On the last day of the session, the Commons assembled at the bar of the House of Lords in the presence of the King himself. Sir Humphrey Wingfield, Speaker of the lower house, made an address of loyalty, after which Sir Thomas Audeley, the Lord Chancellor, read the oath aloud. All those in the chamber subscribed : every squire, every knight, every peer, every abbot and prior, every bishop. A commission had already been issued to Thomas Archbishop of Canterbury, the Lord Chancellor, Thomas Duke of Norfolk and Charles Duke of Suffolk, who were to take the oaths of those who were not present. For Fisher, lying ill at Rochester, the hour was at hand.

Chapter 17

Early in April there came a summons to appear before the commissioners at Lambeth. Fisher knew well enough what this meant. He set about making what provision he could for his household. The little money he had left he divided between his servants and the poor of Rochester. To Michaelhouse, his old college at Cambridge, he sent £100. Next morning he set out for London. As he rode bareheaded through the cathedral city he had served for thirty years, crowds gathered to take leave of him. Many wept openly as he passed, his right hand raised in a gesture of benediction. He had made his choice and he was not afraid. The grief and anxiety he had suffered through long years of discouragement and defeat had now left him. He was more alone now than ever, but that no longer mattered. For five years he had laboured to preserve the liberty of the English Church and he had failed. He had lost much, he had lost everything that mattered most to him. But he still possessed his soul in peace and this could not be taken away from him. It was enough.

At the top of Shooter's Hill he stopped at midday for dinner.

He intended to dine in the open air, he said, as long as he could. Before dark he reached London. On the appointed day, Monday, 13 April, he went to Lambeth Palace, where he met More and Nicholas Wilson. Wilson was one of the handful of clergy who had voted with Fisher in Convocation against the King.[1] As for More, he had not seen Fisher for more than a year. He told his old friend that he hoped they would meet again in heaven. Fisher observed that the way they had chosen was certainly strait and narrow enough to be the way to heaven.

He himself was sent for first. Standing in the presence of the commissioners, he was handed a copy of the oath he was to swear. This is what he read: "Ye shall swear to bear your Faith, Truth, and Obedience, alonely to the King's Majesty, and to the Heirs of his Body, according to the Limitation and Rehearsal within this Statute of Succession above specified, and not to any other within this Realm, nor foreign Authority, Prince, or Potentate; and in case any Oath be made, or hath been made, by you, to any other Person or Persons,[2] that then you to repute the same as vain and annihilate; and that, to your Cunning, Wit, and uttermost of your Power, without Guile, Fraud, or other undue Means, ye shall observe, keep, maintain and defend, this Act above specified, and all the whole Contents and Effects thereof, and all other Acts and Statutes made since the Beginning of this present Parliament, in Confirmation or for due Execution of the same, or of any thing therein contained; and thus ye shall do against all Manner of Persons, of what Estate, Dignity, Degree, or Condition soever they be, and in no wise do or attempt, nor to your Power suffer to be done or attempted, directly or indirectly, any Thing or Things, privily or apertly, to the Let, Hindrance, Damage, or Derogation thereof, or of any Part of the same, by any Manner of Means, or for any Manner of Pretence or Cause. So help you God and all Saints."[3] Fisher offered to swear to the succession as established by law, but as for the rest—and he was required to swear to *"all the whole Con-*

tents and Effects" of the act—he could not, he said, in good conscience oblige them. Thereupon he was given in custody of the Archbishop of Canterbury, in the hope that, before being committed to the Tower, he could be made to change his mind. More gave a similar answer and, after submitting to a second examination the same afternoon, was sent away in custody of the Abbot of Westminster. Wilson also refused the oath and since he was less important to the council than the other two he was sent directly to the Tower.[4]

As the days passed, it became clear that neither Fisher nor More was prepared to yield. On the 17th Cranmer wrote to Cromwell suggesting that both men be allowed to swear to the act without the preamble. "For hereby", he pointed out, "shall be a great occasion to satisfy the princess dowager [Catherine] and the Lady Mary", as well as "the emperor, and other their friends, if they give as much credence to my lord of Rochester and master More, speaking or doing against them, as they hitherto have done and thought that all other should have done, when they spake and did with them. And peradventure it should be a good quietation to many other within this realm, if such men should say, that the succession, comprised within the said act, is good and according to God's laws: for then I think there is not one within this realm, that would once reclaim against it. . . . Which thing, although I trust surely in God that it shall be brought to pass, yet hereunto might not a little avail the consent and oaths of these two persons, the bishop of Rochester and master More."[5] The suggestion was both prudent and humane, but it did not commend itself to the King. He told Cromwell that if Fisher and More were allowed to take the oath with reservations, other men might presume to do the same; "wherefore to thintent that no such thing*es* should be brought into the hedd*es* of the people by the ensample of the said*e* Bisshop of Rochester and Mr. More the king*es* highnes in no wise willeth but that they shalbe sworn aswell to the preamble as to the acte of Succession".[6]

More was committed to the Tower without further delay. Fisher continued at Lambeth a few days longer. While he was waiting there, a delegation from St. John's was allowed to see him. They asked him to confirm a new set of statutes they had prepared for his signature, whereupon he told them he would have to read them first. When they protested that his time was short, he answered that he would attend to their concerns in the Tower as faithfully as any man could; if that were not allowed him, he added, then let God's will be done.[7] What this meant he knew only too well. On 20 April Elizabeth Barton and four of her accomplices were drawn from the Tower on a hurdle to Tyburn and there hanged one by one, cut down alive and quartered. The next day Fisher was brought again before the commissioners. The oath was put to him in the same form as before, and again he refused it. He had made up his mind.

And so at last he was brought to the Tower, which stood waiting for him in dark and eyeless silence on the river's edge three miles from Lambeth. As he climbed the stone stairs leading from the river into the precincts of the Tower, the world closed inexorably around him. Outside these walls, black and dripping and ageless, lay the familiar world, in which the meanest of men is invested with dignity and purpose by virtue of belonging to the community of the living and the dead : within that community he may be a cooper, or an innkeeper or a priest; he is a lover, perhaps, or a husband, or a friend; he may be of Cornish stock, or a Yorkshireman. But here, with the river-gate closed forever behind him, he is none of these; here the best of men is stripped to the bone and left with nothing to sustain him but what he can remember of himself and his past. They took Fisher across the silent, solitary green to a doorway leading to the Bell Tower. Up the winding stairs they led him to a chamber on the upper floor, where he was left alone. He found himself in a bare room with walls of hewn stone ten feet thick. In one corner there was a grate that could be made up in winter for warmth. Lancet windows faced north and west over the city of London and, looking out, Fisher could see the smoke rising in the distance from a thousand chimneys where men and women were living still as if nothing had changed.

He was not forgotten. Indeed, he had been in the Tower for less than a week when bailiffs were sent to Rochester to seize his possessions in the King's name. When the Cardinal of York was deprived, there had been much to gild the cup of royal pleasure. This is what they found in the palace of the Bishop of Rochester: in the bedchamber, a bed and mattress, two chairs, a close stool with an old cushion on it and a fire pan and shovel; in the study, some tables and chairs, fire irons and bookshelves; in the north study, glasses of syrup, some marmalade, a table and bookshelves; in the broad gallery, old hangings of green say, some old carpets, an altar cloth, a head of St. John the Baptist, two old sarcenets and a chair; in the wardrobe, some blankets and divers old trash; in the little study, glasses and syrups and other trash; in the great chapel, eight gilt images, two candlesticks, an old carpet, five wooden images and a crucifix; in the little chamber next to the chapel, old hangings, a broken mirror and an old folding bed; in the great chamber, a table and trestles, a bedstead and andirons in the parlour, five pieces of very old green verdour, a table and trestles, an old carpet and two chairs; in the kitchen, sixteen pewter and several brass pots. At the manor of Halling little was found but some tables and chairs, beds and bedding and working utensils of various sorts. Notes of hand there were, however, in plenty; Fisher had laid out nearly £450 in loans to those who came to him in need.[8]

In Fisher's study the King's agents found something else: a series of letters addressed to the Lady Catherine in an unknown hand.[9] One of these contained a passage that aroused the suspicion of the council. It referred to certain papers carried out of

England by the writer: "what things your Nobleness gave unto me [afterwa]rde by the same father, it needs not [to rehearse] he[re]. That thing only I would your Nobleness should believe, that I will be both so faithful and close in concealing these things that no mortal man shall ever know them besides them whom it behoveth. Of which thing, to the intent your Nobleness may the less doubt, know ye that I have sent over sea, now six days since, one of my servants with that which I received of the bishop of Rochester." The passage is obscure, but the writer is apparently referring to one of the books on the King's marriage prepared by Fisher and secretly conveyed to Spain. At least one of these had been printed and Cromwell already knew that Fisher was the author. No doubt he hoped to discover more by questioning the prisoner. Fisher was examined at length. He protested that the letters had been received so long ago that he could no longer remember the name of the writer or of the messenger who brought them. He could not remember how many books he had written in defence of the Queen, but he thought it was seven or eight. The last two, he said, contained the whole of the matter and one of these he knew to be in the possession of the Archbishop of Canterbury. But he had no way of knowing what copies had been made of the others or what became of them. He denied that he had consented to the publication of any of his books on the King's marriage. Nor had he counselled any other man to oppose the King. He had never given the Queen advice in private except once when she sent to him for comfort in her distress He told her to be of good cheer and to have faith in Christ. Did her distress, he was asked, arise from the fact that she had committed perjury in insisting that she came to Henry a virgin? He answered firmly that it did not.[10]

Meanwhile, Tunstal of Durham and Lee of York had been sent to Catherine to require her to swear to the Act of Succession. Tunstal, a lifelong friend of Fisher and More, a man of learning and integrity, had been for a time a member of the Queen's

council and had written a brief in her favour for submission to
the legates at Blackfriars. Chapuys had learned of Tunstal's
change of heart a few days before, when he attended a meeting
of the King's council at which he was informed of the new act.
Tunstal defended the oath as necessary to the quiet of the realm
and added that Catherine could accept it in good conscience. The
support of so eminent and worthy a man as Tunstal was important to the King and he had spared no pains to secure it. The see
of Durham was worth 15,000 ducats a year, as Chapuys remarked, and to encourage Tunstal in his loyalty to the crown
royal commissioners had been ordered to carry out a search of
his houses in the north while he was on his way to London. The
King lost no time in making use of his services. With Lee,
Tunstal waited on Catherine and explained to her the effects of
the Act of Succession. She replied that the cause having been
decided at Rome in her favour, she would continue to regard
herself as Queen as long as she lived. She spoke scornfully of
Tunstal's irresolution and declared proudly that she for her part
was ready to die for her cause, asking only that she be allowed
to die in public and not in the secrecy of her closet.[11]

Fisher had now been confined for more than a month and
after his return to London from his visit to Catherine Tunstal
was sent to try the effect of persuasion on his old friend. Roland
Lee, bishop-elect of Coventry and Lichfield, had already been
with Fisher and found him ill and weak but unshaken. He was
ready, Lee reported to Cromwell, "to Make hys othe for the
Succession and to swear neuer to medl more yn dissputacon of
the validite of the mariege or ynvalidite with the Lady dow-
eger". But "as for the case of the prohibicon Leuiticall hys
consciens is soo knytt that hee can not put it of frome hym what
soo euer betyde hym". Even Lee, who in most things was amenable enough to the wishes of the Court, was ashamed of what he
saw before him in the Tower. "Sierly", he told Cromwell, "the
man is negh goyne [nigh gone] and dowtlesse can not stynde

onles the kyng and his consell be mercifull to hym for the body can not bere the clothes on hys bake".[12] Tunstal found him in much the same condition. What the two friends said to each other we do not know, but we may suppose that Fisher was touched more nearly by the learning and humanity of Tunstal than by the studied cunning of Cromwell and the commissioners. It was so with More when Margaret Roper laboured to persuade him to yield, and no doubt it was the same with Fisher. With Dr. Wilson, who had also refused the oath when it was first offered to him, confinement had worked a deadlier effect. He sent a message to More in which he confessed that he was suffering from an agony of doubt and asked for his advice. More answered that each man must decide how to answer to the oath in the privacy of his own conscience. When he later learned that Wilson had resolved to take the oath, More sent him good luck, adding that he himself would follow his own conscience without meddling in any other. He asked for Wilson's prayers and offered in turn to pray for him.[13]

So the summer passed without ease or respite for the men in the Tower. They were usually allowed writing materials and when this luxury was withdrawn they wrote with a lump of coal. They had no books but they were allowed to receive letters, and from time to time visitors were admitted. At first they were permitted to take their exercise on the green within the Tower precincts. In those long months More worked first on his *Dialogue of Comfort* and then, as long as he could, on his *Treatise on the Passion*. Fisher composed two meditations for his sister Elizabeth, *A Spirituall Consolation* and a manual on *The Wayes to Perfect Religion*. In them he speaks of the unworthiness of man and of the comfort to be found by the repentant sinner in the love of God. Both men were content to live as they were and content to die, if it came to that.

On 3 November Parliament assembled for the second time in twelve months, and in the next few weeks a series of bills was hurried through the two houses, with the object of strengthening and extending the authority of the King. The first of these confirmed the royal supremacy recognized by the clergy in Convocation almost four years before. A title that had once been explained away by the King and council as an empty form was now found to be great with meaning. The Act of Supremacy provided that "the King our Sovereign Lord, his Heirs and Successors, Kings of this Realm, shall be taken accepted and reputed the only supreme Head in Earth of the Church of *England*, called *Anglicana Ecclesia*". The qualification introduced in Convocation at Fisher's suggestion—"so far as the law of Christ allows"—was now silently dropped, together with all pretence that the Church should be governed by any law other than the will of the prince. The act provided further that the King "shall have and enjoy, annexed and united to the Imperial Crown of this Realm, as well the Title and Stile thereof, as all Honours Dignities, Preheminences Jurisdictions Privileges Authorities Immunities Profits and Commodities to the said Dignity of supreme Head of the same Church belonging and appertaining; and that our said Sovereign Lord, his Heirs and Successors, Kings of this Realm, shall have full Power and Authority from Time to Time to visit repress redress reform order correct restrain and amend all such Errors Heresies Abuses Offences Contempts and Enormities, whatsoever they be, which by any Manner spiritual Authority or Jurisdiction ought or may lawfully be reformed repressed ordered redressed corrected restrained or amended, most to the pleasure of Almighty God".[14] The Act of Supremacy became law on 18 November, little more than two weeks after the session opened. More was to follow. The oath to the Act of Succession had been in use for more than seven months but it had never been given parliamentary approval, having been drawn up and published by letters patent. It was now ratified by both Houses of Parliament.[15] Next a bill was introduced to amend the Annates Act

185

adopted in the previous session. The new bill provided that certain first-fruits hitherto paid to the Bishop of Norwich in his diocese and to the Archdeacon of Richmond in his archdeaconry should cease and the first-fruits of all benefices be paid henceforth to the crown. More important still, it provided that a tenth of all spiritual livings be paid annually to the crown, beginning at Christmas, 1535.[16] Most disturbing of all was a new bill concerning treason. In England treason had until now been defined as an act leading or tending to the bodily harm of the King, the Queen or their heirs apparent. But now, without regard to custom or precedent, it was provided that any person who by words or writing denied the King the dignity, title or name of his royal estate should also be guilty of treason: "if any Person or Persons", the act declared, "after the first Day of *February* next coming, do maliciously wish, will or desire, by Words or Writing or by Craft imagine invent practise or attempt any bodily Harm to be done or committed to the King's most Royal Person, the Queen's or their Heirs apparent, or to deprive them or any of them of their Dignity Title or Name of their Royal Estates, or slanderously and maliciously publish and pronounce, by express Writing or Words, that the King our Sovereign Lord should be Heretick Schismatick Tyrant Infidel or Usurper of the Crown", such person or persons shall be adjudged traitors and shall suffer accordingly.[17] The effect was to make denial of the royal supremacy in words or writing liable to the penalties of high treason. Robert Fisher brought word of the new bill to his brother in the Tower. He had heard that when the bill was first introduced into the House of Commons members were unwilling to pass it, until the council agreed to insert the word "maliciously" into the governing clause. This would make it necessary for the crown to show that where an accused person had denied the supremacy of the King in the Church or deprived him of any other of his titles, he had done so out of malice for the royal person. But if the two brothers supposed that the

King would allow so small a word to stand in his way, they had only to reflect on what had become of the reservations with which the clergy had acknowledged the royal supremacy less than four years before.

Before the session ended Fisher had another reminder of the implacable hostility of the Court. Having refused the oath to the Act of Succession, he was already liable to the penalties provided for misprision of treason. In spite of this, however, a special act of attainder was drawn up and passed by both houses. "For asmoche", it ran, "as John Bysshopp of Rochester", contrary to his "Dewtes of allegiance intendyng to sowe and make Sedicion murmour and grugge within this Realme amongest the Kynges lovynge and obedyent subjectes", since the first day of May last past has been required to take the oath provided by the statute "made for the suertie stablisshement and contynuance of the Kyng our Soveraigne Lorde and his heires in the succession of the imperiall Crowne of this his Realme" and has "obstynatly maliciously and in contempte of the same acte refused to receyve and make the same othes"; now therefore be it enacted "that the said Bysshopp . . . shall stande and be atteynted ajuged and convycted of mesprision of High Treason". The penalties provided by the act were such as were usual in cases of the sort: imprisonment and loss of goods. In addition, Fisher was deprived of his bishopric and the see of Rochester declared vacant as of 2 January, 1535.[18]

The attainder did little to alter Fisher's immediate circumstances. As winter drew on conditions in the Tower became increasingly severe. The two prisoners now knew they were to be held until after the first day of February, when they would be examined again. If they could be induced to give their reasons for refusing the oath, they could perhaps be betrayed into denying the title of the King as "supreme Head in Earth of the Church of *England*". If so, their words could be attributed to malicious intent and the prisoners brought to the block. Meanwhile, both men were suffering from cold and want. Just before Christmas Fisher wrote to Cromwell to ask for relief. He spoke first of his willingness to satisfy the council in the matter of the succession, saving only the necessities of his conscience. "After my most humyl commendacions, where ass ye be content that I shold wryte un to the kyngs hyghness"—apparently Cromwell had urged him to give the King his reasons for refusing the oath, hoping as before to betray him into an incriminating admission—"in gude fathe I dread me that I kan not be soo cir[c]onspect in my wryteng but that sum worde shal eskape me wher with his grace shal be moved to sum farther displeasure aganste me wher of I wold be veray sory. For ass I wyll answer byfor god I wold not in eny maner of poynte offend his grace my dewty saved un to god whom I muste euery thyng prefer. And for this consideracion I am full loth & full of fear to wryte un to his hyghness in this matter. Neuertheless sythen I conceyve that itt is your mynde that I shal so doo I wyl endeavour me to the best that I kann.

"But first hear I must byseche yow gode master Secretary to call to your rememberance that att my last beyng byfor you & the other Commyssionars for takyng of the othe concernyng the kyngs most noble succession I was content to be sworn un to that parcell concernyng the succession. And ther I did rehears this reason whiche I sade moved mee. I dowted nott but the prynce of eny realme with the assent of his nobles & cumons myght appoynte for his succession Royal such an order ass was seen un to his wysdom most accordyng. And for this reason I sade that I was content to be sworn un to that parte of the othe ass concernyng the succession. This is a veray trowth as god help my sowl att my most neede. All be itt I refused to swear to sum other parcels bycawse that my conscience wold not serve me so to doo." He then went on to describe the pitiful condition to which he had been reduced. "I byseche yow", he wrote, "to be good master un to me in my necessite. For I have nather shert nor shete nor yett other clothes that ar necessary for me to wear but that be ragged & rent to shamefully. Notwithstandyng I myght easyly suffer that if tha wold keep my body warm. Butt my dyet allso god knowes how sclendar itt is att meny tymes. And now in myn age my sthomak may nott awaye but with a few kynd of meats which if I want I decaye forthwith & fall in to crases & disseasis of my bodye & kann not keep myself in health.

"And ass our lord knowith I have no thyng laft un to me for to provyde eny better but ass my brother of his own purs layeth out for me to his great hinderance.[19]

"Wherefore gode master Secretarye eftsones I byseche yow to have sum pittie uppon me & latt me have such thyngs ass ar necessary for me in myn age & specially for my health. And allso that itt may pleas yow by your hygh wisdom to move the kyngs hyghness to take me un to his gracioss favour agane & to restoor me un to my liberty owt of this cold & paynefull enprysonment whearby ye shal bynd me to be your pore beadsman for euer un to allmyghty god who euer have yow in his protection & custody.

"Other twayne thyngs I must allso desyer uppon yow. Thattoon is that itt may pleas yow that I may take sum preest with in the touer by the assygnment of master Levetenant to hear my confession aganste this hooly tyme. That other is that I may borow sum bowks to styr my devocion mor effectuelly thes hooly dayes for the comforth of my sowl. This I byseche yow to grant me of your charitee. And thus our lord send yow a mery Chrystenmass & a comforthable to your harts desyer."[20]

What answer Cromwell made we do not know. Fisher was allowed writing materials for some time longer and he may have been permitted a few books. He may also have been given some warmer clothing and perhaps a more adequate diet, though he had still to depend on the help of his friends, especially after the death of his brother Robert later in the winter. Now more painfully alone than ever, and suffering from recurrent illness, Fisher had little cause to thank Cromwell for his attentions.[21] Indeed,

the Secretary had other matters to think of. In January he was
named vicar-general of the Church of England, with authority
to conduct a general visitation of the monasteries and to make
an assessment of their estates and revenues. By the end of the
year, commissions working under the authority of the new
Annates Act had completed an inventory of the wealth of the
secular clergy, showing the income or annual value of every
ecclesiastical benefice and corporation. Already the secular clergy
were required to pay the first-fruits and tenths of their livings
into the royal exchequer. Soon the regulars were to be dispos-
sessed and their wealth appropriated as well for the use of the
King and Court. What was the conscience of a single man to all
this?

Chapter 18

As the long winter turned into spring, Fisher had his answer.
It was now treason to deny the supremacy of the King in the
Church of England. Fisher and More had refused the oath to the
Act of Succession because it involved an acknowledgement of
the royal supremacy, and their refusal had brought them to the
Tower. If they could be made to disclose their reasons, their dis-
closure would cost them their lives.

They were not quite alone. During the latter part of April
Cromwell visited the Charterhouse in London and demanded
that the monks formally submit to the authority of the King.
They had reluctantly taken the oath to the Act of Succession
the year before,[1] but farther than that they would not go. They
refused to yield to Cromwell's demands. The Prior, John
Houghton, was taken to the Tower, together with two other

Carthusians, Robert Lawrence, Prior of the Charterhouse at Beauvale, and Augustine Webster, Prior of the Charterhouse at Axholme in Lincolnshire. On 26 April the three Carthusians were examined by Cromwell in the Tower, along with Richard Reynolds, a Bridgettine of the monastery of Sion. They were each asked whether or not they were willing to obey the King as supreme head of the Church of England, and each answered that they were not. Three days later they were brought to trial in the Court of King's Bench, where evidence was given that they had denied the style and title of the King. A fifth prisoner, John Hale, the Vicar of Isleworth, was charged by one Robert Feron, a clerk of Teddington, with slanderous words spoken against the King on various occasions in May of 1534. The accused at first pleaded not guilty, but later changed their plea to guilty. All five were convicted of high treason and sentenced to be hanged, drawn and quartered at Tyburn.[2] Cranmer interceded with Cromwell in favour of Webster and Reynolds, pointing out, as he had the previous year in the case of Fisher and More, that it would be more profitable to correct the consciences of the prisoners than to allow them to suffer in their ignorance.[3] But Cromwell thought otherwise. He no doubt hoped that if he made an example of the Carthusians Fisher and More and others of a like mind would be brought to submit. On 30 April, the day after the five accused men had been sentenced, he visited More in the Tower, together with several other members of the council. More was asked to declare his mind as to the supremacy, but he refused to say more than that he was the King's good beadsman and daily prayed for him; if that was not enough to keep a man alive, he added, then he wished not to live.[4] If Fisher was examined on the same day, there is no record of what he said.

On Tuesday, 4 May, John Hale, Richard Reynolds and the three Carthusians were led out of the Tower for execution at Tyburn. From a window More watched their departure with his daughter Margaret: " 'doest not thou see, *Megg*' ", he said to her, " 'that these blessed Fathers be now as chearefully going to death, as if they were bridegroomes going to be married? whereby, good daughter, thou maiest see what a great difference there is betweene such as haue in effect spent all their daies in a straight, hard, and penitentiall life religiously, and such as haue in the world like worldlie wretches (as thy poore father hath donne) consumed all their time in pleasure and ease licentiously?' " The five prisoners were drawn to Tyburn on a hurdle and there hanged one by one in their habits. Each in turn was cut down alive and thrown over a block, where his body was ripped open and his bowels torn out and burned. Each was then beheaded and quartered. The quarters were set up on spears and carried off in triumph. One of them was placed over the gate to the Charterhouse. It was the arm of John Houghton, the Prior.[5]

Three days later Fisher and More were examined again by members of the council. Cromwell asked Fisher if he knew what would happen if he persevered in his refusal to take the oath. Fisher answered that he did, adding that " 'this new Acte seemeth to me much lyke a two-edged sword; for yf I answere you directly, with denyall of *th*e kings Supremacie, then am I sure of death; and yf, on the contrarie part, I acknowledge the same contrarie to my owne conscience, then am I sure of the losse of my soule; wherfore (as neare as I can to avoid both daungers) I shall desire *you*r Lord*shi*pps to beare with my silence, for I am not minded to make anie direct answer to it at all.' "[6] His silence could hardly be construed as malicious denial of the title, dignity or royal estate of the King, and so Cromwell determined to resort to devices of a different kind. Later the same day he sent Richard Rich, a young man then rising in the King's service, to the Tower with a message for Fisher. Rich was already well known to More, who said at his trial that he was the last man to whom he would be likely to open his mind, in this or any other matter. But he was probably not known to

Fisher, who in any case was not prepared for what Rich had to say to him. The King, Rich intimated, earnestly desired Fisher to give him his private opinion as to the supremacy, for his own spiritual guidance. Fisher had been confessor to the Lady Margaret and for many years after her death he had continued to enjoy the respect of the young King, her grandson. The appeal went to the heart of his longing for deliverance from the nightmare in which he had been living for so long. It played on his grief, his loneliness and his simplicity. He seized eagerly on Rich's words, in the belief that Henry, sickened by the fruits of his own excess, had sent to him under the seal of confession. He told Rich "to certifie the king Frome hyme, that he belyved directelie in his conscyence, *and* [kn]ewe by his Lernyng preciselie, that it was very playne by the holy scripture, the [la]wes of the churche, the generall counsell, *and* the whole faith *and* generall practise of christ*es* [ca]tholyke churche frome christ*es* Ascension hetherto, That the king was not, nor could be, [by] the Lawe of God supreame head in earthe of the churche of England."[7]

Having obtained an explicit denial of the supremacy from Fisher, Rich tried to practise a similar deception on More. Two months later, at More's trial, he testified that he had put to the prisoner the following case. " 'Admitt there were, *Sir*,' quoth he, 'an Acte of Parliament that all the Realme should take me for king; would [not] you nowe, M*aster* More,' quoth he, 'take me for king?'

" 'Yes, *Sir*,' quoth *Sir* Thomas More, 'that would I.'

" 'I put case further,' quoth M*aster* Riche, 'that there were an Act of Parliament that all the Realme should take me for Pope; would you not then, M*aster* More, take me for Pope?'

" 'For answere, *Sir*,' quoth *Sir* Thomas More, 'to your first case, the Parliament maye well, M*aster* Riche, meddle with the state of temporall Princes; but to make aunswere to your other case, [I will put you this case]. Suppose the Parliament would make a lawe that God should not be God; would you then, Master Riche, say that God were not God?'

" 'No, Sir,' quoth he, 'that I would not, sith no Parliament may make anye suche lawe.'

" 'No more,' saide Sir Thomas More (as Master Riche reported of him) 'could the Parliament make the king Supreme head of the Church.' "[8] More denied under oath that he had made this statement, and indeed it seems unlikely that he did more than ask Rich if Parliament could make a law that God were not God. Denial of the supremacy was implicit in such a question and no doubt Rich, anxious as he was to earn the royal favour, was willing enough to overlook the distinction between what More had implied and what he had said. However that may be, there was no need for perjury in Fisher's case. Fisher had betrayed himself as completely as Cromwell could have wished or hoped for.

The Secretary hesitated, however, to make use of Rich's testimony. With it he knew he could secure a conviction in the Court of King's Bench. But what he wanted was something else: he preferred that Fisher should be brought to submit. If Fisher could be persuaded to take the oath, Cromwell knew, few would then be found to stand out any longer against the King. Hoping that he might yield to the entreaties of his fellows, he sent Stokesley, Gardiner and Tunstal to him in the Tower. Fisher received them gladly enough, but told them that it troubled him to see them playing such a part: " 'me thinketh it had bene rather our partes to sticke together' ", he said, " 'in repressinge these violent and vnlawfull intrusions and iniuries dayly offred to our common mother, the holy Church of Christ, then by any manner of perswasions to helpe or sett forward the same. And we ought rather to seeke by all meanes the temporall distruccion of the so ravenous woolves, that daily goe about wyrryinge and devowringe euerlastinglie, the flocke that Christ committed to our Charge, and the flocke that himself dyed for, then to suffer them thus to range abroade. But (alas) seeing we do it not, ye see in what perrill the *Christ*en State nowe standeth : We are beseeged on all sides, and can hardly escape the daunger of our enemie: And seeinge *that* iudgment is begone at the howse of god, what hope is there lefte (if we fall) that the rest shall stande ! The fort is betrayed even of them that should have defended it. And therfore seeinge the matter is thus begunne, and so faintly resisted on our parts, I feare we be not the men that shall see the ende of the miserie. wherfore seeing I am an ould man and looke not longe to live, I minde not by the helpe of god to trooble my conscience in pleasing the king this waie whatsoeu*er* become of me, but rather here to spend out the remnant of my old daies in prayinge to god for him.' " After the bishops had gone, Fisher's servant, who had been listening at the door, told him that he ought to accept the supremacy, for he could well enough say one thing and think another. Fisher laughed at the suggestion. " 'I tell thee' ", he said, " 'it is not for the Sup*r*emacie only that I am thus tossed and troobled, but also for an oath' (meaninge the oath of the king's succession) 'which yf I would have sworne, I doubt whether I should eu*er* haue bene questioned for the Sup*r*emacie or noe; but god being my good lord I will never agree to any of them both. And thus thou maist saie another daie thou heardest me speake when I am dead and gone out of this worlde.' "[9]

For days Fisher was left alone in the Tower. As the end of May drew near, it almost seemed as if he had been forgotten. Then an event occurred that quickened the King's anger. On 20 May Pope Paul III, who had succeeded Clement VII in the Holy See the previous October, created seven new cardinals. Among them was a name that startled all who knew the King—that of John Fisher, Bishop of Rochester, named *sanctae ecclesiae tituli Sancti Vitalis presbiter cardinalis.* Paul may have been ignorant of Fisher's plight, as he professed himself to be when Sir Gregory Casale objected to the appointment.[10] Or, which is more likely, he may have hoped that the red hat would save

Fisher's life. If this is what he hoped, he could not have made a worse mistake. He sent to Cardinal Du Bellay, asking him to intercede with Francis in behalf of Fisher.[11] But it was too late. When the news reached England, the King sent Cromwell to the Tower to ask Fisher if he proposed to accept the honour. He found the old man still dogged and unafraid. Fisher had already told George Gold, the Lieutenant's servant, that if the red hat were placed at his feet he would not stoop to pick it up, but he had no intention of showing Cromwell how he felt. " 'Sir' ", he told him proudly, " 'I know my self farr vnworthie of any such dignitie, that I thinke nothinge lesse then such matters : but yf he doe send it me, assure your self I will worke with it by all the meanes I can to benefitt the Church of Christ, and in that respect I will receive it vpon my knees.' " When told of Fisher's answer, Henry burst out in a rage; " 'is he yet so lustie?' " he cried. " 'Well, let the Pope send him a hatt when he will, but I will so provide that when soeuer it commeth he shall weare it on his shoulders for head he shall have none to sett it on.' "[12]

He went about his work with despatch. On 1 June a commission was issued to the Lord Chancellor, the Duke of Suffolk, the Marquis of Exeter, the Earls of Cumberland, Rutland and Wiltshire, Thomas Cromwell, Sir John Fitzjames, Sir John Baldwin, Sir William Paulett, Sir Richard Lister, Sir John Porte, Sir John Spelman, Sir Walter Luke, Sir Anthony Fitzherbert, Sir Thomas Inglefeld and Sir William Shelley to try Fisher on a charge of having on 7 May maliciously denied that the King was supreme head on earth of the Church of England. Among these were the very men who had sent four monks and a priest to Tyburn five weeks before.[13] They represented the inherent strength and irresistible will of the royal establishment. Fitzjames was Chief Justice of the Court of King's Bench, Baldwin Chief Justice of the Court of Common Pleas; Lister was Chief Baron of the Exchequer; Porte, Spelman and Luke were all Justices of the King's Bench, Fitzherbert a Justice of the Common Pleas. In such a court, the King had little to fear from a solitary bishop.

The next day Cromwell examined More once again, in the presence of several members of the council. They asked him if he was prepared to accept the King as supreme head of the Church and More replied, much as Fisher had done a few weeks before,[14] that the question was like a two-edged sword: " 'it were a very harde thing', he said, 'to compell me to saye eyther precisely with it against my conscience to the losse of my soule, or precisely against it to the destruction of my body.' " He therefore refused to answer.[15] He had said enough, however, to arouse suspicion. If More and Fisher had not been in communication with each other, how could they explain the similarity of their replies? The council decided to defer Fisher's trial until he had been examined as to his part in the correspondence with More. The inquiry, which was conducted by Sir Edmund Walsingham, Lieutenant of the Tower, began on 7 June and continued for five days. The first to be examined was Richard Wilson, Fisher's servant. Wilson testified that about Candlemas last (2 February) Robert Fisher had come to bring his brother word of the Act of Supremacy. On hearing the news, his master raised his hands and blessed him saying, "Is it so?" Robert Fisher also told his master of how speaking was now made treason, and of how the Commons had been unwilling to pass the bill until the word "maliciously" was added to it. Wilson had also, he said, heard Fisher tell George Gold, the Lieutenant's man, that where there was no malice there was no danger in the statute; whether Fisher asked George to repeat this to More he could not say, but thought it likely. He testified that he himself never took any messages from his master to More, though he did carry presents between them. He took More, he said, half a custard on Sunday last and long since some greensauce. More sent his master an image of St. John—perhaps to replace the image seized at Rochester when Fisher was imprisoned—and apples and oranges after the first snow that winter. On New Year's Day, More sent his master £2000 in gold written on a piece of paper and an image of the Epiphany. He had more than once seen his master burn papers and had burnt them himself at his bidding, but had never read any.

George Gold was the next to be examined. He told the Lieutenant that about ten days before he had brought Fisher word that he was to be made a cardinal, to which the prisoner answered that he cared nothing for that. Two days after the monks had been executed at Tyburn, Fisher told him that he marvelled at their execution, seeing that they had spoken nothing out of malice. Gold admitted that he had carried about a dozen letters between Fisher and More, some of them written with a piece of coal. Fisher, he said, had told him to deny this if he was questioned, unless he was examined upon oath. Five days before he had taken a pot of conserves from Fisher to his friend Antonio Bonvisi, who had sent it back, saying that Fisher needed it more than he did. Until that spring, Bonvisi had sent to More two or three times a week with a parcel of meat and a bottle of wine. Until then he had also sent Fisher a quart of French wine every day and three or four dishes of jelly. There were, Gold added, no letters between them that he knew of.

John a Wood, More's servant, testified that about a fortnight after the council first came to the Tower to question the prisoners, Fisher had sent George to ask More what answer he had made. More replied that he had refused to answer the questions put by the council, adding that he would no longer meddle with such matters. He later sent another message to Fisher, warning him not to use the same words when he was questioned, for fear of revealing their correspondence. After the next visit of the council, Fisher had sent word to More of what had passed. He himself had never carried any letters or messages between them, though on several occasions he had brought them stewed meat.

John Pewnoll or Falconer, who also served Fisher for a time, told the Lieutenant that he had carried a letter from his master to Bonvisi about a sickness he suffered during Lent. Bonvisi consulted Dr. Clement, who sent back word that Fisher's liver was probably wasted and advised him to take goat's milk and other things. His master received money from his brother Robert until he died and then from other friends; from Bonvisi he sometimes received a dish of stewed meat and a bottle of French wine.[16]

On 12 June Fisher was himself examined by Thomas Bedyll and Richard Layton, clerks of the council, in the presence of the Lieutenant of the Tower, Harry Polstede, John Whalley and John ap Rice, notary. He testified that about eight letters had passed between More and himself. More wrote first, he said, to ask what answer Fisher had given the council, and he told him. Some time later George Gold showed Fisher a letter he was to carry to Margaret Roper, in which More told his daughter that he would not meddle with the King's title. Thereupon Fisher sent More a letter by Gold asking what he meant by this. George brought him a reply, but he could remember nothing of what it said. Three or four days later, Fisher wrote to tell More of what he had heard from his brother Robert and offered the opinion that they would be safe in speaking their mind, so they did not speak maliciously. In his reply More warned him not to arouse suspicion by giving answers similar to his. Some time afterwards Gold came from More to ask what reply Fisher had made to the council, and he told him that he had refused to answer to the supremacy one way or the other. All the letters that passed between them were burned, and Gold and Wilson told to keep them secret, but not for any harm that was in them. Not long before Gold had brought Fisher word that he had been made a cardinal, upon which he had told Gold that "yf the Cardinalls hatt were layed at his feete he wolde not stoupe to take it vp, he did sett so litle by it." From time to time, Fisher admitted, he had written to his brother Robert and to Edward White, his half-brother, about the food and drink they brought him, and to my Lady of Oxford for her comfort and to certain of his friends for money to pay the Lieutenant of the Tower for his maintenance. But to none of these did he speak of the King or his title; nor did any of them speak of it to him.[17]

On the 14th More was questioned. He admitted to having exchanged several letters with Fisher. Most of these were intended, he said, to give comfort or to return thanks for sundry presents, usually of meat or drink. But about three months after coming to the Tower, he had, he recalled, written to tell Fisher that he had refused the oath without giving the council his reasons. Fisher replied that he had done the same. After his examination on the Act of Supremacy, he had received a letter from Fisher asking what answer he had made. He sent him word that he had told the council he intended no longer to meddle with earthly things. Later Fisher had sent to tell him that they could speak their minds, so long as they did not speak maliciously. He had replied that the law was unlikely to be interpreted in their favour. Finally, after his last examination, he had written to Fisher that he reckoned on the uttermost and offered to exchange prayers with him. He had also written several letters to his daughter Margaret. None of these was kept, for Gold had always said that the best keeper was the fire. He had suggested that Gold show them to a trusty friend who could testify that they were blameless, but Gold would not do it for fear of the Lieutenant.[18]

At last the long interrogation was over. Nothing had been discovered to indicate that either Fisher or More had made any effort to persuade each other, or anyone else among their acquaintance, to deny the supremacy of the King or to refuse the oath to the Act of Succession. There was no longer any reason for delay. Having answered the questions put to him concerning his correspondence with Fisher, More was asked once again by his examiners whether or not he would obey the King as supreme head on earth of the Church of England. He said he could give no answer. He was then asked if he would recognize the marriage of the King and Queen as good and lawful, to which he answered that he had never spoken against it.[19]

The council came then to Fisher. He was questioned by Thomas Bedyll in the presence of several witnesses. For the last time he was asked, as More had been, if he would obey the King as supreme head on earth of the Church of England, and he answered that he was of the same mind as he had been when the question was last put to him. He was then asked if he would recognize the existing marriage of the King and Queen, to which he replied that he would willingly swear to the succession as set forth in the act but could not answer the question directly: "to answere absolutely to this Interrogatorie, ye, or nae, he desireth to be pardoned". When pressed for an answer, he said he could not say more for fear of falling into "the daungers of the Statutes".[20] And so they left him.

Three days before, on Friday, 11 June, three monks of the Charterhouse in London, Humphrey Middlemore, William Exmewe and Sebastian Newdigate, had been brought to trial. They had been examined by Bedyll five weeks earlier, on the very day their brothers suffered at Tyburn, and all three had refused to acknowledge the supremacy. On 25 May they had been arrested and for seventeen days had been kept in close confinement, standing upright with iron fetters around their necks. All three were convicted and sentenced, like their brothers, to be hanged, drawn and quartered at Tyburn.

Six days later, on Thursday, 17 June, Fisher's turn came. He was brought from the Tower to the bar of the Court of King's Bench in Westminster Hall. He was so weak that he could travel only part of the way on horseback and had to complete the journey by water. Fisher had been deprived of his see by the bill of attainder passed the previous November, and with his see had lost the privilege of trial by his peers. A jury of twelve

commoners, freeholders of Middlesex, were sworn to hear the
evidence and give judgment.[21]

Fisher was charged with having on 7 May maliciously denied
the supremacy of the King in the Church of England. He
pleaded not guilty, whereupon Richard Rich was called to give
evidence. Rich testified that he had visited the accused in the
Tower on the day in question and had asked him his opinion of
the supremacy. The accused had answered, Rich told the court,
that in the sight of God the King neither was nor could be
supreme head of the Church. Fisher was visibly shaken. Apparently it had never occurred to him that he had been deceived:
" 'what a monstruouse ma[tter is] this' ", he cried, " 'to laye
nowe to my charge as treason the thing which I spake not vntill,
[besides] this mans Othe, I had as full *and* as sure a promise
frome the king, by this his trusty [and sure] messeng*er*, as the
king could make me by word of mouthe, that I shuld neu*er* be
empeched [nor hurt] by myne aunswere that I shuld send vnto
hyme by this his messeng*er*, whiche I wold ne[uer haue] spoken,
had it not bene in trust of my prync*es* promyse, *and* of my true
and loving hart tow[ards hyme], my naturall liege lorde, in
satisfyeing hyme with declaraci*on* of myne opynion *and* con-
[science] in this matter, as he ernestlie requyred me by this
messeng*er* *to* signifie playnelie [vnto hyme].' " The court refused to allow Fisher's plea. That he had spoken in confidence
they did not deny, but that he had indeed spoken the very
words put into his mouth he himself had already admitted. It
was enough. Fisher then protested that even if what he had said
in confidence were to be admitted as evidence against him, it
was plain enough that there was no malice in the words he had
used. The " 'very statute that maketh the speakyng agaynst the
kyng*es* supremacie treason' ", he pointed out, " 'is o[nely and]
preciselie lymeted where such speche is spoken malicyously. And
now all y[e, My lordes],' quoth he, 'perceyve playnelie that in
my vttering *and* signifyeing vnto the kyng of my[ne opynyon]

and conscyence, as towchyng this his cleame of supremacie in the churche of Engla[nd, in such] sort as I did, as ye haue hard, There was no man*er* of malice in me at all, and so I co*m*mytted no Treason.' " The Lord Chancellor answered that there could be no such thing as speaking without malice against the supremacy of the King. To deprive the King of his title or estate, or any part of it, was in itself a malicious act.[22]

The jury retired to consider their verdict. They were not long about their business. Everyone knew what to expect, and yet when the single, pitiless word was pronounced there was a moment of shocked silence in the court. The prisoner slowly rose and faced his judges. " 'Truly, my Lo*rds*' ", he said in a quiet, even voice, " 'yf that which I haue before spoken be not sufficient, I haue no more to saie, but only to desire Almightie God to forgeve them that haue thus condemned me, for I thinke they know not what they haue done.' "

His words, for all their gentle simplicity, were scarcely heard; already the Lord Chancellor was pronouncing the terrible sentence: " 'You shall be ledd to the place from whence you came, and from thence shall be drawne through the Cittie to the place of execution at Tyborne, where yo*ur* body shall be hanged by the necke : and beinge half alive, you shall be cutt downe and throwne to the ground, yo*ur* bowells to be taken out of yo*ur* body, and burnt before you, beinge alive; yo*ur* head to be smitten of, and yo*ur* bodie to be devided into four quarters; and after, yo*ur* head and quarters to be set vp where the kinge shall appoint, and god have mercy vpon yo*ur* soule.' "

Fisher was now free at last, after months of silence and confinement, to speak his mind, and this he did. " 'I thinke in deed' ", he told his judges, " 'and alwais have thought, and do now lastly affirme, that his Grace cannot iustly claime any such Supr*e*macie over the Church of god as he now taketh vpon him, nether hath it bene eu*er* seene or heard of, that anie tempo*r*all Prince before his daies hath p*r*esumed to that dignitie. wherfore yf the kinge will now adventure himself in proceedinge in this straunge and vnwonted Case, no doubt but he shall deeply incurre the greevous displeasure of Almightie god, to the great daunger of his owne soul and of manie others, and to the vtter ruine of this realme committed to his charge: wherof will ensewe some sharpe punishment at his hande. wherfore I pray God his grace may remember himself in time, and hearken to good Counsell, for the preservation of himself and his realme, and the quietnes of all Christendome' ".[23] When he had finished speaking he turned from the bar and was led away. He was taken to Westminster stairs, whence he descended the river part way to the Tower, continuing his journey, as he had come, on horseback. At the Tower gate he stopped to thank the guard for their trouble, speaking in a clear, calm voice. As he went in at the gate, those who had gathered to watch noticed that the headsman's axe was borne with its edge towards the prisoner.

For five days he waited for the end. On the 19th, eight days after their trial, the three Carthusians were taken to Tyburn and executed with all the barbarity of the law. On the fourth day word spread through the Tower that Fisher had been taken out for execution. Hearing of it, the cook dressed him no dinner, whereupon Fisher chided him that night: " 'for all that report thou seest me yet alive' ", he laughed, " 'and therfore whatsoeuer newes thou shalt heare of me hereafter, let me no more lacke my dinner, but make yt readie as thou art wont to doe, and yf thou see me dead when thou commest, then eat it thyself; but I promise thee, yf I be alive, I mind by god's grace to eate neuer a bitt the lesse.' "[24] On the morning of the fifth day, Tuesday, 22 June, Fisher was awakened at five o'clock by the Lieutenant, who told him the execution was to take place at nine. By order of the King, however, the Lieutenant explained, he was to be spared the agonies of Tyburn and was instead to be beheaded on Tower Hill. Fisher thanked him and then said he would go back to sleep in the meanwhile, " 'for' ", he added, " 'I have slept verie little this night; and yet, to tell you the truth, not for any feare of deathe, I thank god, but by reason of my great infirmitie and weaknes.' "²⁵ At nine the Lieutenant returned and found him dressing. I will make " 'as convenyent hast' ", he promised, " 'as my weeke *and* syckely aged body will gyve me leave.' "²⁶ He put on a clean shirt and all the best clothes he had, telling his man Richard that this was his " 'mariage daie, and . . . it behooveth vs therfore to vse more clenlinesse for solemnitie of *that* mariage ".²⁷ When he asked for his fur tippet, Richard asked him why he was so careful of his health when he knew he was to live no more than half an hour. " 'I think [none other]wise' ", he answered, " 'but, I pray you, yett gyve me leave to put on my Furred typpett, to ke[pe me warme] for the whyle vntill the verie tyme of execution; for I tell you truth, though I haue, I tha[nk our Lord], a very good stomacke *and* willing mynd to dye at this present, *and* I trust in his goodnesse *and* mercy [he will] styll contynewe it *and* encrease it, yet will I not hynd*er* my health in the meane tyme not a m[inute of an] hower, but will p*re*serue it in the meane season with all suche discrete wayes *and* meanes as a[lmighty God] of his gracious goodnes hath prouyded for me.' "²⁸

He then took up a copy of the New Testament, crossed himself and went out and down the stairs to the courtyard. There he was helped into a chair and so carried between two men, under guard, to the Tower gate, where he was delivered to the sheriffs of London. While he was waiting at the gate, he took his Testament and opened it by chance at the words " '*hec est autem vita eterna vt cognoscant te solum veru*m *deum, et quem misisti Jesu*m *Christum. Ego te clarificaui super terram opus con-sum*m*avi quod dedisti mihi vt faciam: et nunc clarifica tu me pater apud temetipsum claritate qua habui priusquam*' ": in death as in life God is present to all men in the person of Jesus Christ. Whereupon he closed the book and said, " 'Here is even learning ynough for me even to my lives end.' " The procession moved on again, and Fisher was carried slowly up nearby Tower Hill, where a great crowd already surrounded the scaffold. When they came to the scaffold he stood up and took hold of the ladder. He refused help—" 'ye shall see me shifte for myself well ynough' ", he said—and climbed heavily to the top. As he stood there the southeast sun shone full in his face and lifting up his hands he said quietly to himself, " '*Accedite ad eum et illuminamini et facies vestrae non confundentur*' ": come to me and be not troubled.²⁹ The headsman asked his forgiveness and he gave it. " 'I trust [on our Lord]' ", he said, " 'thow shaltt see me dye even lustelie.' "³⁰

His gown and tippet were then taken from him, so that he stood in his doublet and hose—tall, pale and gaunt—before the people. He had been warned by the Lieutenant to speak little, but when he spoke those who crowded the hill below knew at once the familiar voice, still strong and clear and brave in spite of age and sickness. " 'Christian people' ", he began, " 'I am come hither to die for the faith of *Chr*ists holy Catholick Church, and I thanke god hitherto my stomack hath served me verie well thervnto, so that yet I have not feared death : wherfore I do desire you all to helpe and assist me with y*our* praiers, that at the verie point and instant of deaths stroake, I maie in that verie moment stand stedfast without faintinge in any one point of the Catholick faith free from any feare; and I beseech almightie god of his infinite goodnes to save the kinge and this Realme, and that it maie please him to holde his holy hand ou*er* yt, and send the king good Counsell.' "³¹

He then knelt and repeated the *Te deum* and the psalm *In te domine speravi* :

In thee, O Lord, do I put my trust; let me never be ashamed: deliver me in thy righteousness.

Bow down thine ear to me; deliver me speedily : (be thou my strong rock, for an house of defence to save me.

For thou *art* my rock and my fortress. . . .

I am forgotten as a dead man out of mind : I am like a broken vessel.

For I have heard the slander of many : fear *was* on every side : while they took counsel together against me, they devised to take away my life.

But I trusted in thee, O Lord : I said, Thou *art* my God.[32]

When he had finished he was blindfolded with a handkerchief. This done he prayed for a moment in silence. Then he lay down on his belly with his neck on the block. The headsman struck at him and he died at one blow.

The headless body was stripped and left naked on the scaffold all day until eight in the evening. A bystander for pity threw some straw over it. In the evening it was taken up on a halberd by two of the guard and carried to the churchyard of All Hallows, Barking, where a shallow grave was scraped out and the naked body tumbled in and covered over. The head was parboiled and set up on London Bridge next to those of the Carthusians. Two weeks later another head was brought from Tower Hill, that of Sir Thomas More. To make way for it, Fisher's head was taken down and thrown into the river.

Chapter 19

There is no way to measure what Fisher accomplished by his suffering and death. Such things cannot be measured. His execution stunned the people who saw or heard of it and shocked the conscience of Europe. At Rome he was compared to Thomas Becket. King Henry was excommunicated and the kingdom of England placed under an interdict.[1] Henry replied by instructing his agents abroad to publish the "false traiterous dealinges" of the dead man and to explain that he and More were "of suche traiterous hartes and Stomackes" that even while in prison they laboured to raise an insurrection against the lawful government of the King. Sir Gregory Casale notified the Pope, on orders from Cromwell, that the King of England considered himself accountable for his actions to God alone.[2] What he meant by this was clear enough by now.

Already the lines were drawn in a struggle that was to last for more than fifty years. It was not until 1588, when Philip II determined, for the comfort of his own soul and the greater glory of Spain, that he would reconquer England in the name of the Holy Catholic Church, that the moment of decision was at hand. For it was the defeat of the Armada that put the seal of triumph on the policy fashioned by Cromwell and Henry VIII half a century before. And after this first and greatest triumph, Henry's policy was vindicated again and again in the course of history until it became one of the governing myths of the English people.

The new England was no longer a part of the European community, but set apart from it, its people for the first time fully aware of themselves as an island breed. Such men as Drake and Hawkins, Sir Humphrey Gilbert and Sir Richard Grenville of the *Revenge* became the new heroes of English folklore.

> This happy breed of men, this little world,
> This precious stone set in the silver sea,
> Which serves it in the office of a wall,
> Or as a moat defensive to a house,
> Against the envy of less happier lands;
> This blessed plot, this earth, this realm,
> this England. . . .

The Kings and Queens of England looked to no superior but God and to no good but the prosperity of their people.

Against all this Fisher had set his face, and he had failed. For almost four hundred years Englishmen enjoyed a destiny in the making of which he had no share. He had no place in the hearts of the men who adored the Virgin Queen of Shakespeare's England as their fathers had adored the Virgin Mary; no place in the minds of the shrewd, sensible men who made the settlement of 1689 under which England was governed so prosperously for more than a century thereafter. He would have had no place in the comfortable, prudent world of Victorian Barsetshire, nor would he have understood the imperial celebrations of the Diamond Jubilee.

Only now is it possible to consider the legacy of imperial England with anything like detachment. Historians no longer feel sure that the execution of this frail, brave old man was—as it was once called by one of the prophets of Victorian England —"an inevitable and painful incident of an infinitely blessed revolution."[3] It is possible now to see that if Henry spoke for one truth of human nature, Fisher spoke for another.[4] In his own time Fisher was driven out of the counsels of men because he refused to worship the idols of the King. We have learned since then that the King's truth was not the whole truth. We have learned that the last word was not spoken when this helpless man was broken on the wheel, nor when the Armada was driven from the coasts of England, nor even when the map was painted British red in latter days. For we have learned at length that no last word will be spoken as long as any man remains outside the community of history, beyond the reach of pity and love.

Notes

CHAPTER 1

[1] The will of Robert Fisher, dated 19 June, 1477 and proved on 26 June, 1477, is entered in the York Probate Registry, now in the Borthwick Institute of Historical Research.

[2] Since he had been born in 1469. The year of John Fisher's birth was not established until 1934, when A. H. Lloyd reported the discovery in the papal archives of a dispensation issued by Innocent VIII to enable Fisher to take orders while under the canonical age for the priesthood. The dispensation, which is entered in the register under date of June, 1491, states that Fisher had declared himself to be then in his 22nd year. See A. H. Lloyd, *The Early History of Christ's College Cambridge* (Cambridge, 1934), pp. 391–92. Most of the early biographers believed—no doubt because eyewitnesses, misled by Fisher's appearance, reported him to be upwards of seventy at the time of his death—that he had been born several years earlier. The date most often suggested was 1459, and even today the legend persists that Fisher lived to the age of 75 or 76.

[3] The earliest biographer names two of Robert Fisher's four children, *i.e.*, John and Robert. He goes on to say that by her second husband, to whom he gives the name of Wright, Agnes (whom he calls Ann) had four more children, John, Thomas, Richard and Elizabeth (the nun of Dartford). The reliability of this evidence must, however, be considered in the light of the fact that examination of the State Papers and other contemporary records shows the anonymous *Life*, valuable as it is, to be full of errors and inaccuracies. It is important to remember that the English version of the *Life* was not finished—if we are to accept Van Ortroy's carefully considered opinion—until about 1577, 42 years after Fisher's death, and the Latin version not until 1599. Furthermore, it is quite certain, from the nature of the material collected and preserved by the anonymous biographer while he was working on the *Life*, that the author himself had no

personal knowledge of Fisher or his family. These materials are still to be seen, most of them in British Museum MS. Arundel 152. See *Vie de Bienheureux Martyr Jean Fisher*, edited by François Van Ortroy, S.J. (Brussels, 1893). The English version has been edited by the Rev. Ronald Bayne for the Early English Text Society (No. 117) as *The Life of Fisher* (London, 1921). All later biographers, including the most recent (E. E. Reynolds, *Saint John Fisher* [New York, 1955], pp. 1–2), have accepted the account given by their anonymous predecessor. Examination of the Lombard pedigree in the College of Arms indicates, however, that in fact Willus or William White and Agnes Fisher had a son Edward, who married Margaret, daughter of Sir Henry Tutor de Stoke, their grand-daughter marrying William, first of the Lombards. See Philpott's Stemmata, T. no. 11 (1648), fol. 13ᵛ. Many years ago R. von Fischer-Treuenfeld suggested that the Fisher children were John (the bishop), Robert (his steward), Ralph and Elizabeth (the nun of Dartford), that the only child of the second marriage was Edward White (ancestor of the Lombards) and that the John, Thomas, Richard and Elizabeth believed by the early biographer to be Whites were in fact Fishers, children of John's uncle Thomas and so his cousins. See R. von Fischer-Treuenfeld, *Lord Johan Fyssher* (London, 1894). A search of the Heralds' Visitations failed either to confirm or deny this account, but since it seems more likely that a genealogist working from family records in 1648 would have been in possession of the truth than a biographer working from nothing but hearsay more than forty years after Fisher's death, I have come to the tentative conclusion that Fisher had only one brother (Edward) and no sisters by his mother's second marriage. If this is the case, his known sister Elizabeth must have been a Fisher.

[4] See p. 210 n. 2. Most of what little we know of Fisher's boyhood and schooling is derived from the early *Life*. This, as we have seen, is not above criticism, but it is probably accurate enough in essentials.

[5] The early biographer describes Fisher's appearance at some length. There is in addition the terracotta bust, ascribed to Pietro Torrigiano and now in the Metropolitan Museum of Art, New York. This bust, which apparently represents Fisher in his late thirties, was executed, probably in 1509 or a year or two later, as one of a group of three. The other subjects were Henry VII and the young Henry VIII. The former is now in the Victoria and Albert Museum, London, the latter in the Metropolitan Museum. The three busts were at one time in the room over the Holbein Gate of Whitehall Palace, which was built in 1531–32 and demolished in 1759. By 1779 they were in the possession of a Mr. Wright of Hatfield Peverell Priory in Essex, where they were seen and identified by Michael

Tyson the antiquary, who mentioned them in a letter to the Rev. William Cole (British Museum MS. Add. 59993, fols. 152–53ᵛ). They remained at Hatfield Peverell Priory until 1928, when they passed to Arthur Wilson-Filmer, from whose widow the bust of Fisher was acquired by the Metropolitan Museum; the bust of Henry VIII passed first to the Hearst collection and later to the Metropolitan; that of Henry VII was purchased by the Victoria and Albert Museum in 1935. See John Pope-Hennessy, *Catalogue of Italian Sculpture in the Victoria and Albert Museum* (London, 1964), pp. 399–401.

The bust reproduced by Reynolds on the dust-jacket of his life of Fisher is in fact the Torrigiano bust of Henry VII in the Victoria and Albert Museum, and not, as he states, the bust of Fisher in the Metropolitan Museum, which is reproduced here facing p. 8.

CHAPTER 2

[1] When Stanley died in 1504, the Lady Margaret, who was by now entirely devoted to a life of prayer and good works, was sworn by Fisher to a formal vow of chastity. An early manuscript copy of her oath is preserved at St. John's College, Cambridge in the Thin Red Book, fol. 47.

[2] A pound sterling in Fisher's time was probably equivalent in value to about $100 today. Assuming this to be so, the Lady Margaret Readers in Divinity were paid something like $1335 a year.

[3] Thin Red Book, fol. 45ᵛ. Fisher himself took pains to point out, in the prefatory epistle to his treatise on the eucharist, that he owed his bishopric to the King, to whom his name had been suggested by Richard Fox, Bishop of Winchester. See John Fisher, *De veritate corporis et sanguinis Christi in eucharistia aduersus Iohannem Oecolampadium* (Cologne, 1527), fol. [1].

[4] Durham and Winchester were both worth about £3000 (that is, about $300,000) a year. At the height of his career, Thomas Wolsey held first Durham and then Winchester jointly with York and the rich abbey of St. Alban's. His income could hardly have been less than $750,000 a year and was probably far more.

[5] The contemporary *Life* (pp. 12–13) quotes the prefatory epistle to Fisher's treatise on the eucharist, in which Fisher observes that though other bishops have richer sees he has fewer souls to account for, and for

that reason would wish himself none the richer. See his *De veritate corporis et sanguinis Christi*, fol. [1]. Fisher's words were embellished by a later biographer whose striking phrase may well be apocryphal. See the Rev. John Lewis, *The Life of Dr. John Fisher*, edited by T. Hudson Turner (2 vols., London, 1855), I.15–16.

[6] *Calendar of the Patent Rolls Preserved in the Public Record Office: Henry VII* (2 vols., London, 1914–16), II. 388. The proxy was Dr. Thomas Heede, vicar-general of the diocese of Rochester. At the time of his installation, which took place on 24 April, 1505, Fisher was at Cambridge where as President of Queens' he had just received King Henry VII. See p. 18.

[7] Fisher conducted visitations in 1505, 1508, 1511, 1514, 1517, 1520 and 1529. See Diocese of Rochester, Episcopal Register, IV (1492–1542), fols., 42^v, 49^v, 56, 71, 74^v, 102, 145^v. The Episcopal Registers of the Diocese of Rochester, which have never been published, may be examined in the Diocesan Registry.

[8] Register, fol. 41^v (17 May, 1505). St. Nicholas stands next to the Cathedral. It was built in 1423 and thereafter served the town as a parish church. Before that the townsmen had made use of the nave of the cathedral.

[9] Register, fols. 47–47^v, 62 (5 March, 1513), 127–27^v (4 February, 1525), 133–33^v (30 May, 1526), 158 (2 May, 1530), 163–63^v (10 February, 1531), 167 (20 August, 1532), 167–67^v (16 September, 1532). On the persistence of Lollardy in the diocese of Rochester and elsewhere in England, see John A. F. Thomson, *The Later Lollards 1414–1520* (Oxford, 1965).

[10] This was Thomas Batman, Register, fol. 127^v.

CHAPTER 3

[1] See pp. 37–38.

[2] See Lloyd, *Early History of Christ's College*; H. Rackham, *Early Statutes of Christ's College* (Cambridge, 1927). Fisher's statutes remained in force, with minor changes, until they were superseded in 1860.

[3] Oratio habita coram Illustrissimo Rege Henrico Septimo. Cantabrigie, MS. Bodleian 13. It cost the university £40 (about $4000) to receive the King in state. In return, Henry gave his hosts £66 13s. 4d. for their own use and added £40 for the fabric of St. Mary's, then being rebuilt. See British Museum MS. Harl. 7049, fol. 134^v.

[4] *The English Works of John Fisher*, edited by John E. B. Mayor for the Early English Text Society, Extra Series No. 27 (London, 1935), pp. 270, 273, 273–74, 274.

[5] *Ibid.*, pp. 291, 294, 294–95, 295, 303, 302, 303.

CHAPTER 4

[1] *Letters and Papers, Foreign and Domestic, of the Reign of Henry VIII, 1509–47*, edited by J. S. Brewer, James Gairdner and R. H. Brodie (21 vols. in 33 parts, London, 1862–1910), 2.2 (p. 1505). The players used 2643/4 yards of satin, which alone, according to the revel accounts for 6 January, 1516, cost £33 2s. 93/4 d. (about $3315).

[2] The living of Aldington was worth £33 6s. 8d. a year, of which £13 6s. 8d. was left for the vicar. This means that of an income of about $3335 provided for the parish priest, Erasmus received (even after his departure from England) about $2000 a year.

[3] A copy of Fisher's account is preserved in the Thin Red Book, fols. 38–40, from which these extracts have been taken. The original is apparently lost. The copy, which dates from 1541 or 1542, has, however, been printed by J. Hymers in his edition (1840) of Fisher's month-mind sermon for the Lady Margaret, by Mayor in his edition (1869) of Thomas Baker's *History of the College of St. John* and by R. F. Scott in his *Notes from the Records of St. John's College, Cambridge*, published serially after 1889.

[4] The first court is still much as Fisher left it, though the south side was refaced about 1775 and the chapel on the north side torn down in 1863 to make way for a Victorian Gothic improvement.

[5] The statutes were drawn up by Fisher under a commission from the other executors dated 20 March, 1516. The college was formally opened on 29 July under licence from Nicholas West, the new Bishop of Ely, dated 26 July. The statutes were revised, under Fisher's supervision, in 1524 and again in 1530. See Mayor's edition (1859) of the *Early Statutes of the College of St. John*. Perspective was the term used to denote the study of optics; cosmography included both astronomy and geography. See also pp. 63, 121.

[6] Thin Red Book, fol. 219. The letter, which is undated, was probably written between 1519 and 1524.

CHAPTER 5

[1] Henry Hornby to Fisher from Cambridge, 22 [?February, 1512], R. F. Scott, *Notes from the Records of St. John's College, Cambridge*: First Series (Cambridge, 1889–99), *Eagle*, XVI (1890), 10–11. The *Notes* were first published serially in the *Eagle* and the original pagination was retained in the reprint.

[2] Burgavenny and Fisher became friends at this time and Fisher was invited to hunt on Burgavenny's estate, where he was free to follow the greyhounds at his host's expense. On one occasion Fisher sent Burgavenny a salmon, while Burgavenny returned the compliment with a side of venison. See Burgavenny to Fisher from Erige, [1512], Scott, pp. 14–15. This letter, which was reprinted from the *Eagle*, XVI (1890), is undated, but since the subsidy was voted early in 1512 and since Lord Cobham, who is mentioned by Burgavenny, died a few months later, there can be no doubt that it dates from that year. There were five lathes, or administrative districts, in the county of Kent, each containing several hundreds.

[3] Fisher to Erasmus from London [c. 18 November, 1511], *The Epistles of Erasmus*, edited by Francis Morgan Nichols (3 vols., London, 1901–18), II. 75. The Latin original is printed in *Opus Epistolarum Des. Erasmi Roterodami*, edited by P. S. Allen (12 vols., Oxford, 1906–58), I. 485–86. In dating letters to and from Erasmus, I have used Allen's chronology, which often differs from that suggested by Nichols. A few of these letters have been translated afresh by D. F. S. Thomson, with an extensive commentary by H. C. Porter, in *Erasmus and Cambridge* (Toronto, 1963). The letter from Erasmus to which Fisher made haste to reply has not survived, though there is a letter dating from the previous September with which Erasmus enclosed a specimen of his translation of St. Basil (Allen, pp. 469–70).

[4] See *Letters and Papers*, 2.2. Appendix 12 (p. 1527); 2.1. 761–63 (p. 200); 2.1.892 (p. 245). Though he retired as Lord Chancellor in 1515, Warham continued in the see of Canterbury until his death in 1532.

[5] Cambridge University Library, Mm. 2.25, fols. 74^v–77.

[6] *Letters and Papers*, 2.1.1153 (pp. 303–04).

[7] *Praemunire* became a matter of cardinal importance a few years later, after the fall of Wolsey. See pp. 113–14.

[8] Edward Hall, *Chronicle* (London, 1809), pp. 573-80. See E. Jeffries Davis, "The Authorities for the Case of Richard Hunne (1514-15)", *English Historical Review*, XXX (1915), 477-88; Arthur Ogle, *The Tragedy of the Lollards' Tower* (Oxford, 1949). The statues of *praemunire* were passed in 1353, 1365 and 1393 and made it an offence to appeal to the papal curia in matters within the jurisdiction of the King's courts.

[9] Statutes 4 Henry VIII, Chapter 2.

[10] *Letters and Papers*, 2.1.1131 (p. 299). The Abbot of Winchcombe was one of those named in 1512 to attend the Lateran Council at Rome with Fisher.

CHAPTER 6

[1] *Letters and Papers*, 2.1.1652 (pp. 460-61). James V, born on 10 April, 1512, was the eldest surviving son of Henry's other sister Margaret and James IV of Scotland, who was killed at Flodden in the autumn of 1513. A year later Margaret married Archibald Douglas, Earl of Angus; their first child, also called Margaret, was born in October of 1515.

[2] Fisher to Erasmus from Halling, [May, 1515], Allen, II. 90; Erasmus to Fisher from St. Omer, 5 June, [1516]. Nichols, II. 269. Cf. Allen, II. 244-46. Erasmus made amends many years later when, after Fisher's death, he dedicated his treatise *Ecclesiastes sive de ratione concionandi* to his old friend. See Thomson and Porter, pp. 188-89.

[3] More did what he could to persuade Latimer to go to Rochester, but without success. See Thomas More to Erasmus from London, [22 September, 1516], Allen, p. 347; William Latimer to Erasmus from Oxford, 30 January, [1517], *ibid.*, pp. 438-42.

[4] Fisher to Erasmus from Rochester [c. 30 June, 1516], Nichols, II. 292, 293. Cf. Allen, II. 268-69. Fisher may have left his copy with Warham, for a few days later Warham is writing to Erasmus of the approval of several of the bishops to whom he had shown the book (William Warham to Erasmus from Otford, 22 June, [1516], Allen, II. 261-62).

[5] Erasmus to Andrew Ammonius from Rochester, 17 August, [1516], *ibid.*, pp. 317-18. Ammonius replied a day or two later and sent his compliments to Fisher (*ibid.*, pp. 318-19).

[6] Erasmus to Johann Reuchlin, 29 September, [1516], *ibid.*, pp. 350-51; More to Erasmus from London, 31 October, [1516], *ibid.*, pp. 370-72.

[7] Erasmus to More from Antwerp, 1 March, 1517, *ibid.*, pp. 494–95; Reuchlin to Erasmus, 27 March, 1517, *ibid.*, pp. 521–22.

[8] John Colet to Erasmus from London, [c. June, 1517], *ibid.*, p. 599.

[9] Fisher to Erasmus from Rochester, [c. June, 1517], Nichols, II. 569, 569–70, 570. Erasmus replied on 8 September from Antwerp, explaining that Colet had kept Reuchlin's book longer than he ought to have done, and adding, "with your usual good nature you will pardon Colet's avidity; I had given More leave to show it to him, but not to leave it with him" (*ibid.*, III. 41–42; cf. Allen, II. 598; III. 75). He wrote again briefly on 16 September from Louvain (Allen, III. 91). Fisher was not the only one to notice errors in the New Testament. Edward Lee, who was one day to succeed Wolsey as Archbishop of York, made a catalogue of emendations, which he showed to Fisher, More, Latimer and perhaps also to Cuthbert Tunstal, another member of the group who later became first Bishop of London and then Bishop of Durham. He refused to show it to Erasmus, however, apparently because he was afraid that Erasmus would silently correct his mistakes without acknowledging his indebtedness to Lee. In 1520, despite More's efforts to dissuade him, Lee published his *Annotationes* and drew from Erasmus an angry *Responsio ad annotationes*, which appeared later the same year. See *The Correspondence of Sir Thomas More*, edited by Elizabeth Frances Rogers (Princeton, 1947), pp. 137–38.

[10] The events that follow are recorded by the anonymous biographer. No date is given and there is some disagreement as to when they occurred. In his *Life of Blessed John Fisher* (London, 1888, 1890), p. 46, T. E. Bridgett suggested that the indulgence referred to was the bull directed by Leo against Luther and his followers and published in England in 1521. Reynolds follows Bridgett and adds (p. 97n) that in this case "istas" should be read as referring to the doctrines condemned by the bull. It is clear enough from the sequel, however, that the scandalous word was meant to refer to the contents of the proclamation itself and not to anything either approved or condemned by its author. But whether the incident took place in 1517 or at a later date it is no longer possible to determine.

[11] Accounts kept by John Dorne the bookseller show that by 1520 Lutheran books were selling well in Oxford. See Dickens, *The English Reformation* (London, 1964), p. 68.

[12] In his *English Humanists and Reformation Politics* (Oxford, 1965), James Kelsey McConica argues persuasively that the "central tradition" of the English reformation did in fact grow directly out of the New Learning as practised by Erasmus and such of his friends as Fox at Oxford and Fisher at Cambridge. However, such a view—though useful as a corrective to the supposition that the humanists and reformers had nothing essential

in common—underplays the importance of the differences between the two, which are radical enough. Belief in justification by faith and in the sacramental character of the Lord's Supper, for example, were both characteristic of the reformation settlement, but neither had much to do with the kind of textual criticism characteristic of Erasmus. For Fisher at anyrate the distinction was real and essential.

[13] See *Luke* 7. 37–38.

[14] Tournai was returned to France on 3 October, 1518 under the terms of the Treaty of London. Francis bound himself to pay Wolsey a pension for life to compensate him for the loss of the revenues of the see.

[15] Jacques Lefèvre, *De Maria Magdalena, & triduo Christi disceptatio* (1517, 1518, 1519); *Apologię seu defensorij ecclesiae catholicę non tres siue duae Magdalenas sed vnicam celebrantis & colentis* (23 August, 1518); *Scholastica declaratio sententię & ritus ecclesiae de vnica Magdalena per Natalem Bedam studii Parrhisiensis* (18 December, 1518); Fisher, *De vnica Magdalena, Libri tres* (22 February, 1519); Josse van Clichtove, *Disceptationis de Magdalena defensio* (1519); Lefèvre, *De tribus et unica Magdalena, Disceptatio secunda* (1519); Fisher, *Euersio munitionis quam Iodocus Clichtoueus erigere moliebatur aduersus unicam Magdalenam* (n.d.) and *Confutatio Secundae Disceptationis per Iacobum Fabrum Stapulensem* (3 September, 1519). Fisher's first reply to Faber appeared on 8 Kal. March, i.e., 22 February. It was probably on this occasion that More wrote to congratulate Fisher on the publication of a work worthy, as he called it, of the hand of Erasmus. See More to Fisher, [?1519], Rogers, pp. 136–37.

[16] Latimer to Erasmus from Oxford, 30 January, [1517], Allen, II. 438–42; Erasmus to Latimer from Antwerp, [February, 1517], *ibid.*, pp. 485–87.

[17] Erasmus to Fisher from Louvain, [c. 5 March, 1518], *ibid.*, III. 236–38. See also Erasmus to Fisher, 23 April, 23 October, [1518], 2 April, 17 October, 1519, 21 February, 1520, 2 August, [1520], 1 [September], 1522 and 4 September 1524, *ibid.*, pp. 291–92, 427–28, 522–25, IV. 92–94, 191–92, 321–22, V. 122–24, 536–38.

CHAPTER 7

[1] *Letters and Papers*, 2.2.4362 (pp. 1344–45).

[2] There were two ecclesiastical provinces. The southern province was under the jurisdiction of the Archbishop of Canterbury, the northern province (much the smaller of the two) under that of the Archbishop of York. In each Convocation there were two houses: the bishops, abbots and priors sat in the upper house and the inferior clergy or their representatives in the lower house. As Archbishop of York, Wolsey had undoubted authority in the northern province. What he now claimed was jurisdiction over both provinces, in his capacity as legate *a latere*.

[3] Thomas Wolsey to Warham, 14 February, 1519, *ibid.*, 3.1.77 (pp. 21–22); Warham to Wolsey from Otford, 26 February, 1519, *ibid.*, 3.1.98 (p. 28); same to same from Maidstone, 14 March, 1519, *ibid.*, 3.1.120 (p. 38); same to same from Croydon, 18 March, 1519, *ibid.*, 3.1.127 (p. 40).

[4] *Life of Fisher*, p. 35.

[5] *Letters and Papers*, 3.1.702–04 (pp. 235–46). The Bishop of Llandaff from 1517 to 1537 was George de Athequa, a Spaniard.

[6] *Here after ensueth two fruytfull Sermons* (London, 1532), sigs. A2, A2–A2ᵛ. The fullest account of the Field of Cloth of Gold is given by Hall, pp. 605–20.

[7] More to Thomas Cromwell, 5 March, 1534, Rogers, p. 498. Campeggio wrote to Wolsey on 19 September, 1521 to say that the King's book had filled him with joy and was the work of an angel (*Letters and Papers*, 3.1.1592 [pp. 662–63]). The College of Cardinals considered various titles for King Henry, including Protector and Apostolicus; the title of Fidei Defensor was eventually chosen and conferred in full consistory on 11 October (*ibid.*, 3.1.1369 [p. 548]; 3.1.1659 [p. 692]).

[8] Leo X to Wolsey, 17 April, 1521, *ibid.*, 3.1.1234 (p. 468).

[9] See Millar Maclure, *The Paul's Cross Sermons 1534–1642* (Toronto, 1958), pp. 3–4 and frontispiece.

[10] *Letters and Papers*, 3.1.1274 (p. 485).

[11] *English Works*, p. 326. The sermon was printed in the same year by Wynkyn de Worde, with an attractive woodcut of Fisher preaching at St. Paul's.

[12] *A Godlie treatise declaryng the benefites, fruites, and great commodi-*

ties of prayer, translated into English (London, 1560) from the Latin
(first printed in 1576); *Assertionis Lutheranae confutatio* (Antwerp, 1523);
Defensio Regie assertionis contra Babylonicam captiuitatem and *Sacri
sacerdotii defensio* (Cologne, 1525). More also published a defence of the
King's book, under the pseudonym of William Ross; it appeared in
London in 1523. Publication of the *Assertionis Lutheranae confutatio* drew
Fisher into the controversy over the existence of purgatory and the efficacy
of prayer for the dead. In 1528 Simon Fish, a member of Gray's Inn, pub-
lished his *Supplicacyon for the Beggers,* in which he derided the priesthood for deceiving the people and living off the profits of their deception.
More replied the next year in *The supplycacyon of soulys,* which was followed in 1530 by John Rastell's *New Boke of Purgatory.* A year later
John Frith published his *Disputacion of purgatorye* at Antwerp, in
reply to Fisher, More and Rastell. Preoccupied by that time with the
King's great matter, Fisher made no answer to Frith and took no further
part in the controversy. For an admirable account of the struggle between
the established Church and the reformers, see William A. Clebsch, *England's Earliest Protestants 1520–1535* (New Haven, 1964).

13 [Ulrichus Velenus], *In hoc libello grauissimis, certissimisq, & in
sacra scriptura fundatis rationibus narijs probatur, Apostolum Petrum
Roman non uenisse* (n.pl., 1519). See *Matthew* 16. 18–19.

14 *Conuulsio calumniarum Vlrichi Veleni Minhoniensis, quib. Petrum
nunquam Romae fuisse cauillatur* (Antwerp, 1522); Simon Hess, *Apologia
adversus dominum Roffensem, Episcopum Anglicanum, super concertatione eius cum Vlricho Veleno, An Petr. fuerit Romae* (n.pl., n.d.).

15 Thomas [Cresacre] More, *The Life of Sir Thomas More* (London,
1726), pp. 66, 66–67. For the Latin originals of Fisher's letter and More's
reply, see Rogers, pp. 253, 253–54.

16 A copy of the indenture dated 6 March, 1521, is in the Cambridge
University Library, Mm. 1.40, pp. 405–06. An unsigned draft of the indenture of 18 April, 1525 is in the Thin Red Book, fols., 68–72ᵛ. The further
gift of vestments, plate and books is recorded under date of 27 December,
1525 (fol. 72ᵛ). Because they remained in his possession for life, all of
Fisher's books fell into the hands of the King in April of 1534. The library
was broken up and none of the books found their way to St. John's. Earlier
he had given the college £200 for the mortmain of Higham and Bromehall, together with vestments and plate worth £1128 10s. (fols., 65, 66). It is
difficult to assess the value of Fisher's gifts to St. John's, but it is reasonable
to suppose that they were worth in all between $300,000 and $350,000. A
schedule of his gifts to Christ's College is preserved in the Thin Red Book,

fols. 42–43ᵛ. On the eve of his departure for London and the Tower in April of 1534, he sent a gift of £100 to Michaelhouse.

Early in 1529 the university decreed, as a mark of its gratitude and affection, that a yearly requiem should be celebrated on the anniversary of Fisher's death. He accepted, on condition that the name of Lady Margaret be joined with his. The resolution was adopted in spite of the objections of Richard Croke, a fellow of St. John's and lecturer in Greek, who accused Fisher of enriching himself at the expense of the Lady Margaret's estate and of using college revenues for the benefit of his family and fellow Yorkshiremen. Fisher had by this time spoken openly against the divorce proceedings and Croke, who spent several months of the following year in Italy buying up learned opinion in favour of the King, may have felt that it was imprudent for the university to associate itself in such a way with a man who was no longer *persona grata* at Court. Though Fisher had no difficulty in showing that the accusations were groundless, the incident shows how little the younger generation at Cambridge knew of what the university owed to its Chancellor. See Vice-Chancellor and Senate to Fisher from Cambridge (Thin Red Book, fols. 75–76); Fisher to Vice-Chancellor and Senate from Rochester, 25 February, [1529] (fols. 77–78ᵛ); Fisher to Richard Croke from Rochester (fols. 49–50ᵛ).

CHAPTER 8

[1] *Letters and Papers*, 3.2.3504, 3519 (pp. 1456–58, 1465).

[2] This drawing, executed in black and red chalks, brownish wash and India ink on pink paper, is usually thought to have been done during Holbein's first visit to England, probably in 1527. The use of pink paper is, however, unusual in Holbein's drawings of this date, and this suggests that the portrait may have been done after the artist's return to England in 1532. The original, which is in The Royal Library at Windsor (No. 12205), is reproduced facing p. 64; there is also a contemporary copy (possibly by Holbein) in the British Museum (G.g.1–416) and a slightly later copy in oils, somewhat mutilated, in the National Portrait Gallery (2821). See K. T. Parker, *The Drawings of Hans Holbein in the Collection of His Majesty the King at Windsor Castle* (Oxford and London, 1945), p. 13.

[3] Erasmus to Fisher from Basle, 4 September, 1524, Allen, V. 536–38.

[4] When Eck left Rochester on 21 August, 1525, Fisher gave him a com-

plimentary letter addressed to the Duke of Bavaria. For a transcript of the Latin text and a translation into modern English, see Bridgett, pp. 114–15, 115–16n. I have been unable to trace the original of this letter.

[5] *De veritate corporis et sanguinis Christi.* The reply, which was printed at Cologne in 1527, was widely read and three editions were exhausted within a year.

[6] See John Longland to Wolsey, 5 January, 1526, *Letters and Papers*, 4.1.995 (p. 434). Longland was the King's confessor and had been Bishop of Lincoln since 1521. See Allan G. Chester, "Robert Barnes and the Burning of the Books", *Huntington Library Quarterly*, XIV (1951), 211–21.

[7] Robert Barnes, *A supplicatyon vnto the most excellent and redoubted prince kinge henrye the eyght* ([Antwerp, 1531]), fols. 23ᵛ, 24. In his appeal to the King Barnes insisted that he had never spoken "agenst god" or "hys holy worde" but only against the bishops' "abomynable lyuynge and damnable pompe and pryde" (fol. 19). True to his word, he told Wolsey that he should "laye downe his pyllars and pollaxes and coyne them" (fol. 33). The London house of the Bishops of Winchester was in Southwark, near the priory church of St. Mary Overy, now Southwark Cathedral. This part of town, which was the site of a prison called the Clink, was notorious for its brothels. Fox of Winchester was one of Fisher's oldest friends and what he thought of his friend's jest at his expense Barnes does not stop to tell us.

[8] See *Luke* 18. 35–43. The sermon was printed by Thomas Berthelet, probably in 1526. It is reprinted in *English Works*, pp. 429–76. For a highly coloured account of the occasion, see Hall, p. 708.

[9] *Letters and Papers*, 4.1.2002 (p. 901).

[10] In the Record Office, S.P. 1.39, fol. 67, there are three drafts of a letter from Fisher to a Master Draper concerning the visitation. The abbot, he says in one of them, "hathe byne wythe [me] & hathe exhibyt hy[s] accomptes which I haue lokyd vpon somewhat but for by cause I wyll se them with mor delyberacion and dilygence I purpose god wylling to be withe you as lesnes upon thursday next comyng". Wolsey had applied in 1524 for permission to appropriate the revenues of Lesnes Abbey for the benefit of his colleges at Ipswich and Oxford and on 8 February, 1526 the grant was confirmed by the King. Fisher presumably made his visitation that year with a view to winding up the affairs of the community. See Sir William Dugdale, *Monasticon Anglicanum* (6 vols. in 8 parts, London, 1849), VI.1.456.

[11] *Calendar of Letters, Despatches, and State Papers . . . Preserved in the Archives at Simancas* [Spanish Calendar], edited by G. A. Bergenroth, Pascual de Gayangos, M. A. S. Hume, Royall Tyler and Garrett

Mattingly (13 vols. and 2 supplements, London, 1862–1954), 3.2.61 (pp. 171–72).

[12] It is noteworthy that in the surviving records of the negotiations there is no reference whatever to the illegitimacy of the Princess Mary, though it is clear that the English envoys were for their part concerned as to the eligibility of Francis. See *Letters and Papers*, 4.2.3105 (pp. 1397–1415). Here and elsewhere, the word "divorce" is used only for the sake of convenience. Canon law made no provision for divorce as we know it. What Henry wanted was what we would call an annulment, that is, a declaration that his marriage was null and void *ab initio*.

[13] *Leviticus* 18. 16, 20, 21.

[14] Catherine was born on 16 December, 1485, Arthur on 20 September, 1486.

[15] Ferdinand and Isabella, instructions to Hernan Duque de Estrada, 10 May, 1502, *Spanish Calendar*, 1.317–18 (p. 267); Isabella to Hernan Duque, 21 August, 1502, *ibid.*, 1.345 (p. 285); treaty between Ferdinand and Isabella and Henry VII, 23 June, 1503, *ibid.*, 1.364 (pp. 306–08); Ferdinand to Francesco De Rojas, 23 August, 1503, *ibid.*, 1.370 (pp. 309–10); Ferdinand and Isabella, ratification of the treaty with Henry VII, *ibid.*, 1.376, 378 (p. 317); Henry VII, ratification of the treaty with Ferdinand and Isabella, *ibid.*, 1.393 (p. 325). The letter from Ferdinand to De Rojas is printed in full in the original Spanish in *Records of the Reformation: The Divorce 1527–1533*, edited by Nicholas Pocock (2 vols., Oxford, 1870), II. 426–27. This work is cited hereafter as Pocock. Ferdinand is quite explicit in his statement of the case: "y ahun que en el dicho capitulo", he explains, "dize quel matrimonio dela dicha princessa, nuestra hija, con el principe de Gales, Arthur, ya deffuncto, que gloria haya, fue consumado, pero la verdad es que no fue consumado, y que la dicha princesa nuestra hija quedo tan entera como antes que se casasse, y esto es muy cierto y muy sabido donde el la sta; mas ha parecido a los letrados de Inglaterra, que los Scrupulos y dudas que la gente de aquel reyno suele poner en las cosas, que ahun que es assi verdad que la dicha princesa, nuestra hija, quedo entera y ahun que se velaron ella y el principe Arthur, no consummaron el matrimonio, y que por quitar toda duda para adelante en la succession de los hijos que plazendo a nuestro Señor nasceran deste dicho casamiento, que agora seha assentado se deve dezir en la dispensacion que consumaron el matrimonio": although the said chapter [of our agreement] says that the marriage of the said Princess, our daughter, with Arthur Prince of Wales, now deceased, was consummated, the fact is that it was not consummated, for the said princess, our daughter, is still a virgin, as she was before her marriage. This fact is well known in England, but certain of

the English lawyers professed to have doubts and scruples and insisted that though the said princess, our daughter, is still a virgin and though her marriage with Prince Arthur was never consummated, it must be stated in the dispensation that the marriage was consummated, in order to remove all doubts as to the succession of any sons that may, God willing, be born to the union [of the princess with Prince Henry of Wales].

[16] Hadrian de Costello to Henry VII from Rome, December, 1503, Pocock, I. 2. Hadrian quoted Julius as saying *"rem graviorem esse, nec se primâ facie scire, an Pontifici liceat in tali materiâ dispensare"*. Julius wrote to Henry VII on 6 July, 1504 to explain that he wished to give further thought to the case before reaching a decision: "nos expectare in illâ concedendâ tempus magis accommodatum, ut consultius et maturius fieret, cum hujus sanctae sedis et etriusque partis honore" (Pocock, I. 5; see also *Spanish Calendar*, 1.396 [p. 328]).

[17] The text of the statement, which was sworn at Richmond Palace before Richard Fox of Winchester and other witnesses on 27 June, 1505, the eve of Henry's fourteenth birthday, is in Gilbert Burnet, *The History of the Reformation of the Church of England*, edited by Nicholas Pocock (7 vols., Oxford, 1865), IV. 17–18. This work is cited hereafter as Burnet. See also *Spanish Calendar*, 1.435 (pp. 358–59).

[18] *Letters and Papers*, 4.2.3140 (pp. 1426–29).

CHAPTER 9

[1] Don Iñigo de Mendoça to Charles V, 18 May, 1527, *Spanish Calendar*, 3.2.69 (pp. 193–94).

[2] Fisher to Wolsey from Rochester, [c. 31 May], 1527, Record Office, S.P. 1.42, fols. 51–51ᵛ. The Latin original, which is in Fisher's own hand, has been printed by Pocock, I. 9–10.

[3] Wolsey to Henry VIII from Westminster, 2 June, 1527, *State Papers Published under the Authority of His Majesty's Commission: King Henry the Eighth* (11 vols., London, 1830–52), I. 189.

[4] Wolsey to Henry VIII from Feversham, 5 July, 1527, *ibid.*, p. 198.

[5] *Ibid.*, p. 200.

[6] *Ibid.*, p. 199.

[7] *Ibid.*, p. 201.

[8] *Ibid.*, p. 200.

[9] *Ibid.*, pp. 200, 200–01.

[10] Record Office, S.P. 1.42, fols. 165–66ᵛ. The letter is calendared in *Letters and Papers*, 4.2.3232 (pp. 1471–72). The manuscript is not signed, but the hand appears to be that of Fisher's clerk, who must have prepared a fair copy of the letter that was actually sent, probably in the summer of 1527.

[11] Robert Wakefield, *Koster Codicis* (London, n.d.), sigs. Piiii, Piiiiᵛ. Wakefield printed his letter to the King at the end of his book when it appeared the following year. He also published a letter to Fisher and another from Pace to the King.

[12] *Syntagma de hebrẹorum codicum incorruptione.*

[13] *Deuteronomy* 25. 5.

[14] In the British Museum (MS. Cott. Otho C. X, fols. 184–98ᵛ) there is a manuscript copy of another reply, entitled *Eruditi cuiusdam responsio pro regis defensione ad libellum Roffensis ep[iscopi]*, which may be the book prepared for the King by Pace. See also Richard Pace, *Praefatio in Ecclesiasten recognitum ad Hebraicam ueritatem* (?London, ?1530).

[15] *Letters and Papers*, 4.2.3246 (pp. 1475–76).

[16] William Knight to Wolsey, 15 July, 1527, *ibid.*, 4.2.3265 (pp. 1480–81); Charles V to Catherine, 27 August, 1527, *Spanish Calendar*, 3.2.166 (pp. 345–46). See also Mendoça to Charles V, 13 July, 1527, *ibid.*, 3.2.113 (pp. 276–78); Wolsey to Henry VIII from Calais, 19 July, 1527, *Letters and Papers*, 4.2.3283 (p. 1488).

[17] Wolsey to Henry VIII from Abbeville, 29 July, 1527, *State Papers*, I. 230–31.

[18] Wolsey to Henry VIII from Amiens, 11 August, 1527, *Letters and Papers*, 4.2.3340 (p. 1514).

[19] Wolsey to Henry VIII from Compiègne, 5 September, 1527, *State Papers*, I. 267–73; Henry VIII to Wolsey, 11 September, 1527, *Letters and Papers*, 4.2.3419 (p. 1551); Knight to Henry VIII from Compiègne, 12 and 13 September, 1527, *State Papers*, VII. 1–2, 3.

[20] Certainly it is difficult to accept Froude's explanation, which is that the council simply wished to provide for any eventuality. The relevant clauses, which make provision for Anne's betrothal to Henry Percy as well as for the King's liaison with Mary Boleyn, are as follows: "in eventum declarationis nullitatis matrimonii huiusmodi tecum dispensari, ut cum quacunque alia muliere, etiamsi illa talis sit, quae alias cum alio matrimonium contraxerit, dummodo illud carnali copula non consumaverit, etiamsi tibi alias secundo vel remotiori consanguinitatis, aut primo affinitatis gradu ex quocunque licito seu illicito coitu coniuncta, dummodo relicta dicti fratris tui non fuerit, ac etiamsi cognatione spirituali vel legali

tibit coniuncta extiterit et impedimentum publicae honestatis iustitiae sub-sistat, matrimonium licite contrahere et in eo libere remanere ac ex eo prolem legitimam suscipere possis" (*Römische Dokumente zur Geschichte der Ehescheidung Heinrichs VIII. von England*, edited by Stephan Ehses [Paderborn, 1893], p. 15).

21 Knight to Henry VIII from Foligno, 4 November, 1527, *State Papers*, VII. 13-14; same to same, 4 December, 1527, *ibid.*, pp. 16-17; Wolsey to Sir Gregory Casale, 5, 6 December, 1527, *Letters and Papers*, 4.2.3641, 3644 (pp. 1635-37, 1638); Wolsey to Clement VII, ?6 December, 1527, *ibid.*, 4.2.3646 (p. 1639).

22 Two years after his return to Cambridge Bilney resumed his preach-ing. He was examined as a relapsed heretic by officers of the Bishop of Norwich and was burned to death at the Lollards' Pit on 19 August, 1531.

23 Clement VII to Henry VIII from Orvieto, 16 December, 1527, *State Papers*, VII. 27.

24 Wolsey to Sir Gregory Casale, 27 December, 1527, *Letters and Papers*, 4.2.3693 (pp. 1654-55).

25 Knight to Wolsey and to Henry VIII from Orvieto, 1 January, 1528, Burnet, IV. 35-36, 37-39. See also *State Papers*, VII. 36-37.

26 Wolsey to Stephen Gardiner and Edward Fox, c. 11 February, 1528, *Letters and Papers*, 4.2.3913 (pp. 1740-43); Wolsey to Sir Gregory Casale, 12 February, 1528, *State Papers*, VII. 50-51; Wolsey to St. Quatuor, c. 12 February, 1528, *Letters and Papers*, 4.2.3920 (p. 1745).

CHAPTER 10

1 See pp. 53-54.

2 See pp. 76-77. Whether Fisher was sent for in the fall of 1527 or later in the winter of 1528 we do not know. Nor can his letter be dated with any certainty. It is unlikely, however, that he was credulous enough to take Wolsey's story seriously after he had had time to consider it at leisure.

3 *Life of Fisher*, pp. 52, 53.

4 Staphileus to Wolsey from Boulogne, 20 January, 1528, *Letters and Papers*, 4.2.3820 (p. 1701).

5 In a letter to Anne Boleyn, written some months before, the King spoke of having worked for four hours on the book that day and of having a pain in the head as a result (*ibid.*, 4.2.4597 [p. 2003]).

[6] Gardiner and Fox to Henry VIII from Orvieto, 31 March, 1528, *State Papers*, VII. 63–64; Sir Gregory Casale, Gardiner and Fox to Wolsey from Orvieto, 31 March, 1528, *Letters and Papers*, 4.2.4120 (pp. 1819–22).

[7] Gardiner to Henry VIII from Viterbo, 11 June, 1528, *State Papers*, VII. 77–79. The text of the commission is printed in Pocock, I. 167–69.

[8] The Abbess of Wilton having died, Anne Boleyn sought the position for Elinor Carey, Mary Boleyn's sister-in-law. When it was found that she was morally unfit, the King, to do Anne what pleasure he could, promised that neither Elinor Carey nor Isabel Jordon, whom Wolsey proposed, should have the appointment. Wolsey, his mind full of other matters, overlooked Henry's instructions and nominated Isabel Jordon. See *Letters and Papers*, 4.2.4507, 4509, 4513 (pp. 1969–70, 1970, 1972–73).

[9] Anne Boleyn to Wolsey, July, 1528, *ibid.*, 4.2.4480 (pp. 1960–61).

[10] *Ibid.*, 4.2.4735, 4736 (pp. 2054, 2054–55).

[11] *Ibid.*, 4.2.4805 (pp. 2081–82).

[12] Lorenzo Campeggio to Giacomo Salviati, 17 October, 1528, *ibid.*, 4.2.4857 (pp. 2099–2100); Campeggio to Giovanni Battista Sanga, 17 October, 1528, *ibid.*, 4.2.4858 (pp. 2100–02).

[13] *Ibid.*, pp. 2100–02.

[14] Campeggio to Salviati, 26 October, 1528, *ibid.*, 4.2.4875 (pp. 2108–10). For an admirable life of the Queen, see Mattingly, *Catherine of Aragon* (London, 1942; 1950).

[15] See p. 70.

[16] In a letter to Henry VII of 22 February, 1505, Julius II explained at some length why he had agreed to send a preliminary brief to Isabella. See Pocock, I. 7–8. The brief was apparently unknown to Wolsey and the King before it was exhibited by the Queen in 1528, but there is no reason to doubt that copies were sent to England soon after the original arrived in Spain. See Hernan Duque to Isabella, 10 August, 1504, *Spanish Calendar*, 1.398 (pp. 329–30); Ferdinand to Henry VII, 24 November, 1504, *ibid.*, 1.407 (p. 338). Hernan Duque and Ferdinand both speak of a *dispensation*, but since the bull itself was not issued until the following year it is difficult to see how they can be referring to anything but the brief.

[17] Hall, p. 44. Hall prints a complete English translation of the bull. The Latin original is printed by Burnet, IV. 15–16. See Mendoça to Charles V, 18 November, 1528, *Spanish Calendar*, 3.2.586 (pp. 839–49). Relations between England and Spain were governed by the Treaty of Medina del Campo (1489) and subsequent amendments.

[18] The Latin text of the brief is printed by Burnet, IV. 61–62. See Her-

bert Thurston, "The Canon Law of the Divorce", *English Historical Review*, XIX (1904), 632–45.

[19] *Letters and Papers*, 4.2.4842 (p. 2092).

[20] *Ibid.*, 4.2.4841 (p. 2092). The Queen's statement is printed by Pocock, I. 181.

[21] *Letters and Papers*, 4.3.5154.i–ii (p. 2265). See also Charles V to Miguel Mai, 3 March, 1529, *Spanish Calendar*, 3.2.637 (pp. 912–13).

[22] The other witnesses were Warham, Tunstal, Clerk and Standish, all members of the Queen's council. See *Letters and Papers*, 4.3. Appendix 211 (p. 3171).

[23] There are several accounts of the King's address, all in substantial agreement. See Jean Du Bellay to Montmorency from London, 17 November, 1528, *ibid.*, 4.2.4942 (pp. 2144–46); Mendoça to Charles V, 18 November, 1528, *Spanish Calendar*, 3.2.586 (pp. 839–49); *Concilia Magnae Britanniae et Hiberniae*, edited by [David Wilkins] (4 vols., London, 1737), III. 714; Hall, pp. 754–55.

[24] *Letters and Papers*, 4.2.4980 (p. 2162).

[25] Mendoça reported that Warham, Tunstal and two others (both presumably members of the Queen's council) were present with Wolsey on this occasion. See *Spanish Calendar*, 3.2.586 (pp. 839–49); *Letters and Papers*, 4.2.4981 (p. 2163). There is no evidence that Fisher was present.

[26] John Casale to Wolsey from Rome, 17 December, 1528, *ibid.*, 4.2.5038 (pp. 2186–88). John Casale was acting for his brother Gregory, who was ill at Bologna.

[27] *State Papers*, VII. 117–40.

[28] *Letters and Papers*, 4.3.5270 (pp. 2321–22).

[29] Wolsey to Gardiner, Sir Francis Brian, Sir Gregory Casale and Peter Vannes, 6 April, 1529, Burnet, IV. 79–92.

[30] Mai to Charles V, April, 1529, *Spanish Calendar*, 3.2.664 (pp. 971–75).

[31] Brian, Sir Gregory Casale and Vannes to Wolsey, 28 January, 1529, *Letters and Papers*, 4.3.5230 (pp. 2303–06).

[32] Jerome Ghinucci and Edward Lee to Wolsey, 20 April, 1529, *ibid.*, 4.3.5471 (pp. 2409–13).

[33] Clement VII to Henry VIII, 21 April, 1529, *State Papers*, VII. 164–65; Clement VII to Wolsey, 21 April, 1529, *ibid.*, pp. 165–66n; Sanga to Campeggio, 21 April, 1529, *Letters and Papers*, 4.3.5477 (pp. 2416–17); Sir Gregory Casale to Wolsey, 21 April, 1529, *ibid.*, 4.3.5478 (p. 2417).

[34] Wolsey to Gardiner, Brian, Sir Gregory Casale and Vannes, [7 May], 1529, Burnet, IV. 99, 92–102; same to same, 21 May, 1529, *ibid.*, pp. 108–13. For a valuable discussion of the original text of the pollicitation and of the draft containing the "pregnant, fat, and available words" suggested

JOHN FISHER OF ROCHESTER

by Wolsey, see James Gairdner, "New Lights on the Divorce of Henry VIII", *English Historical Review*, XI (1896), 673–702; XII (1897), [1]–16, 237–53.

CHAPTER 11

[1] Sanga to Campeggio, 16 September, 1528, *Letters and Papers*, 4.2.4737 (pp. 2055–56); same to same, 28 December, 1528, *ibid.*, 4.2.5072 (p. 2210); Sir Gregory Casale to Vincent Casale, 16 February, 1529, *ibid.*, 4.3.5302 (p. 2333).

[2] *State Papers*, VII. 177–78; *Letters and Papers*, 4.3.5611 (p. 2483).

[3] *Ibid.*, 4.3.5613 (p. 2483).

[4] *Ibid.*, 4.3.5694 (p. 2520); Pocock, I. 216–18. The text of the Queen's appeal is printed by Pocock, pp. 221–22.

[5] In the Record Office (E.30.1471) there is an affidavit, signed by the Bishops of London, Rochester, Carlisle, Ely, St. Asaph, Lincoln and Bath and Wells and by the Archbishop of Canterbury, acknowledging that the King had consulted the signatories concerning certain scruples as to his marriage. The bishops affirmed that the King's scruples were real enough and allowed that there was reason to refer the case to the judgment of the Pope. The affidavit is dated 1 July, 1529 and so cannot be the document produced by the King two weeks earlier. It may be that after being repudiated by Fisher the original affidavit was destroyed and a new one prepared in such form that Fisher agreed to sign it. Though he had long been suspicious of the King's motives, he may well have felt that he could not refuse his assent to a statement that went no farther than this. In any case, there can be no doubt that he did sign the new affidavit, for traces of his seal are still visible and his signature is entirely convincing. There is a second copy in the Record Office (E.30.1472.2) in better condition than the first, which is partially obscured by damp. It lacks Tunstal's signature, however, though his seal was affixed in the proper place. Room was left in both copies for the hand and seal of the Bishop of Exeter, but for some reason he never executed the instrument. Fisher signed and sealed the second copy as well as the first, and the signatures agree in every particular except for the addition in the second of a period after the customary abbreviation of his given name. His normal signature was *Jo Roffensis* or *Jo Roffs* (John of Rochester).

[6] George Cavendish, *The Life and Death of Cardinal Wolsey*, in *Two Early Tudor Lives*, edited by Richard S. Sylvester and Davis P. Harding (New Haven, 1962), pp. 83–88. The modernized text used here is based on the text prepared by Mr. Sylvester from the manuscript for the Early English Text Society, Original Series No. 243 (London, 1959), pp. 80–85. There are several accounts of the hearing, of which that given by Cavendish is the most complete and probably the most reliable. Though he was partial to Wolsey, Cavendish had less reason than most to falsify or distort the facts. He does, however, elide the events of 18 and 21 June; and he is the only witness to record the Queen's speech or the exchange between Warham and Fisher. Hall's account (pp. 756–58) is much less complete, though his description of the setting is fuller and more colourful. The words he attributes to the King are similar to those recorded at greater length by Cavendish, though (perhaps because of his partiality to the royal cause) he fails to mention the disputed affidavit of the bishops. Fisher's biographer follows Cavendish closely in most respects, though it is interesting to note that he has the Queen accuse Wolsey of pressing the suit out of malice against her nephew Charles for his failure to support Wolsey's election to the Holy See. It is easy to understand why Cavendish might have overlooked an accusation of this sort, and why he might have added instead the King's quite different explanation of his scruples. Fisher's biographer follows Cavendish also in his account of the dispute between Fisher and Warham, though he colours the story here and there. He reports, for example, that the King turned on Fisher "with a frowninge countenance" when the latter denied the truth of Warham's statement; and he adds that, after Fisher had denied that he had given Warham permission to affix his name and seal, he "ment to have said more" (which we can well believe), but the King stopped him (pp. 62, 63). Records kept by officials of the court provide little more than a bare outline of events. See *Letter and Papers*, 4.3.5613, 5694 (pp. 2483, 2520). Burnet denies (III. 120–21) that either the King or the Queen appeared before the legates on 21 June, but if the first-hand reports we have were not enough to substantiate the story the testimony of the King himself would serve. On 23 June Henry sent Sir Gregory Casale, Vannes and Dr. William Benet an account of the proceedings in which he states that on the 21st both "we and the quene appered in person and notwithstanding, that the said judges amply & sufficiently declared aswel the sincerite of thair mynds directely & justely to procede without favour, drede affection or partialite, as also that no suche recusation, appellation, or terme for proving of litis pendentiam coude or might be by them admitted, yet she nevertheless persisting in her former wilfulness layde in her appele, whiche also by the said judges was

likewise recused, and they mynding to procede further in the cause, the quene wolde no lenger make her abode to here what the said judges wolde finally discerne, but incontinently deperted out of the courte, wherfore she was thrice precognisate and called, eftsones to retourne & appere whiche she refusing to do, was denounced by the judges contumax and a citation discerned for her apparance on friday next to make answer to suche articles and positions as shuld be obiected vnto her" (British Museum MS. Cott. Vit. B. XI, fols. 169–69ᵛ). It is not surprising that he said nothing of what the Queen, or he himself, had said.

[7] *Letters and Papers*, 4.3.5716 (p. 2531).

[8] Cavendish, p. 88. The anonymous biographer says that Fisher appealed not to the Scriptural injunction cited by Cavendish but to the authority of Rome, where the question had been thoroughly examined before the dispensation was issued. See *Life of Fisher*, p. 63.

[9] Du Bellay to Francis I, 30 June, 1529, *Letters and Papers*, 4.3.5741 (p. 2543); Florian to Salviati, 29 June, 1529, Ehses, pp. 116–17. See also *Letters and Papers*, 4.3.5732 (pp. 2538–39).

[10] Cambridge University Library, Ff.5.25, fols. 152–97ᵛ. The fragment begins, "Constat inclitissimum Regem Henricum 7ᵘᵐ" and is identified as Fisher's in the Record Office, S.P.1.54, fol. 262, where there is a catalogue of evidence produced before the legates, including two items attributed to the Bishop of Rochester. One is described as beginning, like the fragment at Cambridge, with the words "Constat inclitiss". The other does not appear to have survived. See Gardiner, *Obedience in Church & State*, edited by Pierre Janelle (Cambridge, 1930).

[11] The statement, which begins, "Q ad illud axioma", is in the Record Office, S.P.1.54, fols. 129–65ᵛ. It is identified as Gardiner's in the catalogue of evidence on fol. 262, where it is described as "Libellus d. Stephani Gardineri incipiens Q ad illud axioma". Janelle believes the hand to be that of Gardiner himself.

[12] This brief, like the others, is untitled and begins, "Postquam in hac matrimonij causa". The original, part of which is in Gardiner's hand, is in the Record Office, S.P. 1.54, fols. 166–217ᵛ, and is described in the catalogue of evidence on fol. 262. A fragmentary copy is in fols. 218–29ᵛ. Fisher's comments on his conversation with Wolsey are on fols. 166ᵛ and 168. Gardiner's other brief must have been shown to Fisher as well, for it also contains a number of marginal notations in his distinctive hand.

[13] He admitted as much to Chapuys, though he insisted that he had spoken only in jest. See Eustace Chapuys to Charles V, 16 April, 1533, *Letters and Papers*, 6.351 (pp. 163–69).

[14] *Ibid.*, 4.3.5774 (pp. 2576–81).

[15] Campeggio to Salviati, 13 July, 1529, *ibid.*, 4.3.5775 (pp. 2581–82).

[16] Benet, Sir Gregory Casale and Vannes to Wolsey, *ibid.*, 4.3.5762 (pp. 2565–68); Vannes to Henry VIII, *ibid.*, 4.3.5763 (p. 2568); Vannes to Wolsey, *ibid.*, 4.3.5764 (pp. 2568–69); Benet to Wolsey, Burnet, IV. 122–24. All the despatches are dated 9 July, 1529.

[17] Clement VII to Wolsey, 8 July, 1529, Pocock, I. 249; Clement VII to Henry VIII, 8 July, 1529, *ibid.*, II. 614.

[18] *Letters and Papers*, 4.3.5777, 5780 (pp. 2582, 2583–84).

[19] Clement VII to Wolsey, 18 July, 1529, *ibid.*, 4.3.5785 (p. 2585); Clement VII to Henry VIII, 19 July, 1529, Pocock, II. 615.

[20] Sanga to Campeggio, 29 May, 1529, *Letters and Papers*, 4.3.5604 (pp. 2479–80). On 15 February, 1529, Cardinal Santacroce had confided to Charles V that Campeggio had been instructed not to give judgment.

[21] Cavendish, pp. 92, 93.

[22] *Ibid.*, p. 93.

CHAPTER 12

[1] The King actually spoke in Latin. See Campeggio to Salviati, 7 October, 1529, *Letters and Papers*, 4.3.5995 (p. 2669).

[2] Statutes 21 Henry VIII, Chapters 5, 6, 13. The probate bill provided that on estates worth less than £5 there should be no charge; that on estates worth more than £5 but less than £40 there should be a fee of 3/6; on estates worth more than £40 a charge of 5/-. The schedule of mortuary fees provided that persons dying with less than £6 13s. 4d. should be buried free of charge; that those with more than £6 13s. 4d. and less than £30 should pay 3/4; those with more than £30 and less than £40, 6/8; those with more than £40, 10/-. No fee was to be taken for the burial of women or children.

[3] *Life of Fisher*, p. 35.

[4] Wilkins, III. 717.

[5] William Rastell, "Certen breef notes apperteyning to Bushope Fisher", in Nicholas Harpsfield, *The life and death of Sr Thomas Moore, knight*, edited by Elsie Vaughan Hitchcock for the Early English Text Society, No. 186 (London, 1932), p. 222. The Rastell fragment (cited hereafter as Rastell) is printed as an appendix to Harpsfield's life of More.

[6] *Life of Fisher*, pp. 69, 69–70, 70.

[7] This is the account given by the anonymous biographer. Hall (p. 766) says that Fisher excused himself by pretending that he had meant his words to apply only to the Bohemians. Hall had no love for anyone who opposed the royal cause and there is no reason for us to believe on his account that Fisher would have tried to practise such a shallow deception on the King.

[8] Cranmer's book is printed in Pocock, I. 334–99.

[9] Henry VIII to the University of Cambridge, 16 February, 1530, *Letters and Papers*, 4.3.6218 (p. 2791); Henry VIII to the University of Oxford, 6 March, 1530, Pocock, I. 284.

[10] Gardiner to Henry VIII from Cambridge, c. 27 February, 1530, Burnet, IV. 130–33.

[11] Warham to the University of Oxford, 15 March, 1530, Pocock, I. 284–85; same to same, 28 March, 1530, *ibid.*, pp. 286–88.

[12] Henry VIII to the University of Oxford, c. 4 April, 1530, *ibid.*, pp. 288–90.

[13] Longland, Fox and Dr. John Bell to Henry VIII from Oxford, 5 April, 1530, *ibid.*, pp. 291–93. The decree is given on p. 530. Evidently Fox had joined Longland and Bell after securing the decree at Cambridge.

[14] Similar inhibitions were issued on 21 May and 4 August and were equally ineffective.

[15] Croke kept detailed accounts of his expenditures in Italy and these can still be examined in the British Museum. He normally paid £3 or £4 ($300 or $400) for an opinion favourable to the King. See *Letters and Papers*, 4.3.6375 (pp. 2862–64).

CHAPTER 13

[1] Chapuys to Charles V, 31 December, 1529, *Spanish Calendar*, 4.1.241 (p. 386); same to same, 6 February, 1530, *ibid.*, 4.1.257 (p. 446). See also *Correspondence of the Emperor Charles V*, edited by William Bradford (London, 1850), pp. 298–300. Bradford prints a number of Chapuys' letters in full, together with an English translation.

[2] Tyndale mentions the incident in his *Practice of Prelates* (1530) and again in his *Answer to Sir Thomas More's Dialogue* (1531). See *The Works of William Tyndale*, edited for the Parker Society by the Rev. Henry Walter (3 vols., Cambridge, 1848–50), II. 340; III. 113. The story is

told at much greater length by More in his *Confutacion of Tyndales Aunswere* (1532), *The Workes of Sir Thomas More* (London, 1557), pp. 344–46, and more briefly in *The Apologye of Syr Thomas More* (1533), edited by Arthur Irving Taft for the Early English Text Society, Original Series No. 180 (London, 1930), p. 127. Tyndale's account was adapted to his own purposes by John Foxe, who gave Hitton a minor place in his book of martyrs. See *Acts and Monuments*, edited by the Rev. Josiah Pratt (8 vols., London, 1877), IV. 619. Foxe follows Tyndale in speaking of "sundry torments" inflicted on Hitton during his examination, but Foxe, like Tyndale, was a party man and his work is highly coloured by party feeling. Abuses of this kind are out of keeping with everything we know of the two bishops. More for his part shows no greater charity than Tyndale and Foxe and called Hitton "the deuils stinking martyr, of whose burning Tindall maketh boast" (*Workes*, p. 346).

³ *Life of Fisher*, p. 72. The anonymous biographer says that Fisher told the story while speaking in the House of Lords against the bill for the suppression of the smaller monasteries. Since this bill did not come before the Lords until almost a year after Fisher's death, however, the story must have been used on some other occasion.

⁴ The Latin text is printed by Pocock, I. 429–33.

⁵ Chapuys to Charles V, 15, 29 June, 1530, *Spanish Calendar*, 4.1.354, 366 (pp. 598–602, 616, 619).

⁶ Pocock prints the Latin original, I. 434–37. The letter is dated 27 September. When the papal nuncio presented it to the King, Henry told him that God had shown what he thought of the Pope by causing the Tiber to overflow its banks (Chapuys to Charles V, 13 November, 1530, *Spanish Calendar*, 4.1.492 [p. 797]).

⁷ Henry VIII to Ghinucci, Benet and Sir Gregory Casale, 7 October, 1530, *Letters and Papers*, 4.3.6667 (pp. 3004–05). Ghinucci had been transferred to Rome from the Court of Charles V.

⁸ *Tudor Royal Proclamations*: Volume I, The Early Tudors (1485–1553), edited by Paul L. Hughes and James F. Larkin (New Haven, 1964), pp. 197–98, 197. The proclamation was published on 12 September, 1530.

⁹ The tract is printed in Pocock, II. 385–421.

¹⁰ *De causa matrimonii serenissimi Regis Angliae liber* (Alcala, 1530). There may have been a second printing later the same year. See p. 122.

¹¹ Chapuys to Charles V, 27 November, 1530, *Spanish Calendar*, 4.1.509 (pp. 817–21). See also Bradford, p. 322.

¹² Chapuys to Charles V, 4 December, 1530, *Spanish Calendar*, 4.1.522 (pp. 832–34); same to same, 17 December, 1530, *ibid.*, 4.1.539 (p. 847). See also Bradford, p. 331. These may well have been nothing more than re-

vised drafts of the two works referred to by Chapuys in his letter of 27 November. Writing to Charles V on 23 April, 1531, Dr. Pedro Ortiz referred to only two books by Fisher apart from the work printed the previous August (*Letters and Papers*, 5.207 [pp. 97–98]).

[13] John Stokesley to [Fisher], 8 January, [1531], Pocock, II. 369, 369–70, 370.

[14] This was Chapuys' opinion. He wrote to Fisher and to all the other members of the Queen's council, advising them to use every means to avoid being drawn into such a hearing (Chapuys to Charles V, 21 December, 1530, *Spanish Calendar*, 4.1.547 [pp. 852–53]).

[15] His departure on 11 January is recorded in the Episcopal Register, fol. 160.

[16] Chapuys to Charles V, 23 January, 1531, *Spanish Calendar*, 4.2.615 (p. 39).

[17] Wilkins, III. 725.

[18] Rastell, p. 224. Rochford was Anne Boleyn's brother.

[19] Wilkins, III. 725.

[20] Rastell, pp. 224, 224–25.

[21] Wilkins, III. 725.

[22] Chapuys to Charles V, 14 February, 1531, *Spanish Calendar*, 4.2.635 (p. 63).

[23] Cuthbert Tunstal to Henry VIII, 6 May, 1531, Wilkins, III. 745; Henry VIII to Tunstal, May, 1531, *ibid.*, pp. 762–65.

[24] Chapuys to Charles V, 1 March, 1531, *Spanish Calendar*, 4.2.646 (pp. 79–80); Statutes 22 Henry VIII, Chapter 9. The *Life of Fisher* (pp. 72–73) identifies the dead as Bennett Curwen and a nameless widow. Lewis (II. 73–74) gives the widow's name as Alice Tripit. There are references to a certain Corwen, a messenger in Fisher's service, in correspondence between Fisher and Henry Hornby dating from the years 1510–12. If this is the same man who died of poison in 1531, Curwen must have belonged to Fisher's household for more than twenty years.

[25] *Life of Fisher*, p. 73. He was back in Rochester by 13 March (Episcopal Register, fol. 160v).

CHAPTER 14

[1] Under the title *Grauissimae, atque exactissimae illustrissimarum totius Italiae, et Galliae academiarum censurae.*

[2] The Episcopal Register (fols. 161–62ᵛ) records his presence in Rochester on 15 April, 1 May, 1 June, 3 June, 8 June, 7 August and again on 15 November, 7 December and 12 January, 1532, when he left for the session of Parliament that opened three days later.

[3] Dr. Ortiz to Charles V from Rome, 19 July, 22 August, 1531, *Letters and Papers*, 5.342, 378 (pp. 161–62, 189).

[4] Chapuys to Charles V, 1 October, 1531, *ibid.*, 5.460 (p. 218). During the summer Chapuys had written to Cornelius Agrippa in Brussels, asking him to answer the *Academiarum Censurae.* Agrippa declined the invitation on the grounds that he had nothing new to add to what had already been said. By this time he had seen an early version of Fisher's reply and admired it (Cornelius Agrippa to Chapuys, 21 July, 1531, *Letters and Papers*, 5. Appendix 13 [p. 767]).

[5] Chapuys to Charles V, 6 June, 1531, *ibid.*, 5.287 (pp. 133–38).

[6] Chapuys to Charles V, 9 October, 1531, *Spanish Calendar*, 4.2.805 (p. 261).

[7] Chapuys to Charles V, 16 October, 1531, *ibid.*, 4.2.808 (p. 266).

[8] Chapuys sent it to Charles V on 25 November, 1531, *ibid.*, 4.2.838 (p. 296).

[9] Chapuys to Charles V, 11, 22 January, 1532, *ibid.*, 4.2.883, 888 (pp. 357, 366).

[10] Statutes 23 Henry VIII, Chapter 20. See Chapuys to Charles V, 20 March, 1532, *Letters and Papers*, 5.879 (pp. 412–13). The Earl of Arundel was the only lay peer who opposed the bill in the House of Lords.

[11] Henry VIII to Ghinucci, Benet and Sir Gregory Casale, 21 March, 1532, *ibid.*, 5.886 (pp. 415–16).

[12] Roger Bigelow Merriman, *Life and Letters of Thomas Cromwell* (2 vols., Oxford, 1902), I. 105. There are four drafts of this document in the Record Office (S.P.2.L, fols. 193–202, 203–04, S.P.6.1, fols. 90–103ᵛ, S.P. 6.7, fols. 104–18ᵛ). The numerous revisions and corrections, many in Cromwell's own hand, show clearly enough how much importance was attached to the address by the King and his council. The words in brackets are cancelled in the manuscript, those in italics inserted.

[13] British Museum MS. Cott. Cleop. F.I, fol. 100. There is another copy in the Record Office, S.P.6.7, fols. 119–42[v]. See also Wilkins, III. 751–52.

[14] British Museum MS. Cott. Cleop. F.I, fols. 105, 106. See also Wilkins, III. 752–53.

[15] Richard Watson Dixon, *History of the Church of England* (6 vols., London, 1878–1902), I. 102, 102–03, 103.

[16] Wilkins, III. 747, 748.

[17] *Ibid.*, p. 749.

[18] British Museum MS. Cott. Cleop. F.I, fol. 103. There are three copies of the answer of the clergy. The first (fols. 101–01[v]) is apparently a preliminary draft; the second (fols. 102–02[v]) is the text approved by the upper house, the third (fols. 102[v]–03) the final draft as amended by the lower house. It was the lower house which insisted that the grant be limited to the life of the reigning King. Two other amendments were made at this stage: the King was required to confirm such canons "as do stand with the lawes of almightie god *and holy churche*"; furthermore, ordinaries were expressly authorized to execute any and all existing canons until the King's pleasure was made known concerning them. See also Dixon, I. 107n.

[19] Record Office, S.P.6.3, fol. 62. This is the text of the Submission of the Clergy as it was delivered to the King on 16 May. There is another draft in the Record Office (S.P.1.70, fols. 38–38[v]), which differs in important respects from the draft that was finally adopted. Where in the latter the clergy promised never to "enact put in vre promulge or execute any new canons or constitucion provincial or synodall", in the other version they are made to promise never to "presume to attempt, alege, clayme or yet put in vre, or to enacte promulge or execute any canons Constitucion or ordynaunce" in Convocation assembled. Evidently the more extravagant promises of the rejected draft, which may well have been prepared by the council itself for the approval of the ordinaries, were modified during debate in Convocation, probably at the instance of the inferior clergy, who were on the whole less amenable to the Court than their superiors in the upper house. When the Submission was drafted into law in March of 1534 (see pp. 172–73), the council took care to make use of the preliminary version, knowing it to be more favourable to the King's cause than the text actually approved by the clergy. See Dixon, I. 110–11, 111–12n.

[20] Chapuys to Charles V, 13 May, 1532, *Letters and Papers*, 5.1013 (pp. 466–67).

[21] Gardiner to Henry VIII from Esher, c. 15 May, 1532, *The Letters of Stephen Gardiner*, edited by James Arthur Muller (Cambridge, 1933), p.

49. Gardiner added that in his book against Luther Henry himself had been of the same opinion.

²² Wilkins, III. 746. The statement is dated 24 February.

²³ *Letters and Papers*, 5.1247 (pp. 541–43).

²⁴ Among the papers found in Fisher's possession when he was arrested two years later was a fragmentary discourse, partly in his own hand, on the authority proper to ministers of the Church (Record Office, S.P.6.11, fols. 215–23). A second fragment (Record Office, S.P.6.1, fols. 38–41ᵛ) appears, though not in Fisher's hand, to be another draft of part of the same work. And in the British Museum (MS. Add. 4274, fols. 212–13) there is a brief summary, entirely in Fisher's hand, of the several arguments for clerical immunity, apparently drawn up by Fisher for his own guidance in preparing a longer work. None of these manuscripts is dated, but they probably all relate to the struggle between King and clergy during May of 1532.

²⁵ Chapuys to Charles V, 21 June, 1532, *Spanish Calendar*, 4.2.962 (p. 465).

²⁶ These events were reported by both Capello and Chapuys. See Carlo Capello to the Signory, 13 April, 1532, *Calendar of State Papers and Manuscripts . . . in the Archives and Collections of Venice* [*Venetian Calendar*], edited by Rawdon Brown, Cavendish Bentinck and Horatio Brown (9 vols., London, 1864–98), 4.760 (pp. 331–32); Chapuys to Charles V, 16 April, 1532, *Spanish Calendar*, 4.2.934 (pp. 427–28).

²⁷ Capello to the Signory, 16 May, 1532, *Venetian Calendar*, 4.768 (p. 335).

²⁸ Capello to the Signory, 10 July, 1532, *ibid.*, 4.786 (p. 342). Chapuys also reported the incident to Charles V, 11 July, 1532, *Spanish Calendar*, 4.2.972 (p. 481).

²⁹ See Paul Friedmann, *Anne Boleyn* (2 vols., London, 1884), I. 162–63.

CHAPTER 15

¹ *Life of Fisher*, p. 74.

² Chapuys to Charles V, 27–29 January, 1533, *Spanish Calendar*, 4.2.1043 (p. 585); Edmund Boner to Benet, 31 January, 1533, *State Papers*, VII. 410–16.

[3] Chapuys saw more clearly than Clement what would happen (Chapuys to Charles V, 9 February, 1533, *Letters and Papers*, 6.142 [pp. 62–66]).

[4] For a discussion of the customary oath and the changes introduced by Cranmer, see Dixon, I. 158–59n.

[5] *The Works of Thomas Cranmer*, edited by the Rev. John Edmund Cox for the Parker Society (2 vols., Cambridge, 1844–46), II. 460.

[6] Chapuys to Charles V, 31 March, 1533, *Spanish Calendar*, 4.2.1057 (pp. 625–26).

[7] Wilkins, III. 756–59; Richard Fiddes, *The Life of Cardinal Wolsey* (London, 1724), Collection, pp. 195–204. Where Wilkins and Fiddes differ in their accounts of the voting Fiddes has been preferred. He gives the names as well as the number of those voting on each side of the two resolutions.

[8] Statutes 24 Henry VIII, Chapter 12.

[9] Chapuys to Charles V, 10 April, 1533, *Spanish Calendar*, 4.2.1058 (pp. 629–30); Capello to the Signory, 12 April, 1533, *Venetian Calendar*, 4.870 (p. 392). Though in the custody of the Bishop of Winchester, Fisher must have continued in his own house at Lambeth, since the Episcopal Register (fol. 177^v) contains several entries between 7 April and 5 May, all dated at Lambeth Marsh. On 7 April he admitted William Miles to the rectory of Asshe and Thomas Slater to the rectory of Ridley; on 10 April he admitted William Buckley to the perpetual vicarage of Pepinby; and on 5 May he admitted John Shott to the rectory of Mapistop. The London house of the Bishop of Winchester was in Southwark, which is more than two miles downriver from Lambeth Marsh. Fisher was at Rochester again on 2 June, when he was present in the bishop's palace and admitted Jacob Goldewell to the rectory of Addington (*ibid.*, fol. 178). Since the point is vital to a knowledge of Fisher's movements during these weeks, it is necessary to make it clear that Allen is mistaken when he says (V. 536n) that Rochester House was in Southwark close to the palace of the Bishop of Winchester. His authority is the view of London drawn about 1550 by Anthonis van den Wyngaerde. In point of fact, however, Wyngaerde's view shows nothing of the kind. The building in question is marked "Palace of the Protector Somerset". The last word is faded and must have been overlooked by Allen, leading him to mistake the word "Protector" for "Rochester". In Fisher's day Rochester House (then known as La Place) stood next to the palace of the Archbishop of Canterbury at Lambeth. Originally all the land thereabouts had belonged to the priory of Rochester. Towards the end of the twelfth century, the Bishop of Rochester built himself a town house on part of the site, while the remainder was transferred to the see of Canterbury. John Hilsey, Fisher's successor,

was the last to use the house at Lambeth, which after his removal was occupied by the bishops of Carlisle. It has since been demolished. See the Rev. Samuel Denne, *Historical Particulars of Lambeth Parish and Lambeth Palace* (London, 1795).

[10] Cranmer to Henry VIII, 11 April, 1533, *Works*, II. 237–38. See Jasper Ridley, *Thomas Cranmer* (Oxford, 1962), p. 59.

[11] Henry VIII to Cranmer, c. 12 April, 1533, Cranmer, *Works*, II. 238–39n, 239n.

[12] Wilkins, III. 765–68. There were also 24 proxies voted in favour of the first proposition and five or six in favour of the second.

[13] Cranmer to Henry VIII, 17 May, 1533, *Works*, II. 242. He wrote on Saturday. Monday, Tuesday and Wednesday were rogation days and Thursday the day of Ascension, so the hearing could not be resumed until the Friday.

[14] The Latin text of the sentence is given in Wilkins, III. 759–60.

[15] Cranmer to Henry VIII, 23 May, 1533, *Works*, II. 244. The correspondence between Cranmer and the King has also been printed in full in *State Papers*, I. 390–97, from the originals in the Record Office (S.P.1.75, fols. 86–86ᵛ, 88; S.P.1.76, fols. 42, 66, 101) and the British Museum (MS. Harl. 283, fol. 97).

[16] Cranmer to Nicholas Hawkyns, 17 June, 1533, *Works*, II. 245, 245–46. Hawkyns was Archdeacon of Ely and had succeeded Cranmer at the Court of Charles V. The bishops who assisted Cranmer at the coronation were Lee, Stokesley, Gardiner, Clerk and Standish. The first three had all risen to their present position by serving the King in his suit at Rome. Clerk and Standish had both served as counsel to the Queen in 1529, but Standish had long since changed his mind. Aside from Fisher, Clerk was the only English bishop to vote in Convocation against the King. Standish was Bishop of St. Asaph, but his title was pronounced at the time as Cranmer wrote it.

[17] Chapuys to Charles V, 16 June, 1533, *Spanish Calendar*, 4.2.1081 (p. 706).

[18] The text of the papal bull is given in Pocock, II. 677–78.

[19] *Ibid.*, pp. 502–04.

[20] Cromwell to Henry VIII, 23 July, 1533, Merriman, I. 360, 361.

[21] Stephen Vaughan to [Cromwell], 3 August, 1533, *Letters and Papers*, 6.934 (pp. 407–08).

[22] *Ibid.*, 6.1111 (p. 464).

[23] Chapuys to Charles V, 27 September, 10 October, 1533, *ibid.*, 6.1164, 1249 (pp. 484–87, 510–12).

CHAPTER 16

[1] *Letters and Papers*, 6.1468 (p. 587).

[2] Chapuys to Charles V, 20, 24 November, 1533, *ibid.*, 6.1445, 1460 (pp. 576–78, 582–83). The Bishop of Bangor was John Capon, who had only recently been given the see. In "The Sermon against the Holy Maid of Kent and her Adherents, delivered at Paul's Cross, November the 23rd, 1533, and at Canterbury, December the 7th", *English Historical Review*, LVIII (1943), 463–75, L. E. Whatmore prints the sermon in full from a transcript in the Record Office.

[3] *Articles Devisid by the holle consent of the Kynges moste honourable counsayle*, printed on 26 December, 1533. See Pocock, II. 523–31.

[4] *Letters and Papers*, 5.820 (p. 387). Tunstal's letter is not extant but its contents can be inferred from the King's reply.

[5] Pocock, II. 550, 550–51. The full text of the pamphlet is given in pp. 539–52.

[6] [Fox], *Opus eximium. De vera differentia regiae potestatis et ecclesiasticae* (London: Thomas Berthelet, 1534); translated into English as *The true dyfferens betwen the regall power and the Ecclesiasticall power* by Henry Lord Stafford in 1548. Marsiglio's *Defensor Pacis*, first circulated in Latin in 1324, was translated into English by William Marshall and printed in 1535. Chapuys, who evidently saw Marshall's translation in manuscript, mentions both Fox and Marsiglio in a despatch to Charles V of 3 January, 1534, *Spanish Calendar*, 5.1.1. (pp. 1–4). At some time during this year or the next (the title-page is undated), Richard Sampson produced a similar work, no doubt at the request of the King. Sampson had been resident envoy at the imperial Court from 1522 to 1525 and in 1529 had acted with Dr. Bell as counsel for the King at the legatine hearing at Blackfriars. He was given the see of Chichester on the death of Robert Sherborn in 1536 and in 1543 was translated to Coventry and Lichfield, where he succeeded Roland Lee. His *Oratio, qua docet, hortatur, admonet omnes potissimum anglos, regiae dignitati cum primis ut obediant* was printed for the King by Berthelet. In the following year Reginald Pole published a reply at Rome, *Pro ecclesiasticae unitatis defensione, libri quator*. See Franklin LeVan Baumer, *The Early Tudor Theory of Kingship* (New Haven, 1940), pp. 40n., [225]–37.

[7] Cromwell apparently consulted the King as to whether or not Fisher was to be sent for (*Letters and Papers*, 6.1381 [p. 549]). That he did in fact receive a summons is likely, for he himself wrote to the King on 27 February, excusing himself on grounds of ill-health (see p. 164).

[8] Cromwell to Fisher, between 18 and 28 January, 1534, Burnet, IV. 195, 197–98. The letter is printed in full by Burnet, pp. 195–201, from the draft in Cromwell's own hand in the British Museum MS. Cott. Cleop. E. IV, fols. 101–04.

[9] Fisher to Cromwell from Rochester, 28 January, 1534, British Museum MS. Cott. Vesp. F.XIII, fol. 258. The letter is calendared in *Letters and Papers*, 7.116 (p. 46).

[10] Fisher to Cromwell from Rochester, 31 January, 1534, British Museum MS. Cott. Cleop. E.VI, fols. 155, 155–55^v. See also *Letters and Papers*, 7.136 (p. 52).

[11] Statutes 25 Henry VIII, Chapter 20.

[12] More to Cromwell, 1 February, c. 21 February, 1534, Rogers, pp. 467–69, 470.

[13] Fisher to Henry VIII from Rochester, 27 February, 1534, British Museum MS. Cott. Cleop. E.VI, fols. 156, 156–58. See also *Letters and Papers*, 7.239 (pp. 98–99). More than a year later, Bedyll questioned the monks of Sion concerning Fisher's letter to the King. "I had the father confessor alone in a verey secrete Comunication", he reported to Cromwell, and he "hath confessed to me that the said Fissher sent to him[,] to the said Rainold [i.e. Richard Reynolds, executed on 4 May, 1535 together with three Carthusians and a secular priest] and to one other brother of thers decessed whoes name I remember not the copy of his said letters directed to the kings grace and the copie of the kings aunswer also [which does not appear to have survived] but he hath sworen to me vpon his fidelite that the said copies tarried not *with* thaim but one nyght and that none of his brethern saw thes same but thoes thre affor named. He hath knowleged to me also that the said Fissher sent vnto thaim *with* the said copies a bok of his made in the defense of the kings grace first marriage [evidently one of the several pamphlets then circulating in manscript] whiche he confessed himself to haue in his keeping and whiche he hath willingly deliuerd vnto me" (Thomas Bedyll to Cromwell, 28 July, [1535], British Museum MS. Cott. Cleop. E.VI, fols. 164, 164–64^v). During one of his examinations in the Tower after his arrest in April of 1535, Reynolds had apparently admitted to having seen a copy of Fisher's letter, but Fisher, when later questioned on this point, insisted—if we are to take Bedyll's account at face value—that he had never shown the letter "to any other man nouther wold" (fol. 164). If Fisher was indeed questioned,

as Bedyll says he was, about his correspondence with the monks of Sion, he may have been tempted to conceal the names of those to whom he had sent copies as much for their sake as for his own.

[14] More to Cromwell, c. 1 March, 1534, Rogers, pp. 480–88. More also wrote to the King on 5 March, and again to Cromwell on the same date to clear himself of suspicions that he had encouraged the King to speak too highly of papal authority in his answer to Luther. He explained that on the contrary he had advised the King to temper what he had said in favour of papal authority; he admitted that he had told the King privately of his scruples in the matter of his marriage, but he denied that he had ever spoken of them to anyone else (*ibid.*, pp. 488–91, 492–501).

[15] Fisher to the House of Lords, c. 27 February, 1534, British Museum MS. Cott. Cleop. E.VI, fols. 161–63ᵛ.

[16] *Journals of the House of Lords*: Volume I, 1509–77 (n.pl., n.d.), pp. 58–83. In the act as finally passed (Statutes 25 Henry VIII, Chapter 12), Elizabeth Barton, Richard Master, Edward Bocking, John Dering, Hugh Rich, Richard Risby and Henry Gold were attainted of high treason, and Fisher, Thomas Gold, Thomas Lawrence, Edward Thwaites, John Adeson and Thomas Abell of misprision of treason. Elizabeth Barton and four of those attainted of high treason were executed at Tyburn on 20 April (see p. 180).

[17] Statutes 25 Henry VIII, Chapter 19. The act closely follows a draft version of the Submission of the Clergy in the Record Office (S.P.1.70, fols. 38–38ᵛ). Dixon (pp. 111–12n) suggests that this was a preliminary version prepared in Convocation, but it is more reasonable to suppose that it was in fact prepared by the council itself and then, though it was never approved by Convocation, used as the basis for the later act. See p. 237 n. 19.

[18] Foxe (pp. 208–09) claims that Clement told Francis that he would agree to such a compromise and that when he heard this Henry sent the Bishop of Paris to Rome to notify Clement that it was also agreeable to him. He adds that the compromise failed only because the imperial faction hurried the decision in consistory and Du Bellay arrived two days after the sentence had been pronounced. There is, however, no evidence for any of this, and in fact everything we know about the principals makes it unlikely that either would have accepted such a compromise. Henry had no hesitation in pushing ahead with a series of bills inimical to the Holy See and Clement apparently made no effort to delay the vote in consistory. Chapuys says that the King waited for an answer from Rome before signing the Act of Succession, but since the royal assent was given on the 30th, long before news of the papal sentence could have reached England, this

cannot be true. See Chapuys to Charles V, 25 March, 1534, *Spanish Calendar*, 5.1.31 (p. 92). The papal sentence is printed in Wilkins, III. 769.

[19] *Documents Illustrative of English Church History*, edited by Henry Gee and William John Hardy (London, 1896), pp. 251, 252. It may have been at this time that Fisher, too ill to make the journey to London, began working on a compilation of the arguments from Scripture for the primacy of the Holy See. A Latin fragment on this subject, corrected in Fisher's hand, was found among the papers seized by the King a few weeks later (Record Office, S.P.6.5, fols. 45–83^v).

[20] Statutes 25 Henry VIII, Chapter 22.

CHAPTER 17

[1] See p. 147.

[2] This refers to the oath of canonical obedience to the Pope hitherto taken by bishops at their installation.

[3] *Lords Journals*, p. 82. The oath tendered to Fisher, which was established by authority of letters patent, was confirmed with minor changes by act of Parliament the following November (Statutes 26 Henry VIII, Chapter 2). The most significant change was made in the first sentence, where the phrase "the Heirs of his Body, according to the Limitation and Rehearsal within this Statute of Succession above specified" became "his heires of his body of his most dere and entierly beloued lauful wife Quene Anne begotten and to [be] begotten. And further to the heires of our saide soueraygne lorde, according to the limittation in the statute made for suretie of his succession in the crowne of this realme mencioned and conteyned". The force of the oath was further increased by omitting the qualification, "since the Beginning of this present Parliament", in the original declaration: "ye shall observe, keep, maintain, and defend, this Act . . . and all other Acts and Statutes made since the Beginning of this present Parliament, in Confirmation or for due Execution of the same". See pp. 176–77, 185.

[4] *Letters and Papers*, 7.502 (p. 202).

[5] *Works*, II. 286. Cranmer added, in the hope perhaps of appealing to the shameless cunning of the Secretary, that the reservations could be concealed, so that others would suppose that Fisher and More had sworn to the whole contents and effects of the act.

[6] Cromwell to Cranmer, 17 or 18 April, 1534, Merriman, I. 381.

[7] After his imprisonment, the Master and fellows of St. John's sent Fisher a further message. In their letter, a copy of which is preserved in the Register of Letters at St. John's College (pp. 47–48), they remind him that he is to them both teacher and father. They speak of their grief in his suffering and offer him their daily prayers.

[8] This is a sample of the complete inventory, which is printed in *Letters and Papers*, 7.557 (pp. 221–22). Nothing of consequence has been omitted. Debts due to Fisher are listed, together with an inventory of the few pieces of plate he still possessed, in a memorandum in the Record Office (S.P. 1.93, fols. 126–47). Fisher had lent his brother Ralph £100 (about $10,000); two members of the White family, Robert and John, had borrowed £50 in all. See also *Letters and Papers*, 8.888 (p. 352).

[9] All of Fisher's papers were seized for examination by officers of the crown. In addition to the fragments on clerical immunity, which probably date from May of 1532, and the Latin tract on the primacy of Rome, which is probably later (see pp. 143, 244 n. 19), several other fragments were found, including three English prayers and a commonplace book, all in Fisher's hand (Record Office, S.P.1.93, fols. 99–122), part of an autograph sermon or homily, also in English (S.P.1.239, fols. 181–82), a salutation of the Virgin Mary and part of an autograph commentary on St. Paul, both in Latin (S.P.2.R, fols. 283, 284–84^v; S.P.6.9, fols. 159–64), together with several drafts, some of them corrected by Fisher and one in his own hand throughout, of a Latin treatise on the *Psalms* (S.P.2.R, fols. 28–282). There were also several letters.

[10] Fisher was required to answer no fewer than forty questions. There are three copies of the questions in the Record Office (S.P.1.93, fols. 63–77), two in English and one in Latin, all in different hands. All three have been severely damaged. Fisher's replies were written out in Latin in his own hand. The original, which is still in excellent condition, is in the British Museum MS. Cott. Cleop. E.VI, fols. 169–71^v. See also *Letters and Papers*, 8.859 (pp. 332–37). The letters of Chapuys, which confirm Fisher's testimony that he had written at least seven or eight books (probably nine) in defence of the Queen, give us no reason to suppose that Fisher knew what happened to the manuscript copies that came into the hands of the ambassador, though he must have expected Chapuys to make what use of them he could. For further details, see pp. 122, 126, 133–34, 134–35. One of his books, *De causa matrimonii serenissimi Regis Angliae liber*, was published at Alcala in 1530 (see pp. 126, 154–55). At least two others have been preserved in manuscript. See British Museum MS. Arundel 151, fols. 202–339^v; Record Office, S.P.1.67, fols. 184–280. As for

the advice he gave Catherine, we have her word for the truth of his testimony. See p. 134.

[11] Chapuys to Charles V, 19 May, 1534, *Spanish Calendar*, 5.1.58 (pp. 155–66); Tunstal and Lee to Henry VIII, 21 May, 1534, *Letters and Papers*, 7.695 (pp. 270–71); Chapuys to Charles V, 29 May, 1534, *Spanish Calendar*, 5.1.60 (pp. 169–73). It was natural enough that Catherine and Chapuys should both attribute Tunstal's altered opinion to cowardice or self-interest. In fact, however, there is no reason to doubt that it was in part at least the effect of genuine conviction. Tunstal was not a stiff-necked man and was always ready to adjust his principles to the requirements of circumstance. In this case he had probably come to believe that a sure succession was more important than the preservation of the authority of the Holy See.

[12] Roland [Lee] to Cromwell, c. 1 May, 1534, British Museum MS. Cott. Cleop. E.VI, fol. 160. The letter, which is in Lee's own hand, is extremely illegible and the reading in places is doubtful. Lee's visit cannot be dated with any certainty. He may have seen Fisher at Lambeth after his first examination by the commissioners, though it is more probable that he visited him in the Tower during the first week or two of his confinement. See also *Letters and Papers*, 7.498 (p. 201).

[13] Rogers, pp. 533–38, 532–33. Wilson was not released until after both Fisher and More had been executed. Rogers prints the two letters in the order in which they appear in the British Museum MS. Royal 17 D.XIV, but internal evidence suggests that the letter printed on pp. 532–33 is in fact the later of the two.

[14] Statutes 26 Henry VIII, Chapter 1.

[15] *Ibid.*, Chapter 2. See pp. 176–77, 178, 244 n. 3.

[16] *Ibid.*, Chapter 3.

[17] *Ibid.*, Chapter 13.

[18] *Ibid.*, Chapter 22. More was attainted by a similar bill (*ibid.*, Chapter 23).

[19] The allowance (in Fisher's case, 20 shillings a week) provided for the maintenance of prisoners in the Tower was never adequate, and since Fisher's income and property were forfeit to the crown he had to rely for clothing and provisions on the generosity of his brother and his friends.

[20] Fisher to Cromwell, 22 December, 1534, British Museum MS. Cott. Cleop. E.VI, fols. 168, 168–68ᵛ. See also *Letters and Papers*, 7.1563 (p. 583).

[21] It has been argued, notably by Friedman (II. 48, 340–44), that Fisher was released for about six weeks during the course of the winter. The author of the early *Life* says (pp. 106–07) that both Fisher and More at some time during the course of their imprisonment were told that the other had taken the oath and been released. The council no doubt hoped that

each would be influenced by the other's apparent change of heart. More is said to have suspected the deception, though Fisher seems to have believed the story. In any case, neither was persuaded to submit. Friedmann sees more in this tale than a simple trick, and suggests that Fisher at least may actually have been released for a time early in 1535. Nothing is known of Fisher's circumstances between 22 December, 1534, when he wrote to Cromwell from the Tower, and 7 May, 1535, when he was interrogated by members of the council. That a prisoner of such consequence should have been released from custody is on the face of it, however, highly improbable. Nor is it likely that such a man could have appeared in public without being noticed. Chapuys was in close touch with the English Court and it is impossible to believe that Fisher could have been released without his knowledge; nor is it conceivable that, if he had known of Fisher's release, he would have neglected to mention the fact in one of his despatches to Charles V. For Chapuys, like most of his contemporaries, greatly admired Fisher and considered his safety a matter of importance to the Queen and the Emperor. Furthermore, there is no reference to Fisher's release in any surviving document of the period, with a single ambiguous exception. On 5 February, Palamedes Gontier mentioned in a letter to Philippe Chabot, Admiral of France, that while at Court the previous Monday he had met Fisher in the company of the Dukes of Norfolk and Suffolk and the next day had seen him at a meeting of council (*Les Mémoires de Messire Michel de Castelnau*, edited by J. le Laboureur [3 vols., Brussels, 1731], I. 409, 412). Even if Fisher had been at Court, which was not customary with him except when Parliament was in session, it is quite unlikely that he would have been seen at council (to which he had never belonged) or found in such uncongenial company as that of Norfolk and Suffolk. It has been suggested that Fisher was summoned before the council for examination on the supremacy. This, however, does not account for the fact that no further proceedings were taken against him until 7 May, when members of the council visited him in the Tower. If Fisher made any material denials in February, why did Cromwell not proceed at once to an indictment under the Treason Act, which came into force on the first of that month? If not, why did Cromwell wait for three months before making any further effort to persuade the prisoner to incriminate himself? All the evidence points to the conclusion that after Parliament rose on 18 December, 1534, Cromwell turned his attention to other matters, knowing as he did that he could proceed no further against either Fisher or More until after 1 February. In the event, he appears to have given no further thought to the matter until the end of April, when he visited the Charterhouse and questioned the monks as to the royal supremacy. A few days later the interrogation of Fisher and More was resumed. As for the letter of Palamedes Gontier, it was probably written, not (as Friedmann supposes) in 1535, but in 1536. The date given by le Laboureur (5 February, 1535), if expressed in the Old Style of the original, would fall in February of *1536* New Style. This would explain the references in the letter to the impending ruin of Queen Anne. Anne had given birth to a stillborn child in January of 1536 and when Catherine died in the same month Cromwell urged Henry to take a new wife who would be acceptable to the Emperor. Anne was beheaded on 19 May. If the letter was written in February of 1536 it follows that it could not have been Fisher whom Palamedes Gontier met at Court, for Fisher had then been dead for more than seven months. It may well have been the Earl of Wiltshire. His name, which Gontier would have written as "Wulchier", could easily be mistaken for "Fischer". Having regard to the similarity of the letter "l" and the swash "s", the two names could be readily distinguished only by the initial "w", some forms of which do not differ greatly from the common forms of "f" and "i". This, it is true, does not account for the reference to Fisher as "Chancelier", since Audeley and not Wiltshire was Lord Chancellor at this time. But Fisher himself, though nominally still Chancellor of Cambridge University, was no more likely than Wiltshire to be referred to in such a context as "Chancelier". Gontier probably meant that he met Norfolk, Suffolk, Fisher (i.e., Wiltshire) *and Audeley* (the Chancellor).

There remains the question of the Tower accounts, now in the British Museum (MS. Cott. Titus B.I, fols. 165–66). Sir Edmund Walsingham, Lieutenant of the Tower, kept a record of each of his prisoners and the charges allowed for their maintenance, which he submitted to the exchequer for payment. Fisher's entry reads as follows: "The Bysshope of Rochester for xiiij[th] monthys after xxs le weke Summa lvj li". Fisher was imprisoned for almost exactly fourteen months, from 21 April, 1534 to 22 June, 1535, but in the fourteen months of his imprisonment there were 62 weeks, while the Lieutenant, who claimed £56 at the rate of 20s. a week, charged for only 56. Does this indicate that Fisher was released for six weeks in the course of his imprisonment? Careful examination of the accounts shows that it does not. More was allowed 10s. a week for himself and 5s. for his servant, and for the last three months of his imprisonment the Lieutenant charged £9, which is equal to twelve weeks at 15s. a week. In the last three months of More's imprisonment (*i.e.*, from 6 April to 6 July, 1535) there were thirteen weeks, not twelve; no-one supposes, however, that he was released from the Tower for a week during that period. Similarly, Dr. Wilson was allowed 5s. a week and the charge for his imprisonment of two years and two months came to £28. In other words, the Lieutenant claimed 52 weeks' maintenance for each of the two years of Dr. Wilson's confinement, but only four weeks for each of the two additional months, though any two months taken together in fact contain almost nine (104 × 5s. plus 8 × 5s. = £28). Thomas Abott was imprisoned for two years and four months at 40d. a week and for him the Lieutenant charged £20, which is equal to 104 × 40d. plus 16 × 40d. Here again the Lieutenant claimed 52 weeks' maintenance for each year, but for the four additional months he claimed only sixteen, not seventeen and a half weeks. William Raynoldes was held for one year and two months at 40d. a week and charged £10 (52 × 40d. plus 8 × 40d.). The Lady Anne Hungerford was held for ten months at 10s. a week and charged £20, sufficient for only 40 of the 43 or 44 weeks of her imprisonment. Her sister was held for the same period at 5s. a week and was charged only £10. Dr. Townely was held for eight months at 5s. a week and was charged £8, sufficient for only 32 of the 35 weeks of his confinement. Sir Thomas Percy was held for six months at 10s. a week and charged not £13 (26 × 10s.) but £12 (4 × 6 or 24 × 10s.). The Prior of Dancaster was held for three months at 10s. a week and charged £6 instead of £6 10s.

There are only two possible explanations: either each of Henry's prisoners was released for a portion of his imprisonment, which is nonsense, or else the accounting procedures used by the Lieutenant differed from ours. It appears from the accounts we have that though a year was given its true value of 52 weeks, a month was given an arbitrary value of four weeks or 28 days. Hence the apparent loss of six weeks in the calculation of Fisher's account. The Lieutenant charged for 56 weeks not because Fisher was released for six of the 62 weeks of his imprisonment, but because his confinement lasted fourteen months, for which a charge of only 4 × 14 or 56 weeks was allowed. It is not clear why Fisher's account was not stated, like that of William Raynoldes, as one year and two months, in which case a charge of £60 (52 × 20s. plus 8 × 20s.) could have been made. But if the account was to be stated in months, as it was, there is nothing unusual in the entry, nor is there anything in it to justify the various surmises that have been built upon it.

CHAPTER 18

[1] On 29 May and 6 June, 1534, before Thomas Bedyll and Roland Lee.

[2] *Letters and Papers*, 8.565 (pp. 213–14), 8.609 (pp. 229–31). Feron had also been charged, but he was pardoned as a reward for giving evidence against Hale.

[3] Cranmer to Cromwell, 30 April, 1535, *Works*, II. 303.

[4] More to Margaret Roper, 2 or 3 May, 1535, Rogers, pp. 550–54.

[5] Cresacre More, pp. 233–34, 234. See also Harpsfield, pp. 179–80; *Letters and Papers*, 8.661 (pp. 247–49); Chapuys to Charles V, 5–8 May, 1535, *Spanish Calendar*, 5.1.156 (pp. 452–54).

[6] *Life of Fisher*, pp. 104–05. Rastell (p. 232) gives a similar version of the incident.

[7] Rastell, p. 234.

[8] Harpsfield, pp. 182–83.

[9] *Life of Fisher*, pp. 109, 110. This incident cannot be dated with any certainty. It probably occurred, however, after the execution of the Carthusians on 4 May and before the news of Fisher's elevation to the cardinalate reached London at the end of the month.

[10] Sir Gregory Casale to Cromwell, 29 May, 1535, *State Papers*, VII. 604–05. The decree in which the new cardinals were named is calendared in *Letters and Papers*, 8.742 (p. 277).

[11] The Bishop of Mâcon to Du Bellay, 2 June, 1535, *ibid.*, 8.812 (p. 308); Sir Gregory Casale to Du Bellay, 2 June, 1535, *ibid.*, 8.813 (p. 308). Francis said he would do what he could for Fisher but feared he could not save his life (*ibid.*, 8.837 [pp. 320–21]).

[12] *Life of Fisher*, pp. 111, 111–12, 112.

[13] All of them (except Suffolk and Paulett) had served on the earlier commission, but several of those who had tried the Carthusians (including Norfolk) were omitted.

[14] On the morning of 7 May. See p. 192.

[15] *Letters and Papers*, 8.814 (p. 309); Harpsfield, p. 176. See also Rogers, pp. 555–59.

[16] Record Office, S.P.1.93, fols. 52–61ᵛ. The transcript has been severely mutilated. Most of Wilson's testimony is intact, but large portions of the other depositions are missing or illegible. A summary of what remains is printed in *Letters and Papers*, 8.856 (pp. 325–31).

[17] British Museum MS. Cott. Cleop. E.VI, fols. 165–67ᵛ. The record of the interrogation is in the hand of John ap Rice the notary and signed in Fisher's own hand at the bottom of each sheet. For a summary see *Letters and Papers*, 8.858 (pp. 331–32).

[18] *Ibid.*, 8.867 (pp. 340–42). The original record of the interrogation is in the Record Office, S.P.6.7, pp. 11, 13–16.

[19] Record Office, S.P.6.7, p. 17.

[20] *Ibid.*, p. 10. For a convenient printing of the transcript, see *State Papers*, I. 431–32.

[21] The jurors were Sir Hugh Vaughan, Sir Walter Hunggorford, Thomas Burbage, John Newdygate, William Brown, John Hewes, Jasper Leyke, John Palmer, Richard Harry Yong, Henry Lodysman, John Elryngton and George Henyngham. The official record of Fisher's trial, together with that of the trial of the three Carthusians on 11 June, is preserved in the Record Office, K.B.8.7(2). The record of the trial of John Houghton, Robert Lawrence, Augustine Webster, Richard Reynolds, John Hale and Robert Feron on 29 April is preserved in K.B.8.7(1), that of Thomas More on 1 July in K.B.8.7(3). There are several copies of the indictment of Fisher besides that in K.B.8.7(2). See British Museum MS. Cott. Cleop. E.VI, fol. 172 and MS. Arundel 151, fols. 194–94ᵛ; Cambridge University Library Ee.3.1., fols. 120–21. It was printed by John Bruce in "Observations on the circumstances which occasioned the Death of Fisher, Bishop of Rochester", *Archaeologia*, XXV (1834), 61–99, and later in *Canonizationis Beatorum Martyrum Iohannis Card. Fisher Episcopi Roffensis et Thomae Mori Angliae Cancellarii. Informatio* (Rome, 1934), pp. 14–15. The list of jurors given here has been transcribed from the panel shown in K.B.8.7(2). The list given in the early *Life* contains several minor errors.

[22] Rastell, pp. 238, 238–39, 239.

[23] *Life of Fisher*, pp. 119, 120.

[24] *Ibid.*, pp. 121, 122.

[25] *Ibid.*, p. 122.

[26] Rastell, p. 243. Rastell witnessed the execution and most, though not all, of what we know of the events of that day derives from his account.

[27] *Life of Fisher*, p. 123.

[28] Rastell, p. 243.

[29] *Life of Fisher*, p. 124.

[30] Rastell, p. 244.

[31] *Life of Fisher*, p. 125.

[32] *Psalm 31*, 1–3, 12–14.

CHAPTER 19

[1] *Letters and Papers*, 8.1095, 1117 (pp. 429, 437); Wilkins, III. 792–97.

[2] Record Office, S.P.1.96, fols. 24^v, 25; *State Papers*, VII. 633–36.

[3] J. A. Froude, *The Divorce of Catherine of Aragon* (New York, 1891), p. 344.

[4] Fisher was beatified by decree of Leo XIII on 4 December, 1886, together with More and 52 others executed during the reigns of Henry VIII and Elizabeth; nine more were beatified on 13 May, 1895. Among the 63 men and women so named were John Houghton, Robert Lawrence, Augustine Webster, Richard Reynolds and John Hale, all executed on 4 May, 1535, and Humphrey Middlemore, William Exmewe and Sebastian Newdigate, executed together on 19 June. Fisher and More alone were canonized on 19 May, 1935. For an account of the procedure, see *Lives of the English Martyrs*, edited by Bede Camm (London, 1904).

Bibliography

MANUSCRIPTS

Bodleian Library. MS.13. Oratio habita coram Illustrissimo Rege Henrico Septimo. Cantabrigie. A copy of J.F.'s address of welcome to the King.

Borthwick Institute of Historical Research. York Probate Registry. Will of Robert Fisher dated 19 June, 1477 and proved 26 June.

British Museum. MS.Add.4274, fols. 212–13. Autograph notes on clerical immunity. Mutilated. MS.Arundel 151, fols. 194–94^v. A draft of J.F.'s indictment. MS.Arundel 151, fols. 202–339^v. Copy of a reply by J.F. to the Academiarum censurae. MS.Arundel 152. Contains copies of the English and Latin lives, the Rastell fragment and materials relating to J.F.'s life and work, apparently collected by the author of the early life. Badly damaged by fire. MS.Cott.Cleop.E.IV, fols. 101–04. Autograph letter from Cromwell to J.F., between 18 and 28 January, 1534. MS.Cott.Cleop.E.VI, fols. 155–55^v. A letter from J.F. to Cromwell, 31 January, 1534. Autograph signature. MS.Cott.Cleop.E. VI, fols. 156–58. A letter from J.F. to Henry VIII, 27 February, 1534. Autograph signature. MS.Cott.Cleop.E.VI, fol. 160. Autograph letter from Roland [Lee] to Cromwell, c. 1 May, 1534. MS.Cott.Cleop.E. VI, fols. 161–63^v. A letter from J.F. to the House of Lords, c. 27 February, 1534. Four last words autograph, signature missing. MS. Cott.Cleop.E.VI, fols. 164–64^v. A letter from Bedyll to Cromwell, 28 July, [1535]. MS.Cott.Cleop.E.VI., fols. 165–67^v. Interrogation of J.F., 12 June, 1535. Each leaf is signed by the prisoner. MS.Cott. Cleop.E.VI, fols. 168–68^v. Autograph letter from J.F. to Cromwell, 22 December, 1534. MS.Cott.Cleop.E.VI, fols. 169–71^v. Autograph answers by J.F. to questions submitted to him concerning the E.R. letters. MS.Cott.Cleop.E.VI, fol. 172. Fragment of J.F.'s indictment. MS.Cott.Cleop.F.I, fols. 100–100^v. Fragment of the first answer of the ordinaries to the Commons. MS.Cott.Cleop.F.I, fols. 101–03. Three drafts of the answer of the clergy to the King. MS.Cott.Cleop. F.I, fols. 104–06ᵛ. Draft of the second answer of the ordinaries. MS. Cott.Otho C.X, fols. 184–98ᵛ. A reply to J.F., perhaps by Pace or Wakefield, with a Responsio by J.F. and the author's rejoinder. Damaged by fire. MS.Cott.Titus B.I, fols. 165–66. Accounts of the Lieutenant of the Tower. MS.Cott.Vesp.F.XIII, fol. 258. A letter from J.F. to Cromwell, 28 January, 1534. Autograph signature. MS.Cott. Vit.B.XI, fols. 169–71ᵛ. A letter from Henry VIII to the English agents at Rome, 23 June, [1529]. MS.Harleian 7047. Contains a copy of the early life in English and other narrative fragments. MS. Harleian 7049, fol. 134ᵛ. Materials for a life of J.F. Department of Prints and Drawings. G.g.1–416. Drawing of J.F. A contemporary copy of the Windsor Holbein.

Cambridge University Library. Ee.3.1, fols. 120–21. Draft of J.F.'s indictment. Ff.5.25, fols. 152–97ᵛ. A brief submitted by J.F. to the legates at Blackfriars, 28 June, 1529. Mm.1.40, pp. 405–06. Indenture dated 6 March, 1521. Mm.2.25. Copies of correspondence between J.F. and the Vice-Chancellor and Senate of the university in May of 1514 concerning the nomination of Wolsey as Chancellor (fols. 74ᵛ–77); copies of four letters from the Vice-Chancellor and Senate to J.F. concerning their privileges, dated 1515, 1529 and 1532 (fols. 77–79ᵛ, 82ᵛ–84).

College of Arms. Philpott's Stemmata, T.no.11 (1648), fol. 13ᵛ. The Lombard pedigree.

Metropolitan Museum of Art. No.36–69. Torrigiano bust, probably of J.F.

National Portrait Gallery, No.2821. Oil painting of J.F. A sixteenth-century copy of the Windsor Holbein. Mutilated.

Record Office. E.30.1471, 1472.2. Two copies of a declaration by certain of the bishops as to the King's suit. Both signed by J.F. K.B.8.7(2). Record of the trial of J.F. S.P.1.39, fol. 67. A letter from J.F. to Master Draper, 13 August, [1526]. S.P.1.42, fols. 51–51ᵛ. A letter from J.F. to Wolsey, [c. 31 May], 1527. S.P.1.42, fols. 165–66ᵛ. A letter from [J.F.] to Paul ——, [July,1527]. S.P.1.54, fols. 129–65ᵛ. A brief submitted by Gardiner to the legates at Blackfriars, c. 1 July, 1529. S.P.1.54, fols. 166–217ᵛ, 218–29ᵛ. Drafts of a second brief submitted by Gardiner to the legates, c. 1 July. Marginal notes in J.F.'s hand. S.P.1.54, fol. 262. A schedule of written evidence submitted to the legates. S.P.1.67, fols. 184–280. Autograph fragment of a reply by J.F. to the Academiarum censurae. S.P.1.70, fols. 38–38ᵛ. See also S.P.6.3, fols. 62–62ᵛ. Two drafts of the submission of the clergy to the King. S.P.1.93, fols. 52–61ᵛ. Interrogation of Wilson, Gold and Wood,

7–11 June, 1535. Mutilated. S.P.1.93, fols. 63–77. Three drafts of an interrogation submitted to J.F. concerning the E.R. letters. Mutilated. S.P.1.93, fols. 99–122. Three autograph prayers, much corrected; an autograph commonplace book containing texts from the Scriptures and the Fathers. Two of the prayers are almost illegible; the third has been transcribed by the Rev. J. F. McMahon and printed by Reynolds (q.v.), pp. 297–99. S.P.1.93, fols. 126–47. An inventory of plate and letters seized at the time of J.F.'s arrest, together with a schedule of debts due to him. S.P.1.96, fols. 12–30ᵛ. Instructions given to Edward Fox on his departure for Germany, [31 August, 1535]. S.P.1.239, fols. 181–82. Autograph fragment of a sermon or homily by J.F. S.P.2.L, fols. 193–202; fols. 203–04. See also S.P.6.1, fols. 90–103ᵛ; S.P.6.7, fols. 104–18ᵛ. Four drafts of the supplication of the Commons. The second and fourth are corrected in Cromwell's hand. S.P.2.R, fols. 28–282. Several drafts of a commentary on Psalms 1–51. One is in J.F.'s hand; others contain autograph corrections. S.P.2.R, fols. 283–84ᵛ. Autograph salutation of the Virgin Mary. Much corrected and mutilated. S.P.6.1, fols. 38–41ᵛ. A fragment by J.F. on the authority of the clergy. S.P. 6.3, fol. 62. Final draft of the Submission of the Clergy. S.P.6.5, fols. 45–83ᵛ. Draft of a brief on papal authority. Autograph corrections, S.P.6.7, pp. 9–17. Interrogation of More and J.F., 14 June, 1535. S.P.6.7, fols. 119–42ᵛ. Draft of the first answer of the ordinaries to the Commons. S.P.6.9, fols. 159–64. Autograph fragments of a commentary on St. Paul. S.P.6.11, fols. 215–23. A fragment by J.F. on the authority of the clergy. Partly autograph.

Rochester, Diocesan Registry. Episcopal Register, IV (1492–1542).

St. John's College, Cambridge. Register of Letters. Contains copies of several of the letters and papers in the Thin Red Book. Also contains copies of two letters from the Master and fellows of the college to J.F., one concerning the statutes, the other concerning his imprisonment (pp. 40–41, 47–48). Thin Red Book. Contains J.F.'s account of his difficulties as executor of the Lady Margaret's estate (fols. 38–40); a schedule of J.F.'s gifts to Christ's College (fols. 42–43ᵛ); copy of a letter from Henry VII to the Lady Margaret concerning the see of Rochester (fol. 45ᵛ); the Lady Margaret's vow of chastity (fol. 47); an undated schedule of J.F.'s gifts to St. John's (fols. 65, 66); copy of indentures dated 18 April and 27 December, 1525 (fols. 68–72ᵛ); copy of an undated letter from the Vice-Chancellor and Senate of the university to J.F. concerning his exequies (fols. 75–76); copy of J.F.'s reply, 25 February, [1529] (fols. 77–78ᵛ); copy of a letter from J.F. to Croke (fols. 49–50ᵛ); copy of a letter from the Master and fellows of the college to J.F. dated 1531 (fols. 104–04ᵛ); copy of an undated letter of reference given by J.F. to Wakefield (fol. 219).

Windsor Castle, Royal Library. No. 12205. Drawing of J.F. by Holbein.

PRINTED BOOKS

Apologię seu defensorij ecclesiae catholicę non tres siue duas Magdalenas sed vnicam celebrantis & colentis. N.pl., 1519.

Baily, Thomas. The Life & Death of that Renowned John Fisher Bishop of Rochester. London, 1655. Interpolated text of the early life.

Baker, Thomas. History of the College of St. John. Edited by John E. B. Mayor. 2 vols., Cambridge, 1869.

Barnes, Robert. A supplicatyon vnto the most excellent and redoubted prince kinge henrye the eyght. N.pl., n.d.

Baumer, Franklin LeVan. The Early Tudor Theory of Kingship. New Haven, 1940.

Bowle, John. Henry VIII A Biography. London, 1964; 1965.

Bridgett, T. E. Life and Writings of Blessed Thomas More. London, 1891; 1924.

—— Life of Blessed John Fisher. London, 1888; 1890.

Bruce, John. Observations on the circumstances which occasioned the Death of Fisher, Bishop of Rochester. Archaeologia, XXV (1834), 61–99. Contains transcripts of a number of documents.

Burnet, Gilbert. The History of the Reformation of the Church of England. Edited by Nicholas Pocock. 7 vols., Oxford, 1865.

Calendar of Letters, Despatches, and State Papers . . . Preserved in the Archives at Simancas. Edited by G. A. Bergenroth, Pascual de Gayangos, M.A.S. Hume, Royall Tyler and Garrett Mattingley. 13 vols. and 2 supplements, London, 1862–1954.

Calendar of State Papers and Manuscripts . . . in the Archives and Collections of Venice. Edited by Rawdon Brown, Cavendish Bentinck and Horatio Brown. 9 vols., London, 1864–98.

Calendar of the Patent Rolls Preserved in the Public Record Office: Henry VII. 2 vols., London, 1914–16.

Camm, Bede. Lives of the English Martyrs Declared Blessed by Pope Leo XIII. in 1886 and 1895: Volume I, Martyrs under Henry VIII. London, 1904.

Canonizationis Beatorum Martyrum Iohannis Card. Fisher Episcopi Roffensis et Thomae Mori Angliae Cancellarii. Informatio. Rome, 1934.

Cavendish, George. The Life and Death of Cardinal Wolsey. In Two Early Tudor Lives. Edited by Richard S. Sylvester and Davis P. Harding. New Haven, 1962. Text with modernized spelling based on the edition prepared by Richard S. Sylvester for the Early English Text Society, Original Series No. 243. London, 1959.

Chambers, R. W. Thomas More. London, 1935.

Chester, Allan G. Robert Barnes and the Burning of the Books. Huntington Library Quarterly, XIV (1951), 211–21.

Clebsch, William A. England's Earliest Protestants 1520–1535. New Haven, 1964.

Clichtove, Josse van. Disceptationis de Magdalena defensio. 1519.

Concilia Magnae Britanniae et Hiberniae. Edited by [David Wilkins]. 4 vols., London, 1737. Volume III deals with the period 1350–1545.

Cooper, Charles Henry. Memoir of Margaret Countess of Richmond and Derby. Cambridge, 1874.

Correspondence of the Emperor Charles V. Edited by William Bradford. London, 1850.

Cranmer, Thomas. The Works of Thomas Cranmer. Edited by the Rev. John Edmund Cox for the Parker Society. 2 vols., Cambridge, 1844–46.

Davis, E. Jeffries. The Authorities for the Case of Richard Hunne (1514–15). English Historical Review, XXX (1915), 477–88.

Denne, Rev. Samuel. Historical Particulars of Lambeth Parish and Lambeth Palace. London, 1795.

Dickens, A. G. The English Reformation. London, 1964.

—— Thomas Cromwell and the English Reformation. London, 1959; 1964.

Dixon, Richard Watson. History of the Church of England. 6 vols., London, 1878–1902.

Doernberg, Erwin. Henry VIII and Luther: An Account of their Personal Relations. London, 1961.

DuBellay, Jean. Ambassades en Angleterre: La Première Ambassade. Edited by V.-L. Bourrilly and P. de Vaissière. Paris, 1905. Contains despatches dating from September, 1527 to February, 1529.

Duggan, G. H. The Church in the Writings of St. John Fisher. Napier, 1953.

Erasmus, Desiderius. The Epistles of Erasmus from his Earliest Letters to his Fifty-first Year. Edited by Francis Morgan Nichols. 3 vols., London, 1901–18.

—— Erasmus and Cambridge: The Cambridge Letters of Erasmus.

Translated by D. F. S. Thomson with an introduction, commentary and notes by H. C. Porter. Toronto, 1963.

—— Opus Epistolarum Des. Erasmi Roterodami. Edited by P. S. Allen. 12 vols., Oxford, 1906–58.

Ferguson, Charles W. Naked to Mine Enemies: The Life of Cardinal Wolsey. Boston, 1958.

Fiddes, Richard. The Life of Cardinal Wolsey. London, 1724. Prints a number of important documents.

Fischer-Treuenfeld, R. von. Lord Johan Fyssher. London, 1894. The genealogy of the Fisher family.

Fisher, John. Assertionis Lutheranae confutatio. Antwerp, 1523.

—— Confutatio Secundae Disceptationis per Iacobum Fabrum Stapulensem. Paris, 1519.

—— Contio [in Ioh. xv.26] . . . uersa in Latinum per Richardum Pacaeum. Cambridge, 1521.

—— Conuulsio calumniarum Vlrichi Veleni Minhoniensis, quib. Petrum nunquam Romae fuisse cauillatur. Antwerp, 1522.

—— De causa matrimonii serenissimi Regis Angliae liber. [Alcala, 1530].

—— The Defence of the Priesthood. Translated from the Latin by the Rt. Rev. Msgr. P. E. Hallett. London, 1935.

—— Defensio Regie assertionis contra Babylonicam captiuitatem. Cologne, 1525.

—— De veritate corporis et sanguinis Christi in eucharistia adeursus Iohannem Oecolampadium. Cologne, 1527.

—— De vnica Magdalena, Libri tres. Paris, 1519.

—— The English Works of John Fisher. Edited by John E. B. Mayor for the Early English Text Society, Extra Series No. 27. London, 1935.

—— Euersio munitionis quam Iodocus Clichtoueus erigere moliebatur aduersus unicam Magdalenam. Louvain, [1519].

—— The Funeral Sermon of Margaret Countess of Richmond and Derby. Edited by J. Hymers. Cambridge, 1840. Contains transcripts of a number of important documents.

—— A Godlie treatise declaryng the benefites, fruites, and great commodities of prayer. London, 1560. A translation of the Tractatus de orando deum.

—— Here after ensueth two fruytfull Sermons. London, 1532.

—— Mornynge remembraunce had at the moneth mynde of the noble prynces Margarete countesse of Rychemonde & Darbye. London, 1509.

—— Opera, Quae hactenus inueniri potuerunt omnia. Wurzburg, 1597.

—— Sacri sacerdotii defensio. Cologne, 1525.

—— A sermon had at Paulis . . . vpon quinquagesom sonday, concern-ynge certayne heretickes. London, ? 1526.

—— Sermon . . . made agayn the pernicyous doctryn of Martin luuther. London, 1521.

—— Sermon . . . sayd in the Cathedrall chyrche of saynt Poule . . . the body beynge present of the moost famouse prynce kynge Henry the .vij. London, 1509.

—— A spirituall consolation. The wayes to perfect Religion. A Sermon . . . Preached vpon a good Friday. N.pl., n.d.

—— Tractatus de orando deum. Douai, 1576.

—— Treatyse concernynge . . . the seuen penytencyall psalmes. London, 1509.

[Fox, Edward]. Opus eximium. De vera differentia regiae potestatis et ecclesiasticae. London, 1534. Translated into English as The true dyfferens betwen the regall power and the Ecclesiasticall power by Henry Lord Stafford. London, 1548.

Foxe, John. The Acts and Monuments. Edited by the Rev. Josiah Pratt. 8 vols., London, 1877.

Friedmann, Paul. Anne Boleyn. 2 vols., London, 1884.

Frith, John. A disputacion of Purgatorye. Münster, 1533. The third book is a reply to J.F.

Froude, J. A. The Divorce of Catherine of Aragon. New York, 1891.

Gairdner, James. The Draft Dispensation for Henry VIII's Marriage with Anne Boleyn. English Historical Review, V (1890), 544–50.

—— The English Church in the Sixteenth Century. London, 1902.

—— Henry the Seventh. London, 1889.

—— New Lights on the Divorce of Henry VIII. English Historical Review, XI (1896), 673–702; XII (1897), [1]–16, 237–53.

Gardiner, Stephen. The Letters of Stephen Gardiner. Edited by James Arthur Muller. Cambridge, 1953.

—— Obedience in Church & State: Three Political Tracts. Translated into English by Pierre Janelle. Cambridge, 1930. Contains Si sedes illa and De vera obedientia. Valuable introduction.

Gee, Henry and Hardy, William John. Documents Illustrative of English Church History. London, 1896.

Grauissimae, atque exactissimae illustrissimarum totius Italiae, et Galliae Academiarum censurae. London, 1530.

Hall, Edward. Chronicle. London, 1809.

Harpsfield, Nicholas. The life and death of Sr Thomas Moore. Edited by Elsie Vaughan Hitchcock for the Early English Text Society, No. 186. London, 1932. Contains Rastell's Breef notes.

—— A Treatise on the Pretended Divorce between Henry VIII. and Catherine of Aragon. Edited by Nicholas Pocock for the Camden Society. London, 1878.

Henry VIII. Assertio septem sacramentorum aduersus M. Lutherum. London, 1521.

Hess, Simon. Apologia adversus dominum Roffensem, Episcopum Anglicanum, super concertatione eius cum Vlricho Veleno, An Petr. fuerit Romae. N. pl., n.d.

Hughes, Philip. The Reformation in England. 3 vols., London and New York, 1951–54.

Ingram, T. Dunbar. England and Rome: A History of the Relations between the Papacy and the English State and Church. London, 1892.

Journals of the House of Lords: Volume I, 1509–77. N.pl., n.d.

Lefèvre, Jacques. De Maria Magdalena, & triduo Christi disceptatio. Paris, 1517; 1518; 1519.

—— De tribus et unica Magdalena, Disceptatio secunda. Paris, 1519.

Letters and Papers, Foreign and Domestic, of the Reign of Henry VIII, 1509–47. Edited by J. S. Brewer, James Gairdner and R. H. Brodie. 21 vols. in 33 parts, London, 1862–1910.

Lewis, Rev. John. The Life of Dr. John Fisher. Edited by T. Hudson Turner. 2 vols., London, 1855.

The Life of Fisher. Edited by the Rev. Ronald Bayne for the Early English Text Society, Extra Series No. 117. London, 1921.

Lloyd, A. H. The Early History of Christ's College Cambridge. Cambridge, 1934.

Lupton, J. H. A Life of John Colet. London, 1887; 1909.

Mackie, J. D. The Earlier Tudors 1485–1558. Oxford, 1957.

Maclure, Millar. The Paul's Cross Sermons 1534–1642. Toronto, 1958.

Mattingly, Garrett. Catherine of Aragon. London, 1942; 1950.

Mayor, John E. B. Early Statutes of the College of St. John. Cambridge, 1859.

McConica, James Kelsey. English Humanists and Reformation Politics under Henry VIII and Edward VI. Oxford, 1965.

Les Mémoires de Messire Michel de Castelnau. Edited by J. le Laboureur. 3 vols., Brussels, 1731.

Merriman, Roger Bigelow. Life and Letters of Thomas Cromwell. 2 vols., Oxford, 1902.

More, Thomas. The Apologye of Syr Thomas More. Edited by Arthur Irving Taft for the Early English Text Society, Original Series No. 180. London, 1930.

—— The Correspondence of Sir Thomas More. Edited by Elizabeth Frances Rogers. Princeton, 1947.

—— The Workes of Sir Thomas More. London, 1557. A new edition of the works of More is now in course of preparation by the Yale University Press. The edition begun in 1931 was never completed.

More, Thomas [Cresacre]. The Life of Sir Thomas More. London, 1726.

Mozley, J. F. William Tyndale. London, 1937.

Muller, James Arthur. Stephen Gardiner and the Tudor Reaction. New York, 1926.

Mullinger, James Bass. The University of Cambridge from the Earliest Times to the Royal Injunctions of 1535. Cambridge, 1873.

Oecolampadius, Iohannis. Quid de eucharistia veteres tum Graeci, tum Latini senserint, Dialogus. N.pl., 1530.

Ogle, Arthur. The Tragedy of the Lollards' Tower. Oxford, 1949.

Pace, Richard. Praefatio in Ecclesiasten recognitum ad Hebraicam ueritatem. [London, 1530].

Pole, Reginald. Pro ecclesiasticae unitatis defensione, libri quatuor. Rome, 1536.

Pollard, A. F. Henry VIII. London, 1902; 1905; 1913.

—— Thomas Cranmer and the English Reformation 1489-1556. London, 1904; 1926.

—— Wolsey. London, 1929; 1953.

Pollard, A. W. and Redgrave, C. R. A Short-Title Catalogue of Books Printed ... 1475-1640. London, 1926.

Rackham, H. Early Statutes of Christ's College, Cambridge. Cambridge, 1927.

Read, Conyers. Bibliography of British History Tudor Period, 1485-1603. Oxford, 1933; 1959.

Records of the Reformation; The Divorce 1527-1533. Edited by Nicholas Pocock. 2 vols., Oxford, 1870.

Reynolds, E. E. Saint John Fisher. New York, 1955.

Ridley, Jasper. Thomas Cranmer. Oxford, 1962.

Römische Dokumente zur Geschichte der Ehescheidung Heinrichs VIII. von England, 1527-1534. Edited by Stephan Ehses. Paderborn, 1893. Contains the despatches of Campeggio.

Sampson, Richard. Oratio, qua docet, hortatur, admonet omnes potissimum anglos, regiae dignitati cum primis ut obediant. London, n.d.

Scholastica declaratio sententie & ritus ecclesiae de vnica Magdalena per Natalem Bedam studii Parrhisiensis. Paris, 1519.

Scott, R. F. Notes from the Records of St. John's College, Cambridge: First Series. Cambridge, 1889–99. There is a typescript index to all four series of Notes in St. John's College Library.

State Papers Published under the Authority of His Majesty's Commission: King Henry the Eighth. 11 vols., London, 1830–52.

The Statutes of the Realm: Volume III, 1509–45. London, 1817.

Strype, John. Ecclesiastical Memorials . . . Shewing the Various Emergencies of the Church of England, under King Henry VIII. Oxford, 1822.

Sturge, Charles. Cuthbert Tunstal. London, 1938.

Surtz, Edward. S.J. The Works and Days of John Fisher. Cambridge, 1967. A careful study of Fisher's controversial writings.

A Survey of the Ecclesiastical Archives of the Diocese of Rochester. [London, 1952].

Thomson, John A. F. The Later Lollards 1414–1520. Oxford, 1965.

Thurston, Herbert. The Canon Law of the Divorce. English Historical Review, XIX (1904) 632–45.

Tudor Royal Proclamations: Volume I, The Early Tudors (1485–1553). Edited by Paul L. Hughes and James F. Larkin. New Haven, 1964.

Tyndale, William. The Works of William Tyndale. Edited by the Rev. Henry Walter for the Parker Society. 3 vols., Cambridge, 1848–50.

Van Ortroy, François. Vie du Bienheureux Martyr Jean Fisher. Brussels, 1893. Contains the English and Latin texts of the early life. The introduction is useful and important.

[Velenus, Ulrichus]. In hoc libello grauissimis, certissimisq, & in sacra scriptura fundatis rationibus narijs probatur, Apostolum Petrum Romam non uenisse. N.pl., 1519.

Vetera Monumenta Hibernorum et Scotorum. Edited by Augustinus Theiner. Rome, 1864. Reprints documents from the papal registers dating from 1216 to 1547.

Wakefield, Robert. Kotser Codicis. London, n.d.

—— Syntagma de hebręorum codicum incorruptione. N.pl., n.d.

Whatmore, L. E. The Sermon against the Holy Maid of Kent and her Adherents. English Historical Review, LVIII (1943), 463–75.

These are the most important sources, in print and manuscript, for a study of Fisher's life and work. Others are indicated in the notes. Fisher has, in addition, become the subject of a considerable body of folklore. Works of this kind, whatever their value as human documents, are of no immediate interest to the historian and no attempt has been made to list them.

Index

For a list of the more important sources, which are not included in the index, see pages 253–62. Other sources are indicated in the notes.